China's
New Political Economy

China's New Political Economy

REVISED EDITION

Susumu Yabuki

Stephen M. Harner

Westview Press

A Member of the Perseus Books Group

Copyright © 1999 by Westview Press, A Member of the Perseus Books Group

Published in 1999 in the United States of America by Westview Press, 5500 Central Avenue, Boulder, Colorado 80301-2877, and in the United Kingdom by Westview Press, 12 Hid's Copse Road, Cumnor Hill, Oxford OX2 9JJ

Library of Congress Cataloging-in-Publication Data
Yabuki, Susumu, 1938–
  [Zusetsu Chugoku no keizai. English]
  China's new political economy / Susumu Yabuki and Stephen M. Harner.—Rev. ed.
    p. cm.
  Includes bibliographical references and index.
  ISBN 0-8133-9036-2 (hardcover).—ISBN 0-8133-9037-0 (pbk.)
  1. China—Economic policy—1976– . I. Harner, Stephen M.
II. Title.
HC427.92.Y327813 1999
338.951—dc21
                                                                        98-40786
                                                                        CIP

The paper used in this publication meets the requirements of the American National Standard for Permanence of Paper for Printed Library Materials Z39.48-1984.

10   9   8   7   6   5   4   3   2   1

For our wives,
Yasuko Yabuki and Annie Lai Harner

Contents

**Part 3
State Finances, Financial Institutions and Markets,
and Government Institution Reform**

Direct Investment of Japan and Other Countries in China, 277
Japanese Economic Cooperation with China, 278

Tables
and Illustrations

Maps

Figures

Preface to
the English Language Edition

The years 1997 and 1998 are likely to be seen as turning points in the development of modern Asia. It seems that Asia, having attended the epochal changes in Russia and Eastern Europe in the late 1980s as observer, is getting its turn a decade later.

Nowhere is this more true than in China. To live in China in 1998, as this coauthor does, is to feel the tensions and excitement of change—and the expectation of change. China, which has changed so much, is changing again. The authors have no doubt that the passing of China's leadership from the second to the third and fourth generations of leaders means that economic reforms will be pursued more steadfastly and effectively than ever in the past. The authors have no doubt that the result will be China's continuing rapid advance to higher levels of prosperity, international importance, and national strength.

It is against this backdrop that we have produced a new version of *China's New Political Economy*. Although first published in Japan in early 1998, this book was written with its translation into English for a U.S. audience in mind. After the publication in Japan, the authors and the Japanese publisher, Sososha Ltd., collaborated in April and May 1998 to update and revise the book in light of developments in the first part of the year, especially the Ninth Chinese National People's Congress, the elevation of Zhu Rongji to premier, and the new plans for government, financial system, and state-owned enterprise restructuring.

The reality of China is exceptionally complex, and understanding it is difficult. To facilitate understanding, this book's approach (as in the first edition) is to offer to the extent possible easily grasped illustrations— charts, graphs, and maps—that both support and elucidate the analysis. At the same time, we present and discuss broadly the realities of China's political economy, from China's size and population, through its agriculture, to industry, industrial reform, labor and unemployment, consumerism, trade, state finances and banking, balance of payments, government institution reform, U.S.-Chinese relations, and, of course, the political structure, particularly the role of the Communist Party.

For the book published in Japan, Professor Yabuki translated my chapters into Japanese. In the current English translation, I have returned the favor. The original author of each chapter is indicated at its end. During editorial meetings and correspondence concerning this book, Professor Yabuki and I shared ideas and insights, and we have used some of these in our individual chapters. On a number of chapters the collaboration was more formal, and in these cases there is joint attribution.

As in the case of the previous edition, producing this book has been a gargantuan task, primarily because of the number of illustrations used. Our thanks go to the staff of Sososha Ltd., particularly its president, Nakamura-san, and Ms. Yamada Kaori. Our particular thanks to Ms. Sharron Y. Bao, in Shanghai, for her dedication and skill in producing the graphics. We wish Xiao Bao success in her future career in banking.

Stephen M. Harner
Shanghai

Preface to
the Japanese Edition

The predecessor of this book, *The Economy of China—Illustrated, First Edition*, was published by Sososha Ltd. in August 1992. It was half a year after Deng Xiaoping's remarks during his southern tour; a time when the wounds of the Tiananmen Incident had healed and China was returning to the policy of reform and liberalization. The approach of the first edition—that is, to use many charts and graphs to present an analysis of the constantly changing Chinese economy from numerous perspectives, so as to make the analysis more readily comprehensible—was, fortunately, well received.

Although the current book, the second edition, follows the style of its precursor, it is completely revised and, in terms of content, may be said to be an entirely different book.

First, the statistics have been updated. The main source is the *China Statistical Yearbook* (1997), which provides figures ending in the year 1996. Also some 1997 data from statistical bulletins are used.

Second, there has been a structural change in the Chinese economy during the first half of the 1990s. This change is huge, and in order to reflect this it has been necessary to significantly change the format of the structure of this edition.

Third, I have received the estimable assistance of my coauthor, Stephen M. Harner (chief representative of Deutsche Bank AG in Shanghai) to strengthen analysis of finance, public finance, and Sino-U.S. relations.

The first edition was translated into English by Mr. Harner and was published in the United States (*China's New Political Economy: The Giant Awakes*, Boulder: Westview Press, 1995). Happily, the English translation was widely read. Most importantly, it was selected by *Choice* magazine as "Outstanding Academic Book for 1995." Additionally, it received numerous highly favorable reviews (not only in English but also in French and Italian).

The authors hope that this second edition will follow the first edition into the possession of many readers. If this book can serve readers as a guide to understanding the Chinese economy's advance from slumbering potentiality, to takeoff, and now to continued rapid growth, then we shall be gratified.

Susumu Yabuki
Tokyo

Acronyms

ABC	Agricultural Bank of China
ASEAN	Association of Southeast Asian Nations
BOC	Bank of China
CCB	China Construction Bank
CCP	Chinese Communist Party
CITIC	China International Trust and Investment Company
CNPC	China National Petroleum Corporation
CSRC	China Securities Regulatory Commission
EU	European Union
FIEs	foreign-invested enterprises
GATT	General Agreement on Tarrifs and Trade
GDP	gross domestic product
GNP	gross national product
ICBC	Industrial and Commercial Bank of China
ICP	International Comparison Program (United Nations)
IMF	International Monetary Fund
IPOs	initial public offerings
ITICs	international trust and investment companies
MITI	Ministry of International Trade and Industry
MOF	Ministry of Finance
MOFTEC	Ministry of Foreign Trade and Economic Cooperation (Japan)
NPC	National People's Congress
PBOC	People's Bank of China
PLA	People's Liberation Army
PRC	People's Republic of China
RMB	renminbi (Chinese currency)
S&P	Standard and Poor's
SAFE	State Administration of Foreign Exchange
SAIC	Shanghai Automotive Industrial Corporation
SAR	Special Administrative Region
SDPC	State Development Planning Commission

SETC	State Economic and Trade Commission
Sinopec	China Petrochemical Corporation
SOEs	state-owned enterprises
SPC	State Planning Commission
TICs	trust and investment companies
TVEs	township and village enterprises
VAT	value-added tax
WTO	World Trade Organization

China's
New Political Economy

Introduction

Six Realities and Unrealities About the Chinese Economy

"When China awakes, the world will tremble," warned Napoleon III. This book's first English edition, published in 1995, was subtitled "The Giant Awakes." In the few years since then, the giant has unmistakably awakened.

Now, like a jumbo jet, China is beginning to take off. Its ascent is causing turbulence that seems to create an apparition. It is like an echo of the preamble of the classical *Communist Manifesto*; a specter is haunting Asia; it is the specter of China.

This book is written with the intention of clarifying and demystifying the reality of the Chinese economy through thorough and objective analysis. In this spirit we begin by examining six frequently heard propositions.

The Proposition of China's Impending Collapse (or China's Strategic Threat)

The first proposition is the view of some commentators that China will break up or collapse. Evidence offered includes the breakup of the former Soviet Union. These commentators aver that a corpus of fraternal countries cannot withstand the separation of one of them, and China therefore will not stand alone. It is true that Chinese socialism is based on a nation-building model learned from the former Soviet Union. However, in the process of freeing citizens from socialism and the planned economy, Chinese-style pragmatism—"feeling the stones while crossing the river"—has succeeded. It is wrong to conclude that the precedent of breakup in the former Soviet Union bears significant similarity to the situation of China.

Another justification offered for the proposition of China's impending collapse is sentimentalism over the notion that China is naturally impelled by the dynamic romanticized in the *Three Kingdoms*: "What is long united, must divide; what is long divided, must unite." Considering the fifty-year history of unity of the People's Republic of China (PRC), it is

1

averred that the hands of China's historical clock have reached "time." This is a somewhat philosophical point of view; however, it manifests a misapprehension of reality. Indeed, it is more correct to see China as being in a "unification" period. We observe that the forces militating toward greater centralization and unity are far stronger than those militating toward devolution or separation of powers. One only needs to observe the portrayal of the handover of Hong Kong—Hong Kong's "return to the motherland"—to appreciate the unifying power of Chinese nationalism.

The corollary, converse proposition is that China is a strategic threat: A unified China is a threat. This argument has several threads. The first is the view of anticommunists who maintain that China retains a totalitarian character. The second is the belief that China, possessing nuclear weapons, seeks to be the regional hegemonic power. The third is the contention that as an economic power China will become a source of instability in the global economy. In addition, there is the "clash of civilizations" school. This is the argument that Confucian civilization will join with Islamic civilization to challenge Christian civilization. Finally, there is the "neighboring country threat" hypothesis: By its very existence, China presents a threat to its neighbors.

It is certainly true that politically and militarily China is consciously and deliberately becoming a great power. This is partly because China feels it is a weak country and itself feels threatened. The crux of the problem is a vicious cycle of mutual suspicion. With an increase of dialogue on national defense issues, the futility of mutual hostility will become evident. The proposition of a Chinese strategic threat is replete with misunderstanding and bias. Economically, China's rapid economic growth is not a threat to the Asian region; rather, it should be taken as an opportunity to join in dynamic development.

The Proposition of China's Food Crisis

This theme got much play immediately after the publication of *Who Will Feed China?* by Lester Brown, director of the World Watch Institute. It happened that in 1994, due to natural disasters, Chinese grain production dropped 11.39 million tons below the previous year. Further, prices rose dramatically due to the error in judgment of pushing too quickly to commercialize the grain distribution system. A series of countermeasures were implemented to deal with the situation, including suspension of corn exports and import of a large volume of wheat. Against this backdrop the mistaken view that Mr. Brown's warning was valid spread. However, as we point out in Chapter 7, a study of the concrete figures on population, arable land, and consumption of animal protein clearly shows that the "food problem" is not a "crisis" or even a "threat." If agricultural problems were disregarded and left unattended for a long period, then descent into crisis is conceivable. However, we can observe in actual performance the fruits of Chinese authorities' diligent attention to these problems. Incidentally, in 1996 grain production volume exceeded 500 million tons for the first time in history; per capita grain production reached 414 kilograms. These were targets previously set by the Chinese government for the year 2000.

The Proposition of a Chinese Energy Crisis or Environmental Crisis

The third proposition is that of a Chinese energy crisis or environmental crisis. This is a variant of the food crisis. Although basic self-sufficiency in food is not a problem, there does exist a problem with supply of energy (see Chapter 8). Imports of oil are increasing, and acid rain and carbon dioxide levels are inevitably increasing due to continued high use of coal. To say that the burden to the world's environment of the economic take-off of 1.3 billion people is unsustainable is ridiculous. And to single out China's energy problem for attack is unfair. It is no more unfair to say that the clamor for global environmental protection reflects developed-country egoism. The contradiction between development and despoliation of nature is serious, but we should see that only through economic development will the material conditions to deal with environmental problems be created. An environmental protection policy that seeks to leapfrog the development of these conditions is impractical.

The Proposition of a Chinese Economic "Bubble"

Here the reality is more complex. Since China embarked on its reform and liberalization policy in 1979, we have seen spurts of frenetic economic activity, rising prices, and widespread speculative behavior followed by slowdowns (see Chapter 6). To date the slowdowns—including the most important, the one being seen as this book goes to press in 1998—have been generally successful "soft landings." It is certainly true that the system of market socialism is fundamentally flawed in that it is, in a real sense, capitalism without capitalists. Its actors are usually playing with other people's money (OPM), which means that they are not as risk-averse as are people who place their personal assets at risk. The result of the OPM mentality (not just in China, but anywhere) is almost always overinvestment and, later, severe correction. This happened in the U.S. real estate market during the late 1980s, even when there were real capitalists involved.

Overinvestment and excess capacity (often for the first time in Chinese history) are now a feature of the Chinese economy. The situation in real estate, especially in the major cities, certainly qualifies under the description of "bubble." The correction in real estate has begun and will be a factor for the next few years.

Overinvestment and excess capacity, and the resulting economic corrections, usually take a heavy toll from providers of credit, notably banks. This is certainly true in China, where, as we see in Chapter 19, the banking system has been the key conduit for investment funding. Chinese banks have huge portfolios of bad loans and meager or negative capital resources. And as reform of state-owned enterprises (SOEs) proceeds with bankruptcies and mergers, the Chinese banks will have to recognize losses and seek new capital resources.

Notwithstanding the above, the Chinese economy as a whole is not a bubble about to burst, for two reasons. First, with a savings rate of 40 percent of gross domestic product (GDP), the economy's ability to renew itself is enormous. Most Western economists, particularly U.S. economists, having no experience with such high domestic savings rates, have difficulty fathoming this reality. Second, China will continue to grow quickly. The Chinese economy now appears to be catching up with the Japanese economy during its high-growth period. We see the economy going through a stage like that seen during the first half of Japan's thirty-year high-growth era. At least for the next twenty to thirty years, there is a very strong possibility of continuing with close to double-digit growth. The Japanese bubble burst, but the basic tempo of Chinese growth will continue.

The Proposition of China's Huge Domestic Market

Here we will join the "realists" against the "visionaries." It is probably true that most companies that have ventured into China to manufacture and sell goods have been disappointed. Somehow, the market they expected was not there.

The reasons are multiple and complex. First, as we point out in Chapters 10 and 11, China is a country of vast disparities in income among regions and between cities and the countryside. Most of China's people remain poor in terms of cash income translatable into purchases of goods and services. For most Chinese consumers, therefore, the types of goods many foreign companies want to sell are out of reach. A famous example is automobiles. The entire Chinese market for passenger sedans in 1997 was some 500,000 vehicles. It is said that individuals become buyers of cars when family income reaches US$4,000 per year. In this case, instead of a market of China's 1.2 billion people, the potential market is roughly 5–6 million people, about the size of the market in Massachusetts.

A second reality that has visited itself harshly on some foreign firms is that China at present, for all practical purposes, is not one vast market but dozens, hundreds, even thousands of small markets. This high level of market segmentation results from the "protectionist" behavior of local officials who favor local firms and block the products of firms outside their cities, districts, or provinces; from highly varied local consumer tastes and preferences; from very high price elasticities of demand for many products; and from logistical and distribution barriers and problems.

A third reality is that local Chinese companies can be fiercely and successfully competitive. During the late 1980s and early 1990s foreign, particularly Japanese, manufacturers of household appliances, including color TVs, entered China expecting to repeat the success they achieved in dominating markets in Southeast Asia, except on a record-breaking scale. After early gains, they rapidly lost market share and money to local competitors. In 1997 China's leading color-TV manufacturer was Changhong Electronics from Sichuan, with close to 40 percent market share. In 1998 Changhong's market share approached 50 percent. Listed on the Shanghai stock exchange, Changhong has been able to raise huge amounts of capital to invest in capacity and to lower unit costs while leading price competition. Foreign competitors, afraid to risk too much capital, have increasingly been marginalized in the competition.

The bottom line is that China's market is a tough market and a smaller market than is often believed and touted (not least by Chinese officials seeking investment or new concessions).

The Proposition of Chinese "Country Risk"

Periodically, and particularly since the Asian financial crisis, we have heard much concern expressed about "country risk" for China. The reality is that in terms of standard measures of country or sovereign risk, China is a very low risk country (see Chapter 28). However, if we take a more comprehensive approach to risk and look at overall business investment risk, then China is, if anything, highly risky.

To gauge standard country risk—the holy trinity of war and revolution, expropriation, and inconvertibility and nontransferability—we consider issues of political stability, government policy, and national accounts, especially net foreign debt and the balance of payments. At the end of 1997 China's foreign debt stood at US$131 billion, making China the world's third largest debtor. However, at the same time, China's official foreign exchange reserves exceeded US$140 billion, meaning that as a holder of foreign exchange reserves China is in second place worldwide behind Japan. Unofficial foreign exchange holdings, primarily by Chinese individuals, in the form of bank deposits are of a similar magnitude. This means that China could without difficulty repay its entire foreign debt in cash. Add to this continuing strength in the balance of payments due to strong and stable exports and large inflows of direct foreign investment, and the picture must objectively be considered excellent.

Yet for companies investing and doing business in China, there is another reality. It is the fragmented, often protected domestic market, intense competition (including from rampant smuggling), operational problems caused by the prevalent joint-venture form of investment, logistical and distribution barriers, changing regulations, often arbitrary government actions, an unreliable legal system, and, in general, the distortions and pernicious economic consequences of the socialist market system. Taken together, these conditions produce risks that are exceptionally difficult to measure, and even more difficult to mitigate. So China, as a place to do business, is very risky. Many (if not most) companies will lack the ability to manage such risks, and, in any event, cannot expect potential returns from investments to be high enough to justify taking the risk in the first place.

What we see from these seven propositions is that China is not a specter threatening the West; neither is it the El Dorado for world business in the twenty-first century. China is an exceptionally large and increasingly politically, militarily, and economically important country in the world, particularly in the Asian region. We would hazard to suggest those propounding the "China threat" and predicting the "China collapse" are evidencing a specter within themselves. What they offer is nothing more than a slightly retouched version of the long discredited "yellow peril" theory. When exposed to the light of evidence the specter will be banished. This book is intended to help readers to understand the realities of the Chinese economy, to help them form an objective view of China's role in the world of the future.

—*Yabuki and Harner*

Part One

Toward a Basic Understanding of the Chinese Economy

1

A Huge Country

An Amalgamation of "Small Countries"

China's Area and Population
in Global Perspective

When Mao Zedong was young he admitted to dreaming of founding the "Republic of Hunan." After the founding of the People's Republic of China, Mao repeatedly revived this youthful dream. In the essay "On the Ten Great Relationships" (1956) he spoke of the proper relationship between the provinces and Central as being one of limited local autonomy. During the Great Leap Forward (1958–1960) the dream of a communal system was realized in the people's communes. During the Cultural Revolution period (1966–1976) he spoke of establishing a Shanghai commune.

The origin of Mao's dream is the notion of "small nations with few people" in a "titular ruler republic."

> In the end, a titular ruler republic is best. Both the queen of England and the emperor of Japan are titular rulers in titular ruler republics. In the end, it is best for Central to be a titular ruler, responsible only for the setting of broad political policy. The broad political policy should be formulated based on opinions collected from the localities. Central should make policy as though it were a processing factory using raw materials from the regions. Central can only set policy after actively eliciting the opinions from the provincial and county levels. In other words, Central should manage "form" only, and not "substance." (Mao Zedong, *Long Live Mao Zedong Thought*, p. 638)

> What would happen if no one died? If today, Confucius were still living, the earth could not support humanity. We should applaud the behavior of Zhuang Zi who joyfully beat a tray when his wife died. We should hold celebrations at funerals and toast the victory of the dialectic. Isn't this a celebration of the destruction of old things? (Mao Zedong, "Talks on Some Philosophical Questions," in *Long Live Mao Zedong Thought*, p. 559)

Anyone contemplating the hugeness of China becomes a philosopher.

9

Another United Nations: "The Chinese Confederation of States"

Figure 1.1 presents China's land area and population shares of the world's totals. With land area covering more than 7 percent of the globe, China is second after Russia, followed by Canada, the United States, and Brazil. What about population? Of the world's 5,673 million people, more than 21 percent are Chinese. In other words, one-fifth of the people on the planet are Chinese. However, China has implemented a rigid, one-child-per-family restriction, and it is forecast that by the middle of the twenty-first century the population of India will surpass that of China. With 21 percent of the world's people occupying just 7 percent of total land area, China's population density is three times the world average.

Comparing Shanghai and Singapore, we see that Shanghai's land area is ten times that of Singapore, whereas its population is nearly five times greater. Comparing the industrial province in China's northeast, Liaoning, to South Korea, we see that it is about 50 percent larger in land area yet has roughly 10 percent fewer people. Guangdong province is China's southern gateway. It has a land area some 60 percent of that of the Philippines, whereas the population is almost equal (roughly 70 million). The formerly combined administrative areas of Chongqing municipality and Sichuan province (separated in 1997 as Chongqing became a municipality directly subordinate to Beijing) had a population of more than 100 million, nearly equal to that of Japan (whereas Sichuan's land area was some 50 percent greater than that of Japan). The directly administered municipality of Chongqing has a population of some 30 million, so the population of former Sichuan is reduced by this number.

We may allow ourselves to imagine that within a single country, China, we have entities like Singapore, South Korea, the Philippines, and Japan. Were we to continue, we could draw parallels for more than thirty "countries." Mao Zedong at one time compared China to "another United Nations." There is, indeed, this aspect of China.

China has more than 54 minority peoples, and even the Han race differs significantly in language and eating habits from north to south and east to west. It is impractical to apply common perceptions of the modern nation-state when speaking about this huge a country.

China's Provinces—Like Separate Countries

Let us take this idea further and compare the land areas of China's province-level administrative units with those of other Asian countries. With the largest area of all China's provinces, the Xinjiang Uigur Autonomous Region is smaller than Indonesia but larger than Iran. The Tibet

FIGURE 1.1 China's Share of World Territory and Population

World territory: Total 130,310,000 sq. km. (1994)

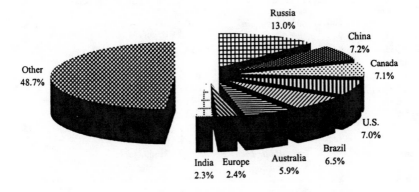

World population: 5,673,000,000 persons (1995)

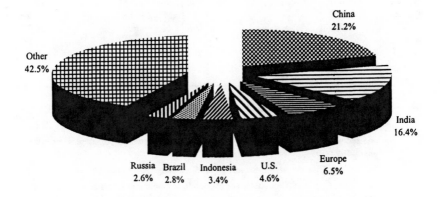

Source: The World Bank, *World Development Indicators, 1997.*

and Inner Mongolia Autonomous Regions are smaller than Mongolia but larger than Pakistan. Qinghai province is between Turkey and Myanmar, Sichuan province is between Afghanistan and Yemen, Heilongjiang and Gansu provinces are between Turkmenistan and Uzbekistan. The area of Yunnan province is slightly larger than Japan's total area, Guangxi Autonomous Region is roughly the size of Laos. Among the smaller regions, Ningxia Hui Autonomous Region is larger than Butan. Beijing, Tianjin, and Shanghai municipalities are about the same size as Kuwait, Qatar, and Brunei, respectively.

TABLE 1.1 Comparison of Per Capita GNP of Asian Countries and China's Province-Level Administrative Units   (unit: U.S. dollars)

Low Income		Shanxi	505	Jordan	1,510
Nepal	200	Inner Mongolia	510	Tianjin	1,529
Vietnam	240	Hubei	613	Beijing	1,801
Bangladesh	240	Jilin	618	Lebanon	2,660
Guizhou	251	Xinjiang	619	Shanghai	2,667
Yemen	260	China (whole)	620	Thailand	2,740
Cambodia	270	Hebei	640	Turkey	2,780
Mongolia	310	Hainan	659		
Tibet	327	Sri Lanka	700	Upper Middle Income	
India	340	Armenia	730	Malaysia	3,890
Gansu	347			Oman	4,820
Laos	350	Low Middle Income		Saudi Arabia	7,040
Shaanxi	397	Heilongjiang	774	Bahrain	7,840
Butan	420	Shandong	818		
Yunnan	445	Turkmenistan	920	High Income	
Jiangxi	445	Liaoning	926	South Korea	9,700
Ningxia	`447	Uzbekistan	970	Taiwan	12,439
Qinghai	449	Fujian	974	Israel	15,920
Sichuan	451	Indonesia	980	Kuwait	17,390
Pakistan	460	Jiangsu	1,011	Hong Kong	22,990
Anhui	465	Philippines	1,050	Singapore	26,730
Azerbaijan	480	Syria	' 1,120	Japan	39,640
Henan	483	Zhejiang	1,132		
Guangxi	489	Guangdong	1,139		
Hunan	495				

Notes: • Chinese province-level units and whole China in italics.

• Chinese provincial 1995 per capita GDP converted at the 1995 average RMB/US$ rate.

• Asia and whole China per capita GNP rate converted at average exchange rate for three years, 1993–1995.

• Whole China GNP converted at average 1995 exchange rate equals US$569.

• The following is the differentiation of economic development levels according to the United Nations (in US$): (a) low income country—below $765; (b) lower middle income country—$766–$2,895; (c) upper middle income country—$3,036–$9,385; (d) high income country—above $9,386.

Sources: For China: *China Statistical Yearbook* 1997; for Taiwan: *Taiwan Statistical Data Book* 1996; for Asia: *World Bank Indicators*, *1997*.

What if we compare the populations of China's province-level administrative units with those of Asian countries (data for China from *China Statistical Yearbook* 1966; data for other countries from United Nations publications)? Starting from the smallest, Tibet (2.38 million) is close to Mongolia (2.46 million), Qinghai province (4.74 million) and the Ningxia Hui Autonomous Region (5.09 million) are close to Laos. Hainan province and Tianjin municipality are close to Azerbaijan. Beijing (12 million) and

Shanghai (14 million) municipalities are at the same level as Yemen. The Xinjiang Autonomous Region is a little smaller than Kazakhstan. Inner Mongolia, Gansu, Jilin, Shanxi, Fujian, Guizhou, Shaanxi, Heilongjiang, Yunnan, Jiangxi, Liaoning, and Zhejiang provinces have populations between 20 and 40 million, falling between North Korea (24 million) and South Korea (45 million). The Guangxi Autonomous Region (45 million) is on par with Myanmar; Hubei (57 million) and Anhui (60 million) provinces with Iran (68 million); and Hunan, Hebei, and Guangdong provinces with the Philippines (70 million). Jiangsu (70 million), Shandong (87 million), and Henan (91 million) provinces are close to Vietnam (74 million).

Table 1.1 is an attempt to present a comparison in terms of per capita gross national product (GNP). China as a whole, with per capita income of US$620 (U.S. dollars are used throughout this book unless otherwise specified), is ranked as a "low income country" (below US$765). Twenty province-level administrative units could be assigned to the "low income country" category. The lowest is Guizhou province at US$251, followed by Tibet at $327. At the same time, however, ten province-level units have reached the "low middle income country" ($776–$2,895) level: Heilongjiang, Shandong, Fujian, Jiangsu, Guangdong, Zhejiang, Liaoning, Tianjin, Beijing, and Shanghai. At the top is Shanghai with $2,667 (this reached $3,000 in 1997). Of course, Hong Kong, now returned to the motherland, is in the "high income country" category. In short, China's regions have attained income levels ranging from among the highest to among the lowest by world standards. Thus, China is an amalgam of "small countries" constituting a whole, distinct world.

—Yabuki

2
Population Pressure

The Challenge of
1.6 Billion People in 2030

The Chinese Population Pyramid

Let us look at China's population pyramid as of October 1, 1995 (Figure 2.1).

Generation Born During the Anti-Japanese War

There was previously a clear compression during this war period. What appears now is a only a pattern of virtually no population growth.

Period of Economic Recovery

This was the postwar baby boom. Population grew rapidly as the economy of the newly established state enjoyed rapid recovery under political stability after the long war.

Period of Natural Disasters

This is the period of the so-called three consecutive years of natural disasters (actually manmade disasters) following the Great Leap Forward. The reality of widespread famine-related deaths in the weakest—newborns—is visible. A spokesman for the State Statistics Bureau stated on September 13, 1984, that more than 10 million people died from starvation due to manmade factors and natural disasters during the Great Leap Forward. Knowledgeable estimates place the death toll at roughly 20 million.

Cultural Revolution Period

From the period of economic adjustment that began in 1962 through the first half of the Cultural Revolution, in the context of growing political

16

FIGURE 2.1 Population Pyramid from the October 1, 1995, Census
           (1 percent sampling)

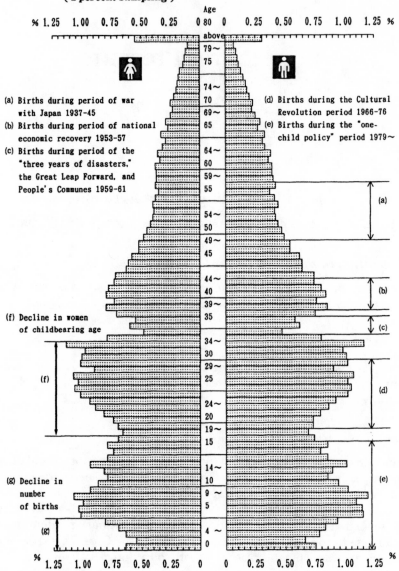

Source: China Statistical Yearbook 1996, p.72.

disorder, the birthrate rose substantially (the second baby boom). A birth control system was instituted during the second half of the Cultural Revolution, and the effects of state-mandated birth control began to surface.

The One-Child Policy

In the first half of the Deng Xiaoping era, starting in 1978, a fairly coercive one-child-per-family policy was implemented. There followed a striking drop in the population's growth rate. By the second half of the 1980s opposition to the population control policy compelled the state to grant a policy exception, in villages only, permitting families to have two children if the firstborn was a girl. Also there was an increase in "black children" (*hei haizi*)—children not registered under the family registration (*hukou*) system and therefore unrecognized—which further shook the population control regime. However, during the 1990s, birthrates have rapidly declined. The drop in births in 1994 was particularly remarkable. That reflected the firm grounding of the one-child policy together with a drop in the childbearing population of eighteen- to thirty-two-year-old women (State Statistics Bureau, *China Population Yearbook* 1995, p. 347).

Population Trends Since 1949

Figure 2.2 presents in graphic form the increase in both rural and urban populations. Starting at 540 million in 1949, China's population reached 600 million in 1954, 700 million in 1964, 800 million in 1969, 900 million in 1974, and broke 1 billion in 1981. In 1988 it surpassed 1.1 billion, and in 1995 1.2 billion. The 1.2-billion level had been a population control policy target for the year 2000; a new target of 1.3 billion has been substituted. At the end of 1996 the population stood at 1,223,890,000.

If we try to create a rough model of the PRC's population growth, we find that during the 1950s the average annual increase was 20 million (a total of 200 million for the decade), during the 1960s 25 million (total 250 million), during the 1970s 20 million (total 200 million), and during the 1980s 15 million (total 150 million). In aggregate, in just more than forty years there were some 800 million births; subtracting deaths, population increased by 600 million.

Figure 2.3 presents the natural population growth rate (birthrate minus death rate) divided into four phases. Phase one is the first period of growth from 1950 through 1957. The birthrate remained high while the death rate steadily dropped, thus producing a high 2 percent rate of natural increase. The second phase, 1958 to 1961, was an abnormal period that included a drop in the natural increase rate to a negative in 1960. This was because of the economic crisis. The third phase, 1962 to 1971, was the

18

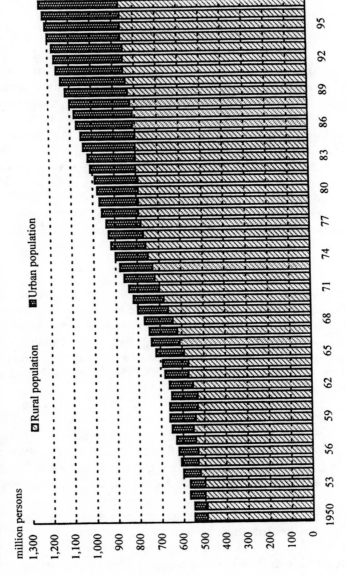

FIGURE 2.2 Trends in China's Total Population, 1950–1997

million persons

☒ Rural population   ▣ Urban population

Sources: China Statistical Yearbook 1991, 1997; "Bulletin on National Economic and Social Development for 1997," *Economic Daily*, March 5, 1998.

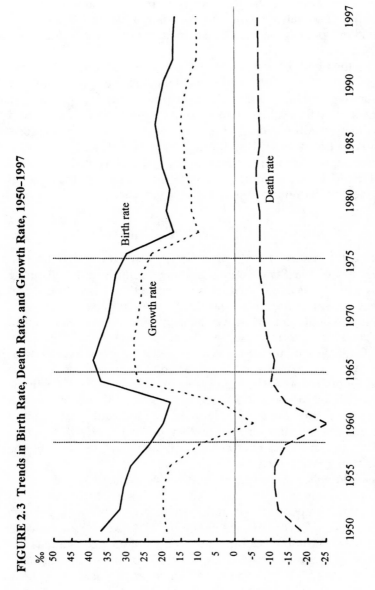

FIGURE 2.3 Trends in Birth Rate, Death Rate, and Growth Rate, 1950–1997

Sources: China Statistical Yearbook 1991, 1997; "Bulletin on National Economic and Social Development for 1997," *Economic Daily*, March 5, 1998.

second period of rapid population growth. The birthrate recovered strongly after the previous period while the death rate remained fairly stable. The result was a natural increase rate as high as 3 percent (this was the turning point from a society of "many births and many deaths" to "few births and few deaths"). The fourth phase was 1971 to 1997, a period of stable and low population growth. During this period the birthrate fell to developed-country levels.

Observing the trends of population, we recognize that during the forty-seven years from 1950 to 1997 China has followed the general rule for countries undergoing rapid economic development, moving from a stage of high rates of births and deaths to a stage of low rates of births and deaths. We may view this process as having been compressed by the coercive population policy. From 1992 through 1994 the natural increase rate was 1.1 percent; in 1995 to 1996 the rate fell to 1.0 percent. China's is a successful model for birth control. However, this means that the aging of China's society will soon progress at a frightening pace.

China's Model for Birth Control

Let us review the history of birth control in China. At the end of the Mao Zedong era in 1973 the State Council Leading Group for Birth Planning (i.e., birth control) was established. This came at a time when official policy was yet critical of theories regarding "population explosion" and "global resource depletion." However, a real population explosion was in clear view, and birth control soon began in earnest. In February 1978, Premier Hua Guofeng announced the goal of "reducing the rate of population's natural growth rate to less than 1 percent within three years" in his government work report to the National People's Congress (NPC). In the constitution ratified in March 1978, article 53 specified that "the state advocates and shall promote family planning." At a meeting of local and Central heads of the Office for Family Planning in January 1979, in the first proposal of a one-child policy, "the ideal family of a couple and one child" was strongly endorsed.

The one-child policy was implemented relatively smoothly in the cities. This had much to do with the prevalence of both spouses working outside the home, cramped living conditions, and the retirement pension system for workers. In contrast, the policy encountered stiff resistance in the countryside. Traditional Chinese thinking that "four generations under one roof" (i.e., a big family) is a source of happiness and "the more sons, the more blessings" is deep-rooted. Moreover, the "family responsibility system" in agriculture means that the more laboring hands, the easier for all. Even today, implementing the one-child policy in the countryside requires desperate efforts.

Let us examine the success of China's birth control program as evidenced in the statistics.

Table 2.1 presents the rate of receipt of the "one-child certificate." The national average rate of receipt is 20 percent. That is to say, one in five married women has received the certificate. However, there is much disparity beneath the national average figure: In general, we see that the higher the income level of the locality, the better performance, and the poorer the region, the worse the performance. The rate of "late marriage" (calculated by figuring the percentage of women over the age of twenty-three in the total number of women being married for the first time) is

TABLE 2.1 Ratio of Receipt of One-Child and Late-Marriage Certificates

(unit: thou. persons, %)

Province, City, or Auto. Region	Married Women of Childbearing Age (a)	Recipients of One-Child Certificate (b)	Certificate Receipt Rate (b) / (a)	Total First Married Women (c)	Of Which 23 Years Old or Over (d)	Late Marr-iage Ratio (d) / (c)
Beijing	2,290	1,390	60.5	71	60	85.5
Tianjin	1,980	1,000	50.6	59	37	62.8
Hebei	12,980	1,480	11.4	348	180	51.8
Shanxi	5,770	800	13.8	189	122	64.5
Inner Mongolia	4,760	690	14.4	171	125	72.5
Liaoning	9,010	3,850	42.7	266	164	61.6
Jilin	6,700	1,750	25.1	163	80	49.1
Heilongjiang	7,800	2,370	30.4	232	113	48.9
Shanghai	2,790	1,950	70.0	72	45	62.4
Jiangsu	14,960	6,760	45.2	426	300	70.6
Zhejiang	9,540	2,240	23.4	332	245	73.7
Anhui	11,240	1,220	10.8	465	315	67.7
Fujian	6,400	850	13.3	227	113	49.7
Jiangxi	7,800	750	9.6	300	88	29.6
Shandong	17,250	4,530	26.3	634	628	99.1
Henan	18,060	1,840	10.2	663	444	67.0
Hubei	10,540	1,810	17.2	333	164	49.3
Hunan	12,580	1,390	11.1	503	209	41.7
Guangdong	12,650	1,160	9.2	504	361	71.6
Guangxi	7,560	490	6.5	272	167	61.5
Hainan	1,130	90	7.6	36	24	66.9
Sichuan	23,260	7,750	33.3	957	328	34.4
Guizhou	5,960	410	6.8	207	108	52.5
Yunnan	7,150	590	8.3	280	120	42.9
Shaanxi	6,600	780	11.8	218	125	57.3
Gansu	4,930	490	10.0	170	80	47.1
Qinghai	900	110	12.2	30	16	53.7
Ningxia	990	120	12.3	40	18	45.5
Xinjiang	2,960	400	13.4	104	85	82.4
Total	236,840	49,060	20.7	8,270	4,867	58.9

Source: China Population Statistics Yearbook 1996, pp. 419–421.

TABLE 2.2 Methods of Contraception in China, 1995

(unit: thou. persons, %)

Method	Vasectomy	Female sterilization surgery	IUD	Implant	Pills	Condom	Diaphragm	Other	Total
Number	22,630	85,480	89,190	670	6,260	8,050	1,110	730	214,110
Proportion	10.6	39.9	41.7	0.3	2.9	3.8	0.5	0.3	100.0

Source: China Population Statistics Yearbook 1996, pp. 422-423.

near 60 percent on national average. But, as we expect, there is great regional disparity, with rich regions having a higher figure.

Table 2.2 presents methods of contraception in China. The most popular is the intrauterine device (IUD) at about 42 percent, followed by surgical sterilization of women at about 40 percent, showing that women are making the greatest efforts at contraception. Vasectomies for men constitute only about 10 percent, and condoms and birth control pills, together, are less than 7 percent.

FIGURE 2.4 Forecast of the World and China's Population Growth by the United Nations (middle-level case)

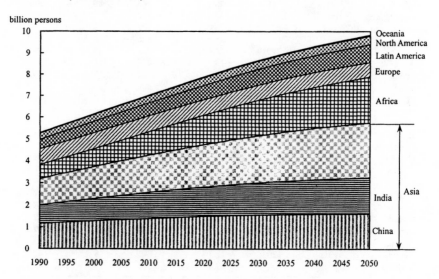

Source: UN, *World Population Prospects* (1994 revision).

Population Projection for
the Twenty-first Century

According to the UN's midrange population projection for China (UN, *World Populations Prospects*, 1994 rev.), China's population will peak at 1.6 billion in 2050. China itself forecasts reaching the 1.6 billion peak in 2030, declining thereafter. In terms of timing, these forecasts diverge by 20 years, but, based on the one-child policy, they arrive at the same population peak: 1.6 billion. The population of India is expected to overtake that of China between 2040 and 2050. The rates of increase of China and India are in stark contrast, evidencing the success of China's birth control regime.

Figure 2.4 presents the UN forecast for the five continents, distinguishing India and China in Asia. Whereas the parameter for Europe remains virtually unchanged, we see that Africa experiences a great expansion. The largest population is in Asia, particularly India and China. In considering the future global environment, we should realize that population is one of the most important factors.

—Yabuki

3

The Volatile History of "Chinese Socialism"

The Mao Zedong and Deng Xiaoping Eras

Founded on October 1, 1949, the People's Republic of China in 1999 will celebrate the fiftieth anniversary of its birth. To use the metaphor of a human's life span, this is the age of robust strength. In the context of China's long history, however, it is hardly more than the blink of the eye. The PRC's history can be divided into the Mao Zedong era (1949–1976) and the Deng Xiaoping era (1979–1997), with the Hua Guofeng regime briefly sandwiched between the two. In fact, due to Deng Xiaoping's weakening health, the period after 1994 is actually the Jiang Zemin era (Figure 3.1).

The twenty-seven years of the Mao Zedong era were marked by the periods of the Great Leap Forward (1958–1960) and the Cultural Revolution (1966–1976). During these, Mao Zedong took personal command in attempting to realize "utopian socialism." Preceding these two cataclysmic periods, in the mid-1950s and the first half of the 1960s, there were intervals of stable development in which Zhou Enlai, Liu Shaoqi, Chen Yun, Deng Xiaoping, and other moderates were collectively dominating policy. The radicalism advocated by Mao Zedong was in conflict with the policy of steady advance advocated by pragmatists. The situation was one in which Mao Zedong's influence was dominant, and the pragmatists found themselves in a position of opposition.

Entering the Deng Xiaoping era, the previously dominant utopian socialism ideology was rejected, and in its place "seeking truth from facts" and "reform and liberalization" became the dominant lines. In the beginning this change occurred quietly, sometimes imperceptibly. However, Deng Xiaoping's line—abandoning central planning and moving toward a market economy—became clear when the "theory of the early stage of socialism" was adopted at the Thirteenth Party Congress, convened in October 1987, yet further when the "theory of the market socialism" was adopted by the Fourteenth Party Congress in 1992. In November 1993 the

FIGURE 3.1 Vicissitudes in Line Since the Establishment of the PRC — from the Revolution Generation to the Third Generation

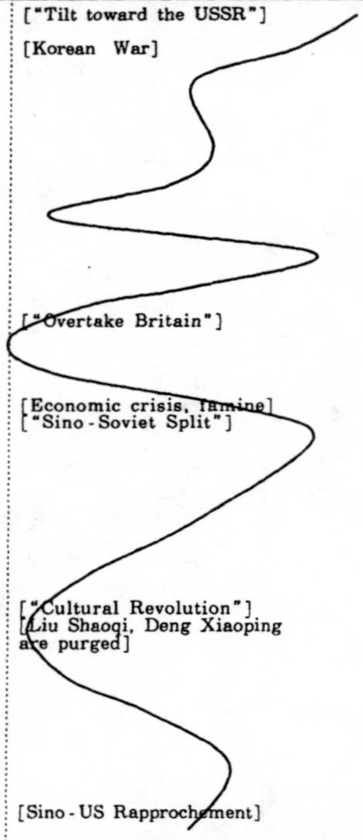

Year	Five Year Plan Period	Period	<-Left Tilt	Line	Right Tilt->
1949		Period of Recovery		["Tilt toward the USSR"] [Korean War]	Oct. 49 Establishment of the People's Republic of China
1950			Oct. 50 Oppose America Aid Korea Campaign		
1951			Nov. 51 Three-Anti Five-Anti Campaign		
1952					
1953	First Five Year Plan		Aug. 53 General Line for transition period		
1954			Dec. 53 Agricultural production cooperatives		
1955			May 55 Criticism of Hu Feng		
1956			1955 Collectivization of agriculture		May 56 "Hundred Flowers"
1957			Jun. 57 Anti-Rightist struggle		Sep. 56 Eighth Party Congress
1958	Second Five Year Plan	Great Leap Forward Period	Aug. 58 People's Commune Campaign	["Overtake Britain"]	
1959					Apr. 59 Liu Shaoqi becomes president [Liu Shaoqi Line]
1960					
1961				[Economic crisis, famine] ["Sino-Soviet Split"]	
1962	Period of Readjustment				Jan. 62 Mao Zedong's self-criticism. Debate over class struggle
1963			1963-64 Sino-Soviet Debate		1962 Deng Xiaoping's "White Cat, Black Cat" doctrine
1964			1964 Four Purity Campaign		
1965			Nov. 65 Criticism of "The Dismissal of Hai Rui"		
1966	Third Five Year Plan	Cultural Revolution	Aug. 66 Decision on the Great Proletarian Cultural Revolution	["Cultural Revolution". Liu Shaoqi, Deng Xiaoping are purged]	
1967					
1968					
1969			Apr. 69 Ninth Party Congress [Lin Biao designated successor]		
1970					
1971	Fourth Five Year Plan			[Sino-US Rapprochement]	Sep. 71 Lin Biao dies while escaping after attempted assassination of Mao Zedong
1972					Sep. 72 Japan and China restore diplomatic relations

Year	Five Year Plan Period	Period	Left Tilt	Line	Right Tilt
1973	Fifth Five Year Plan		Aug. 73 Criticism of Confucius (The Gang of Four criticize Zhou Enlai)		Oct. 74 Deng Xiaoping is rehabilitated
1974					
1975			Aug. 75 Criticism of The Water Margin (The Gang of Four criticize Deng Xiaoping)		
1976			Apr. 76 '76 Tiananmen Incident (Deng Xiaoping purged, Hua Guofeng designated Successor)	[Mao Zedong Dies]	Jan. 76 Zhou Enlai dies / Oct. 76 Gang of Four arrested
1977		Deng Xiaoping Era			Jul. 77 Deng Xiaoping rehabilitated
1978				Deng Xiaoping Leads Main Faction [The Four Modernizations] [Foreign Opening, Domestic Revitalization]	Dec. 78 Third Plenum 11th Party Congress Central Committee
1979			Jan. 79 Four Basic Principles / Dec. 79 Democracy Wall prohibited		Jul. 79 Special economic zones established
1980					May 80 Liu Shaoqi's reputation restored
1981	Sixth Five Year Plan		Apr. 81 Criticism of Bai Hua's "Kulian"		Jun. 81 Historic decisions of the Sixth Plenum of the 11th Central Committee
1982					Sep. 82 12th Party Congress [Hu Yaobang made general secretary, Deng Xiaoping becomes chairman of Military Affairs Committee]
1983			Oct. 83 Decision to reform the Party, oppose spiritual pollution		
1984					Apr. 84 Fourteen cities opened to foreign investment / Oct. 84 Decision on Reform of the Economic System
1985					Sep. 85 Party Congress
1986	Seventh Five Year Plan		Oct. 86 Decision on spiritual culture / Dec. 86 Student demonstrations		
1987			Jan. 87 Hu Yaobang purged, antibourgeois liberalism		Oct. 87 13th Party Congress [Zhao Ziyang becomes general secretary, generational transfer of leadership]
1988			Summer 88 Erratic price movements, panic buying		
1989			Jun. 89 Tiananmen Incident Zhao Ziyang purged, Jiang Zemin made general secretary		
1990					Jan. 90 Martial law in Beijing lifted
1991	Eighth Five Year Plan		Dec. 91 Soviet Union collapses		
1992				[Reform and liberalization line revived]	Oct. 92 14th Party Congress
1993			Anti-corruption struggle		
1994		Jiang Zemin Zhu Rongji Regime	1994 Consumer prices increase 24 percent	Jiang Zemin consolidates power [Reform, development, stability]	Sep. 94 Jiang Zemin becomes the Third Generation leader
1995			Apr. 95 Beijing mayor Chen Xitong resigns under corruption cloud		1995 GNP quadrupling plan achieved
1996	Ninth Five Year Plan				1996 Start of Ninth Five Year Plan
1997			Feb. 97 Deng Xiaoping dies	Hong Kong reverts to China	Sep. 97 15th Party Congress
1998				Zhu Rongji becomes premier	Mar. 98 Ninth National People's Congress

Third Plenum of the Fourteenth Party Congress Central Committee convened and adopted the "Decision of the Party Central Concerning Some Issues with the Establishment of a Socialist Market Economic System" (the "Fifty Articles"). This was the grand design for conversion to a market economy and institutionalizing the Deng Xiaoping line; its implementation has become the main theme of the current Jiang Zemin regime.

Distinct Periods Within the Mao Zedong Era

Let us attempt to explain the Mao Zedong era in very simple terms.

Phase One: Agricultural Collectivization

First was the agricultural collectivization campaign launched in the mid-1950s. Individual farms were reorganized into low-level cooperatives, high-level cooperatives, and finally into people's communes. The system was enforced for more than twenty years before the communes were broken up during the early 1980s, the farmlands being returned to individual family units under a "production responsibility system."

Phase Two: The Great Leap Forward Campaign (1958–1960)

In the din of voices shouting "overtake and surpass Britain" and "the road to communism is in sight" the people's communes were organized; crude technologies called "traditional Chinese methods" and mass mobilization of labor were employed—all in a frenetic pursuit of increased production. Mistakes in policy and natural disasters combined to create extreme food shortages, and deaths from starvation were recorded on a massive scale.

Phase Three: Period of Readjustment

Readjustment policies were implemented in response to the food and economic crises. Deng Xiaoping's famous "White Cat, Black Cat" doctrine (the cat that can catch a mouse is a good cat; the method that can raise production is a good method) expressed in vivid terms the essence of the readjustment policies. (It may be said that the "early stage of socialism" theory of the 1980s is actually a restatement of Deng Xiaoping's "theory of productive forces." At the same time, we know that the 1980s theory is more profound, having been evoked and informed by awareness of the gap in economic power compared with Taiwan and Hong Kong.)

Phase Four: The "Great Proletarian Cultural Revolution" (1966–1976)

"Pure socialism"—involving theories of "class struggle" and "priority of productive relations"—was pursued by Mao's adherents as a counterattack against revisionism; the ensuing turmoil and the extremes that were reached greatly impeded economic development.

Phase Five: The Hua Guofeng Period as the Post–Mao Zedong Period

With the death of Premier Zhou Enlai on January 8, 1976, the penultimate skirmishes in the palace revolution began. Shortly after the Qingming Festival in April, Deng Xiaoping was the first to fall. At first the extreme leftist Cultural Revolution faction was victorious. On September 9, in parallel with Mao Zedong's death, the moderate faction of Hua Guofeng (party chairman) enlisted the support of the faction of former actual power holders, including Ye Jianying (party vice chairman), to arrest the "Gang of Four," including Mao's wife, Jiang Qing. Thus was the extreme leftist faction defeated. Hua Guofeng avowed "the two alls" (i.e., respecting Mao Zedong's decisions in all matters) and advocated continuation of the Mao Zedong line, but the rehabilitation of Deng Xiaoping was only a matter of time. Rehabilitation occurred in July 1977, and by December 1978 Deng was leading the dominant faction.

Distinct Periods Within the Deng Xiaoping Era

Broadly speaking, the Deng Xiaoping era extended for eighteen years, from December 1978 to February 1997. Narrowly speaking, it extended for fifteen years, from 1979 to 1994. In the former, the period began with Deng Xiaoping's assuming leadership of the dominant faction at the Third Plenum of the Eleventh Party Congress Central Committee and ended with his death on February 19, 1997. The latter covers the period when Deng Xiaoping was directly orchestrating political and economic affairs. The Southern Excursion Talks during the spring of 1992 were Deng's "last call to battle," after which he gradually withdrew from the political scene, but he continued to have a strong influence on affairs. Jiang Zemin continued until the Fourth Plenum of the Fourteenth Party Congress Central Committee in September 1994 to seek Deng's approval on the major important policy decisions. In other words, it can be said that the post–Deng Xiaoping era (the Jiang Zemin era) actually began when the Fourth Plenum approved Deng's request that he "henceforth not be involved" in policy decisionmaking.

Figure 3.2 presents indicators explaining the basic currents of the Deng Xiaoping era. The top panel shows introduction of foreign capital and dependency on foreign trade. Both indicators show continuous increases. The middle-panel bar graph shows each year's GNP growth rate while the line graph indicates the rate of increase in retail prices. The bottom panel charts important events during the period.

The Deng Xiaoping era is divided into four phases: the five years of reform in the countryside; the five years of high growth in the mid-1980s; three years of economic adjustment; and the high growth period of the 1990s.

The first phase was a reform effort carried out primarily in the countryside during the first half of the 1980s. The main element was the dismantling of the people's communes. The people's commune system, organized along lines of "socialist collective agriculture," was touted as "a shortcut to communism." After collective agriculture floundered for more than twenty years, however, the decision was taken to return to a family-based "production responsibility system." In the beginning this contributed to township and village enterprise development and to the revitalization of the countryside. During the second phase, in the second half of the 1980s, reform and liberalization were begun in the cities and in industry. The most important component was the introduction of foreign capital through the establishment of foreign-invested enterprises (FIEs), principally in the coastal region. A large volume of capital was received from Hong Kong, the United States, Japan, and other sources. This funded the production of high-quality goods that were exported in exchange for foreign currency, and also satisfied a certain volume of domestic demand. The third period was the interval of tightening during the economic adjustment following the Tiananmen Incident. The fourth period is that of high continuous growth during the first half of the 1990s. Such was the advance of China's economy during the 1990s that China actually became an engine of growth for the world economy.

The Jiang Zemin System and the Path of "Reform and Liberalization"

Table 3.1 presents a view of generational succession among Chinese leaders. The era of Mao Zedong's first generation and its special characteristics are well known. It is possible to characterize the Deng Xiaoping generation as one that renounced the Cultural Revolution and launched reform and liberalization. During this period a major incident was the fall

FIGURE 3.2 Vicissitudes After the Policy of Reform and Liberalization

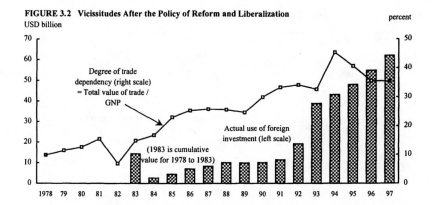

USD billion / percent

Degree of trade dependency (right scale) = Total value of trade / GNP

(1983 is cumulative value for 1978 to 1983)

Actual use of foreign investment (left scale)

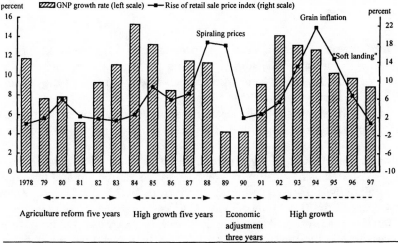

percent — GNP growth rate (left scale) — Rise of retail sale price index (right scale) — percent

Spiraling prices

Grain inflation

"Soft landing"

Agriculture reform five years   High growth five years   Economic adjustment three years   High growth

1978	Third plenum of the 11th CCP Central Committee. Deng Xiaoping takes control.	1991	Martial law lifted in Beijing and Lhasa.
1979	Establishment of special economic zones.	1992	Deng Xiaoping's remarks during his Southern Excursion restart reform and liberalization.
1980	Zhao Ziyang becomes premier.	1993	Fifty Articles program for transformation to a market economy adopted.
1981	Hu Yaobang in as general secretary.		
1983	Campaign against "spiritual pollution."	1994	Jiang Zemin succeeds Deng Xiaoping as preeminent leader.
1984	Fourteen coastal cities opened to the outside world.		
1987	"Resolution on spiritual civilization."	1995	Ninth Five Year Plan adopted.
1988	Zhao Ziyang becomes general secretary. Li Peng becomes permier.	1997	Fifteenth Party Congress. Beginning of Jiang Zemin-Zhu Rongji partnership.
1989	Tiananmen Incident. Jiang Zemin becomes general secretary.		

TABLE 3.1 Generational Change in China's Leadership

Generation	Core Leader	Characteristic	Main Challenges	Associate Leaders	Period
First	Mao Zedong (1893–1976)	Revolutionary	Revolution, nation-building	Zhou Enlai, Liu Shaoqi, Zhu De, and others	1949–1976
Second	Deng Xiaoping (1904–1997)	Pragmatist	Close Cultural Revolution period, reform and liberalization	Chen Yun, Yang Shangkun, Hu Yaobang, Zhao Ziyang, and others	1978–1992
Third	Jiang Zemin (1926–)	Technocrat	Conversion to a market economy	Li Peng, Qiao Shi, Zhu Rongji, Li Lanqing, and others	1992–

Source: Economic Daily, March 12, 1997.

(in the context of student demonstrations demanding democracy) of Hu Yaobang in January 1987 and (following the Tiananmen Incident) the purge of Zhao Ziyang in June 1989. In each case we observed the conservative faction applying a brake to the progress of reform and liberalization. For about three years after the Tiananmen Incident the process of reform and liberalization was arrested. The Southern Excursion Talks by Deng Xiaoping during an inspection of the Shenzhen and Zhuhai special economic zones in Guangdong province just before the 1992 Spring Festival were exploited as a basis upon which to revive the reform and liberalization policy. This ushered in high growth from 1992 to 1997. Deng Xiaoping observed firsthand the problem of succession to Mao Zedong, and he suffered in the process. After the experience, he was careful in grooming a successor. His final selection, Jiang Zemin, as a technocrat, has undertaken the task of transforming to a market economy. Jiang was party secretary in Shanghai in June 1989 when he was picked as general party secretary. Until the 1992 Spring Festival, a period when the conservative faction had dominant influence, Jiang busied himself exclusively with restoring stability. After the Southern Excursion Talks, Jiang's political stance changed, and he emerged as a proponent of the reform and liberalization program, eventually consolidating his leadership position in the post–Deng Xiaoping era. This leadership position was further buttressed by result of the Fifteenth Party Congress in September 1997.

—*Yabuki*

4

The Political System

The Role of the Chinese Communist Party as the "Conservative Party"

The Chinese Communist Party as the "Economic Development Party"

The Chinese Communist Party (CCP) was formed in 1921, swearing allegiance to the Communist revolution. After the founding of the PRC, the CCP pursued the goals of modernization through economic development and establishment of pure communism through repeated trial and error.

After the 1989–1991 collapse of socialist systems in the Soviet Union and Eastern Europe, the overwhelming emphasis of CCP policies became the economic development of China. This is seen in the emphasis on the market economic system as opposed to the socialist economic system, distribution according to capital and asset inputs as opposed to distribution according to labor inputs, and the call for efficient utilization of capital. In other words, despite adamantly maintaining the name of socialism, the CCP effectively blurred the distinctions between socialism and capitalism (the "Black Cat, White Cat" doctrine and criticism of the "surname capitalist, surname socialist" debate) and has adopted economic development of China as its highest policy priority. In this sense, the Chinese Communist Party is nothing other than the "Chinese Economic Development Party."

The organization of the CCP is roughly depicted in Figure 4.1. It is separated into three tiers: the Central organizations, provincial-level (county-level) organizations, and basic-level organizations. The key personnel are appointed directly by the respective superior levels; additional personnel decisions are made by the subordinate levels after the consent of the superior level. Through this personnel system, effective control and direction are exercised through the organizational structure from the Central

33

FIGURE 4. 1 Chinese Communist Party Organization Chart

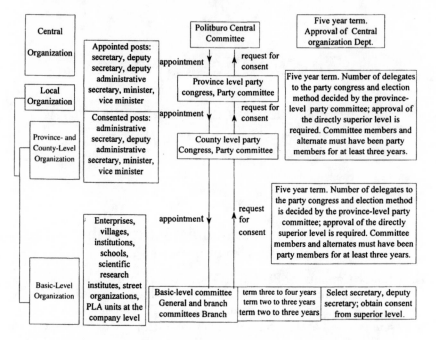

Source: Sun Benyao et al., *Record of the Fourteenth Party Congress*. Beijing: CCP Central Party School Press, 1992.

Politburo at the extreme top to the most basic organization level. The term of appointment for cadre at the basic organization level is two to four years; at and above the county level it is five years. In other words, the appearance is given that every five years a congress is held and the key cadres at various levels are elected by decision of the congress delegates, but in reality the congresses are rubber-stamping personnel appointments. From time to time these rubber-stamp ceremonies witness organized opposition to the decisions of the higher levels and force a "nomination" to be withdrawn. This evidences that superior levels are not able to simply exercise dictatorial power; discussion is also necessary.

Control Over Nonparty Organizations

Figure 4.2 attempts to depict the ways in which the CCP exercises control over noncommunist organizations.

First, with respect to governmental administrative institutions, within the State Council (comprising the premier, vice premiers, and other State Council members—equivalent to the cabinets in Japan or the United

FIGURE 4.2 CCP Central Control Over Non-CCP Units, 1990

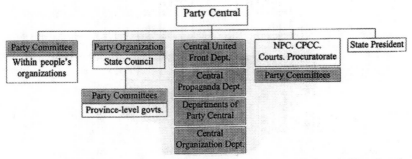

Source: CCP Organization Dept., *Chart of Cadre Assignments for Positions Under Control of Party Central* (doc. 2, 1990).

States), and the State Council plenary meeting organization (including, apart from the standing committee members, the ministers of the finance, foreign affairs, and other ministries), a distinct "party organization" exists, and all-important decisions must be approved by the party organization before being implemented. In the provinces, provincial party committees parallel provincial government organizations, and all government decisions must be approved by the party committees before any action can be taken.

With respect to lawmaking institutions, within the National People's Congress (equivalent to the Japanese Diet or the U.S. Congress) and the complementary National Political Consultative Congress (comprising noncommunist "democratic party" representatives), Communist Party committees are established and provide "guidance." Communist Party committees are established within the courts and the procuratorate, as they are within such mass organizations as trade unions, women's organizations, and youth organizations.

The CCP organization extends to all corners of Chinese society and can be perceived as the way that order is maintained in China.

Figure 4.3 shows that the Chinese civil service system is divided into fifteen ranks, from the premier to the lowest level. Provincial governments and the eight large city governments are one rank apart.

The Communist Party organizations that control these governmental personnel carry out "management of different levels" through a three-level hierarchy: the Politburo level, the Central Organization Department, and province-level party organization departments (including party organizations in each ministry under the State Council).

The People's Liberation Army (PLA) is ranked one level above the local or civilian departments.

FIGURE 4.3 Relationship Chart for Centrally Appointed and Consented Positions

Official rank	State Council = Central Gov't — Appointed post	State Council = Central Gov't — Consented post	Provincial Level = Local Gov't — Appointed post	Provincial Level = Local Gov't — Consented post	Eight cities — Appointed post	Eight cities — Consented post	CCP central — Dept. responsible for personnel	(Military level)	People's Liberation Army — Revision	Previous gov't rank Revision	Previous gov't rank
1	Chair. Premier Vice Chair.						Central Politburo	Military Affairs Commission	Chairman	1	1-3
2	Vice Premier State Councilor								Member	2	4
									Mil. Region commander	3	5
3	Minister		Provincial governor		Mayor		Central Organization Dept.	Corps level	Mil. reg. vice cmdr.	4	6
									Corps dep. cmdr.	5	7
4	Vice Minister		Vice governor			Vice mayor	Party provincial level organization	Group level	Full group cmdr.	6	8
									Dep. group cmdr.	7	9
									Group sub-cmdr.	8	10
5		Div. chief		Office head		Vice mayor level	Party organization in all State Council ministries	Division level	Full div. cmdr.	9	11
6	Appointment down to vice minister level	Deputy division chief	Consent down to vice minister level	Deputy office head		Consent down to vice mayor level			Deputy div. cmdr.	10	12
7		Consent down to deputy division head level		Consent down to deputy division head level					Division sub-cmdr.	11	13
8								Regiment level	Full reg. cmdr.	12	14
									Deputy reg. cmdr.	13	15
									Reg. sub-cmdr.	14	16
9								Battalion level	Full battalion cmdr.	15	17
									Deputy bat. cmdr.	16	18
10								Company level	Full co. cmdr.	17	19
									Deputy co. cmdr.	18	20
11								Squad level	Squad cmdr.	19	21
									Dep. squad cmdr.	20	22
12								Platoon level	Platoon cmdr.	21	23
									Dep. platoon cmdr.	22	24
13								Soldiers	Worker-soldier	23	25
14									New recruit	24	26
15										25	27
										26	28
										27	29
										28	30

Sources: For PLA, compiled from *Summary of the Cadre System* (Beijing: Military Science Press [internal distribution], 1988, p. 313). For government administration, compiled from Li Weiyi, *China's Wage System* (Beijing: China Labor Press, 1991, pp. 153, 224), and "Provisional Regulations Governing State Public Servants," *People's Daily*, August 19, 1993.

China has been traditionally, and remains, a class society. In the past it was said that "punishment cannot reach an official," meaning that a mandarin who had passed the imperial examination could not be punished under the law. These mandarins considered themselves subject only to the direct authority of the emperor from whom they had received appointments. This tradition still lives. It is rare that senior government officials are punished under law.

The National People's Congress's Role of Confirming the Decisions of the Communist Party

Figure 4.4 illustrates the process by which the National People's Congress has formally adopted governmental policies in accordance with the Communist Party's decisions on basic concepts and strategy. This is the essence of the leadership of the Communist Party.

Lessening of Direct Control of the Central Organization Department

In the process of reform and liberalization in the 1980s, control of the Communist Party through personnel assignments underwent substantial change. For example, in the spring 1987 reform the Central Organization Department's direct appointment of personnel was reduced to twenty-six enterprises, ten universities, and eleven scientific and technical institutions. Before the reform the various units had totaled more than one hundred (Wu Guoguang and Zheng Yongnian, *A Discussion of Central-Local Relations*, 1996, p. 170). Before the Thirteenth Party Congress in fall 1987, Cao Zhi, deputy director of the Central Organization Department, revealed that cadres directly managed by the Central Organization Department had totaled about 130,000 before the reform. These were reduced to some 2,700 persons. Included were the "deputy" positions (deputy secretary, deputy provincial governor, deputy committee chairman) at the province-level party committees, provincial government, and Provincial People's Congress standing committees (Wu Guoguang and Zheng Yongnian, *A Discussion of Central-Local Relations*, p. 171).

The Significance of the Variance Vote

After the Thirteenth Party Congress, through the initiative of Zhao Ziyang, a "variance vote" was conducted against Communist Party members at all levels of party and governmental leadership. As a result, persons not intended by Central were elected provincial governor in both

FIGURE 4.4 Connection Between the CCP Central Committee and the National People's Congress

Period	Important CCP Meetings	Connec-tion	National People's Congress
Oct. 12-18, 1992 Oct. 19, 1992	*14th CCP Congress.* Establishment of a socialist market economy proposed. *First plenum of 14th Congress Central Committee.* Jiang Zemin re-elected general secretary.		
Mar. 3-7, 1993	*Second plenum of the 14th Congress Central Committee.* Decisions on adjustment of targets for the 8th Five Year Plan and reorganization of party and government organs.		*First session of the 8th NPC.* Upward revision of GDP growth rate in 8th Five Year Plan. Approved amendment of Constitution to include transformation to a socialist market economy.
Mar. 15-31, 1993			
Nov. 11-14, 1993	*Third plenum of the 14th Congress Central Committee.* Party Central decision on "Some Issues concerning Reform of the Socialist Market Economic System."		
Mar. 10-22, 1994			*Second session of the 8th NPC.*
Sep. 25-28, 1994	*Fourth plenum of the 14th Congress Central Committee.* Party Central decision of several important issues concerning strengthening party construction. Huang Ju appointed member of the Politburo, Wu Bangguo and Jiang Chunyun to the Party Central secretariat.		
Mar. 5-18, 1995			*Third session of the 8th NPC.* Wu Bangguo and Jiang Chunyun elected vice premiers of the State Council.
Sep. 25-28, 1995	*Fifth plenum of the 14th Congress Central Committee.* "Party Central Proposal Regarding the 9th Five Year Plan and Adoption of Long Term Goals for 2010" adopted.		
Mar. 5-17, 1996			*Fourth session of the 8th NPC.* "Ninth Five Year Plan and Outline of Long Term Goals for 2010" and summary of Premier Li Peng's report adopted.
Sep. 12-18, 1997	*15th CCP Congress.* Continuation of Deng Xiaoping line and enterprise reform through the shareholding system accepted.		
Sep. 19, 1997	First plenum of the 15th Congress Central Committee. Zhu Rongji elected number-three.		
Mar. 5-19, 1998			*First session of the 9th NPC.* Zhu Rongji elected premier. Government institutions reform plan adopted.

Zhejiang and Guizhou provinces. This incident delivered a huge shock to persons inside and outside the Communist Party. It compelled leaders sent from Central to the provinces to promise "loyalty" to the localities. For example, in 1992 Minister of Coal Hu Fuguo was transferred to Shanxi province as acting governor. When the Provincial People's Congress was officially voting, he was compelled to declare that his purpose in taking up office "is to be of service to the people of Shanxi province. The interests of Shanxi province will be my greatest interest" (article by Yan Xiaoming, *People's Daily*, March 23, 1992). Regarding this situation, Wu Guoguang commented as follows: "Looked at from the orthodox ideological standpoint of Central, it is easy to find fault with this pronouncement. However, regional interests and regional authority have formulated ideological opposition to such orthodoxy" (Wu Guoguang and Zheng Yongnian, *A Discussion of Central-Local Relations*, p. 172).

—*Yabuki*

5

Economic System Reform

The Progress of the
Market Economy Program

The Fifty-Point Program for
the Market Economy (1993)

The Chinese Communist Party adopted the "Decision on Some Issues Concerning the Establishment of a Socialist Market Economic System" (the "Fifty Articles") at the Third Plenary Session of the Central Committee of the Fourteenth Party Congress, convened in Beijing on November 11–14, 1993. The "Fifty Articles" encapsulated China's approach to attaining a market economy. To slightly overgeneralize, there were five main elements:

Conversion of State-Owned Enterprises into Stock Companies

The significance of converting state-owned enterprises into joint stock companies was explained as follows. Creating a legal corporate person would facilitate transforming enterprise operations by effectively separating the ownership rights of the investors from the property rights of the corporation as well as the government from the enterprise. The enterprise would be removed from the purview of government administrative institutions, and the government's unlimited responsibility for the enterprises would be ended. Capital would become easier to raise, and risk would be diversified.

Several types of companies were proposed: (1) wholly owned companies (only one investor); (2) limited liability companies; and (3) limited stock companies (multiple investors). The "Fifty Articles" also provided for the following:

41

A limited number of limited stock companies will be permitted to list on the stock exchanges, following stringent auditing of their operations. The percentage of shares which shall continue to be held by the state will be decided according to industry and degree of shareholder concentration. Some companies producing specialized products and defense industry enterprises will be wholly invested and operated by the state.

The state would hold a controlling percentage of shares in the main enterprises in key industries and basic industries. The change in the enterprise system was not to be a change in name only or just a fund-raising exercise. Rather the emphasis was on changing how enterprises were managed and operated.

National-scale holding companies were to be organized. These companies were to bring different ownership and operational forms of enterprises into a group, where state ownership was in a controlling position, to develop large-scale enterprises across territorial and product sector lines, introduce advanced technology, create new products, and work toward achieving international competitiveness. Although it went unstated, this was essentially the model of the huge Korean enterprise groups. (By 1998 this model was being questioned, because it had proven highly deficient in China and because the Korean companies that had provided the model were in crisis and were restructuring.)

Operation of small-scale SOEs would preferably be taken over by private interests on a fixed-return basis, or leased out, or restructured into a cooperative shareholding system whereby employees would become shareholders. It was also acceptable to sell to collectives or private individuals.

Reform of the Financial System

Converting the People's Bank of China (PBOC) into a functioning Central Bank had long been planned. Now specifics for the central banking system were provided, such as the Central Bank's operation of a deposit reserve ratio and lending (discount window) facility. Also specified was the establishment of a monetary policy committee to adjust policy for money and finance.

Separation of policy banks and commercial banks was advocated. The State Development Bank and the China Export-Import Bank would be newly established as policy banks, and the existing Agricultural Bank of China (ABC) would be transformed in its entirety into a policy bank. The existing specialized banks (the Industrial and Commercial Bank of China [ICBC], the China Investment Bank, the Bank of China [BOC], and the

People's Construction Bank of China) would gradually be relieved of government-directed policy lending responsibilities and become pure commercial banks; agricultural cooperative banks and urban cooperative banks would also be established. Commercial banks would adopt asset-liability and risk-management disciplines. Nonbanks (e.g., leasing and finance companies) would be brought under strict regulation.

The Central Bank would adjust a prime rate according to demand and supply of funds, and commercial banks would be permitted to raise or lower lending rates within a regulated range. The management system for foreign exchange would be improved. A floating exchange rate system based upon market forces would be established; the foreign exchange market would be unified; the renminbi (RMB; called CNY in international markets) would gradually be made convertible. In tandem with building the banking system's electronic and telecommunications infrastructure, credit (debit) card settlement systems would be introduced, facilitating a reduction in the amount of currency in circulation.

Reform of the Investment System

Policy with respect to the investment system is specified in article 20 of the "Fifty Articles." The principle is that the entity undertaking investment should be a "legal person" that will assume the risk and rewards. Borrowed funds will come from banks that will assume credit risks and gain profit therefrom. This was a reform of the old planned economy system under which SOEs and state-owned banks evaded responsibility for the outcome of investment decisions. The policy made clear that enterprises should act like profit-seeking, legal persons and that the banks' responsibilities and support toward the enterprises should be subject to limitations.

Problems with Fiscal Reform

With respect to fiscal and tax reform, we can point to three major issues:

Dual Tax System. The "local fiscal responsibility system" would be replaced by a dual tax system. Central and local authorities would establish separate administrative structures, and Central and local taxes would be separated. Taxes required to support national interests and those necessary for macroeconomic control would be designated Central taxes; taxes that could meet local needs would be local taxes; taxes that directly affected economic development would be "joint taxes" shared between Central and the localities.

The new system was designed to raise the proportion of fiscal revenues to GNP; to rationally fix the proportionate shares of Central and local fiscal revenues; and to bring into effect a system for returning fiscal funds and fiscal transfers from Central to localities. The latter was important especially for regions with undeveloped economies and for reforming old industrial bases.

Introduction of the Value-Added Tax (VAT).   A distribution tax, with a value-added tax as the main element, would be introduced. For some commodities a consumption tax would still be assessed, whereas most non-goods enterprises would be assessed a business (gross receipts) tax. The income tax rate on SOEs would be lowered. The allocation of profit between the state and enterprises would be further rationalized, most importantly through the abolition of assessments for the energy and key transportation construction funds and the budget adjustment fund. Enterprises and personal income taxes would be unified and tax rates standardized.

Establishment of a Dual Budgetary System.   Together with the establishment of a government public works budget and a state-owned assets operations budget, social welfare budgets and other budgets would be drafted. The state fiscal deficit would be strictly controlled. Making up deficits in the Central budget by borrowing from banks would be discontinued; government short-term bonds would be issued. There would be unified management of the government's domestic and foreign debts.

Reform of the Trade System

The basic concept held that modern enterprises would have the right to engage in international trade. At the same time, the development of general trading companies was also discussed. The state would manage enterprises' trading activities by means of economic levers such as exchange-rate policy, taxation, and policies governing bank credit. This was clearly a different approach from the previous system, where the government interfered through direct control of imports and exports as well as through planning and administrative fiat.

Status of Economic System Reform (1997)

From 1994 through 1997, proceeding along lines of the "Fifty Articles" program, China took great strides in realizing a more market-oriented economy.

Reform of the financial system provides one of the most concrete examples. Three policy banks were established in succession: the State Devel-

TABLE 5. 1 Implementation of the Fifty Articles Program for a Socialist Market Economy

	Fifty Articles Program	*Implementation Status (March 1998)*
SOEs	1. Convert to a corporate form separating ownership rights from property rights. 2. Reorganize to wholly-owned companies, limited liability companies, and limited stock companies. 3. Establish holding companies, develop large-scale groups. 4. Operate large-scale enterprises under contract responsibility, leases, cooperative stock arrangements. Sales of enterprises.	1. Company Law implemented (July 1994). 2. Formation of the China Technology Group (Dec. 1994). Formation of the Electronic Industry Group (April 1994). Formation of the State Electric Power Corporation, Xinxing Oil Company, and others. 3. Decision to increase number of large-scale groups from 57 to 120 (May 1997). 4. 15th Party Congress adopts "mixed economic" model (September 1997).
Market system	1. Nurture the market system in resource distribution. 2. Deepen price reform. 3. Reform of the commodity distribution system. 4. Nurture financial, labor, real estate, technology, and information markets. 5. Develop market mediation organizations. 6. Strengthen and improve management and supervision of markets.	1. Implementation of antidumping and antikickback regulations (March 1997). 2. Temporary measures for management of convertible bonds announced (April 1997). Temporary measures form management of the labor market announced (March 1996). Temporary rules for managing itinerant farm labor between provinces implemented--"itinerant employment certificate." China property market and land mediation service established (May 1994). Urban real estate management law (July 1997). 3. Arbitration law (August 1994). Audit supervision law (August 1994). Advertising law (September 1994).
Fiscal system reform	1. Introduce dual tax system. 2. Reform tax system. 3. Reform fiscal system.	1. Implementation of the dual tax system (January 1994). 2. Budget law promulgated (January 1995). Implementing regulations for personal income tax (January 1993). Publication of "Corporate Accounting Standards and Consolidation Disclosure"--increased transparency of listed companies (June 1997).
Financial system	1. Convert PBOC to a central bank. 2. Establish policy banks. 3. Develop commercial banks. 4. Liberalize interest rates and establish foreign exchange market. 5. Computerize banks and popularize credit cards.	1. Law of the People's Bank of China promulgated (March 1995). Regulations governing the Monetary Policy Committee announced (April 1997). 2. State Development Bank (March 1994). China Export-Import Bank (July 1994). Agricultural Development Bank of China (November 1994). 3. Commercial Bills Law (May 1995). China Minsheng Bank (January 1996). 4. Announcement of Temporary Regulations on Prohibited Securities Trading (prohibiting insider trading) (March 1997).
Social security	1. Provide old age, unemployment, and medical insurance. 2. Establish social security management institutions.	1. The 87 Anti-Poverty Action Plan (February 1994). 2. Labor Law (July 1994). 3. The 40-hour week introduced (May 1997).
Foreign economic affairs	1. Implement comprehensive opening to the outside world. 2. Construct a trade system compatible with international rules. 3. Introduce foreign capital, technology, people, and management know-how.	1. Foreign exchange certificates abolished (January 1994). Unification of airline tariffs between local and foreign passengers (July 1997). 2. Lowering of some tariffs (January 1994). Foreign trade law and state compensation law (May 1994). Implementation of IMF article 8 (December 1996).

opment Bank (March 1994), the China Export-Import Bank (July 1994), and the China Agricultural Development Bank (November 1994). With policy lending now entrusted to these banks, it became possible for the People's Bank of China to function as a central bank.

The Law of the People's Bank of China was promulgated in March 1995. At about the same time (May 1995) the Commercial Banking Law of China was promulgated, providing a legal basis for the commercialization of specialized banks like the Industrial and Commercial Bank of China and the People's Construction Bank of China (which later changed its name to China Construction Bank). In January 1996 the first joint-stock company bank, China Minsheng Bank, was founded. The Commercial Bills Law of China was adopted in May 1995. However, preceding this, in September 1994 the coal, electric power, metallurgical, chemical, and railway sectors had implemented, on an experimental basis, a bills-based settlement system. This helped solve the problem of "triangle debts."

Reform in foreign trade was also remarkable. First, in January 1994 "foreign exchange certificates" were abolished, and tariffs for a large group of products were reduced by a further step. In May 1994 the foreign trade law was established. In December 1996 the long-desired goal of complying with article 8 of the International Monetary Fund (IMF), ending restrictions on exchange transactions on current account, was realized. (This meant that RMB was freely convertible into foreign currency and vice versa in connection with an actual trade or service transaction.) In July 1997 the premium tariff applied to foreigners on trains and airlines was reformed, and a uniform tariff was adopted for locals and foreigners.

Fiscal system reform, including introduction of the dual tax system, commenced in January 1994. The budget law was implemented in January 1995.

As part of market system reform, the China property market was established in May 1994, and three years later the law governing urban real estate management was implemented. In March 1996 temporary regulations for management of the labor market were adopted. In August 1994 the arbitration law was promulgated, followed by the advertising law in September.

Although it was not clearly elucidated in the "Fifty Articles" program, the development of the securities market during this period has been remarkable (see Table 5.1). By the end of 1997 the market value of stocks on the Chinese exchanges was equivalent to more than one-fourth of GDP.

—*Yabuki*

Part Two

Some Domestic Economic Problems

6

Economic Growth

A Low-Income Country on a Fast-Growth Path

China's GDP in Global Perspective

In 1995 China's GDP was US$744.8 billion, seventh in the world. At the time, the GDP of the United States was US$6.95 trillion, Japan US$5.10 trillion, Germany US$2.41 trillion, France US$1.53 trillion, Great Britain US$1.10 trillion, Italy US$0.8 trillion, then China. Following China were Brazil at US$688 billion, Canada US$568.9 billion, Spain US$558.6 billion, South Korea US$455.4 billion, the Netherlands US$395.8 billion, Australia US$348.7 billion, Indonesia US$198.0 billion, and Switzerland US$300.5 billion.

In terms of volume of national production, China is among the top seven countries in the world, but considering its huge population, the volume is rather small. What has riveted the attention of the world is not the size of China's economy but its growth rate. During the first half of the 1990s China jumped to the top in GDP growth rate. Also remarkable were the growth rates of countries in the Association of Southeast Asian Nations (ASEAN) such as Singapore, Malaysia, and Thailand.

Table 6.1 presents a comparison of Asian countries in terms of per capita GNP. The left column is calculated according to exchange rates, whereas the right column presents a calculation against the "international dollar" used for comparisons by the United Nations. This is a comparison based on purchasing power parity. By this latter measure, China's per capita GNP is immediately elevated fivefold to close to US$3,000. Due to the high cost of living in Japan, Singapore, and Hong Kong, these countries fair worse when compared by prevailing exchange rates only. Figure 6.1 presents a comparison of purchasing power based on "actual living requirements." By this measure China remains a poor developing coun-

TABLE 6. 1 GNP of Some Asian Countries and GNP Per Capita, 1995

Country/ region	GNP		GNP Per Capita				Income level
	US$ billion	index	US$	index	Int'l $	index	
Vietnam	17.6	0.02	240	0.4	---		low
India	319.7	0.43	340	0.5	1,400	0.5	low
China	744.9	1.00	620	1.0	2,920	1.0	low
Indonesia	190.1	0.26	980	1.6	3,800	1.3	lower middle
Philippines	71.9	0.10	1,050	1.7	2,850	1.0	lower middle
Thailand	159.6	0.21	2,740	2.8	7,540	2.6	lower middle
Malaysia	78.3	0.11	3,890	6.3	9,020	3.1	higher middle
So. Korea	435.1	0.58	9,700	15.6	11,450	3.9	high
Taiwan	263.6	0.35	12,439	20.1	---		high
Hong Kong	142.3	0.19	22,990	37.1	22,950	7.9	high
Singapore	79.8	0.11	26,730	43.1	22,770	7.8	high
Japan	4,963.6	6.66	39,640	63.9	22,110	7.6	high

Notes: [1] International dollar is a parity unit intended to express purchasing
power developed by the United Nations International Comparison
Program (ICP). It is a measure of the amount of currency needed in
each country to purchase the same volume of goods and services as
could be bought with US$1.00 spent in the United States.
[2] Income level is according to World Bank categories:
Low income = under US$765, lower middle income = US$766-3,035,
higher middle income = US$3,036-9,385, high income = over US$9,386.
Sources: *World Bank Atlas* 1997; Taiwan: *Taiwan Statistical Data Book* 1997.

try. However, when the low per capita figure is multiplied by the vast
population, we find again that China is a GNP power. In terms of purchasing power parity, China's GDP in 1995 was 3,504 billion international
dollars, second after the United States (7,096 billion international dollars)
and ahead of Japan (2,764 billion international dollars).

The Dream of Quadrupling GDP Is Realized

On January 16, 1980, in a speech entitled "Concerning the Current Situation and Tasks," Deng Xiaoping said the following:

> By the end of this century, if we can attain an average per capita GNP of
> US$1,000, we can say that we have reached a level of being well off.... Now
> we are only at something over $200. To reach $1000 will require a quadru-
> pling. Singapore and Hong Kong have both exceeded $3000. It will not be
> easy for us to achieve the $1,000 level. (Deng Xiaoping, *Selected Works of Deng
> Xiaoping*, 1993)

FIGURE 6. 1 Per Capita GNP of Asian Countries in Purchasing Power
Prices, 1995

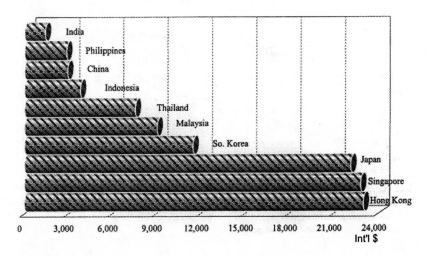

Source : Table 6.1.

The term used by Deng Xiaoping was *xiaokang,* meaning "fairly well off." Deng Xiaoping later explained that this idea was born during a conversation with Japanese Prime Minister Ohira Masayoshi during the latter's visit to China in December 1979. Deng Xiaoping died on February 19, 1997, before the end of the century. Let us look at realization of his dream.

As can be seen from Figure 6.2, China's GDP doubled by 1987 and, in 1995, achieved the dreamed-for quadrupling. In other words, on the basis of GDP, Deng Xiaoping's vision was realized five years earlier than expected. What about the result on a per capita basis? By 1996 it was already approaching a fourfold increase.

There is no doubt that by the end of this century, the quadrupling of GDP on a per capita basis will be achieved.

This is certainly something to be applauded, but as we see in Figure 6.3 progress toward this goal has not always been smooth. In the first half of the 1980s there was a "reform leap" phenomenon, but in the late 1980s the pace cooled dramatically as a consequence of the Tiananmen Incident.

Deng Xiaoping set off on his "southern excursion" and appealed for a revitalization of the reform and liberalization programs. And as if a sorcerer had conjured up some magical power, his appeal brought about high growth during the first half of the 1990s. The average annual growth

FIGURE 6.2 Process of China's GDP Quadrupling, 1980-1997

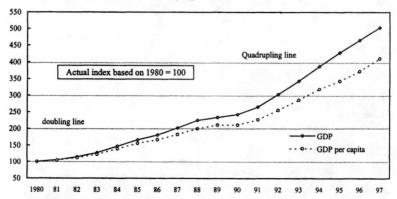

Note: According to the "Outline of the Ninth Five Year Plan and Goals for the Long Term Plan for the Year 2010,"
(1) GDP per capita by 2000 should be four times that of 1980, and (2) as a "goal of struggle" GDP per capita
should double from 2000 to 2010.

Source: *China Statistical Yearbook* (each year).

FIGURE 6.3 Year-on-Year Growth Rate of China's GDP, 1980-1997

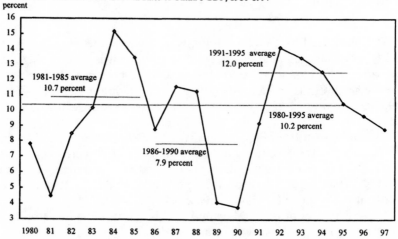

Sources: Mitsubishi Research Institute, *China Information Handbook* 1997 (figures from
China Statistical Yearbook each year); "Bulletin on National Economic and Social
Development for 1997," *Economic Daily*, March 5, 1998 .

rate during the fifteen years from 1981 to 1995 was a lofty 10.2 percent. By virtue of this growth the structure of the Chinese economy underwent huge change. In 1980 primary industry occupied 30 percent of GDP; by 1995 this had declined to 20 percent. Conversely, tertiary industry in 1980 accounted for only 20 percent of output, but by 1995 it had risen to more than 30 percent. Although the share of secondary industry did not change, it changed greatly in content, as the previous overemphasis on heavy industry has been gradually corrected.

Long-Term Outlook for the Chinese Economy: Continued Fast Growth

But how long can China's rapid growth continue? Table 6.2 presents the record of rapid growth in Japan, South Korea, and Taiwan. The numbers diverge at different periods, but each country managed to grow at an average annual rate of close to 10 percent over a period of some thirty years. If China is able to follow this "precedent," then it is likely that it can continue to achieve high growth for another fifteen to twenty years. The Japanese Economic Planning Agency's research report, *Scenario for China in the Twenty-First Century* (1997), boldly proffered such a prognosis. The author (Yabuki) was one of the report's researchers and strongly supported this outlook.

Let us consider several other similar forecasts.

The first is a research report, *China in the Year 2020,* a World Bank analysis of the Chinese economy in seven volumes including a synopsis, released on the occasion of the IMF World Bank annual meeting in Hong Kong in September 1997. In the synopsis, "The Challenge of Development in the New Millennium," it was forecast that by 2020 China's per capita GDP on a purchasing power parity basis will reach the current level of Portugal.

Switch from Volume-Based Growth to Quality-Based Growth

Let us consider another graph from *China in the Year 2020.* Figure 6.4 explains the decisive factors behind China's growth. It is now virtually common knowledge that a large volume of capital accumulation and an elevation in labor productivity are two highly significant factors in determining China's rate of growth. Underpinning the contribution of these factors are, first, reform of the economic system, and, second, political and social stability. If these two conditions were lacking, the basis for

TABLE 6. 2   Continuation of High Growth in Japan, South Korea, and Taiwan

(unit: %)

	Period	Years	Ave. Growth Rate Per Year	Period	Years	Ave. Growth Rate Per Year	Period	Years	Ave. Growth Rate Per Year
Japan	1947-1958*	11	8.9						
	1947-1973*	26	9.7						
	1958-1973	15	9.7						
	1958-1988	30	6.6	1973-1988	15	3.6			
	1958-1993	35	6.1	1973-1993	20	3.5	1988-1993	5	3.0
So.	1962-1977	15	9.6						
Korea	1962-1987	25	9.0	1977-1987	10	8.0			
	1962-1992	30	8.9	1977-1992	15	8.1	1987-1992	5	8.3
	1962-1995	33	8.8	1977-1995	18	8.1	1987-1995	8	8.1
Taiwan	1962-1977	15	10.1						
	1962-1987	25	9.5	1977-1987	10	8.7			
	1962-1992	30	9.0	1977-1992	15	8.0	1987-1992	5	6.7
	1962-1995	33	8.8	1977-1995	18	7.7	1987-1995	8	6.6

Origin notes: [1] Real growth rates.
   [2] 1-3 produced from the following sources.
   Source 1:   Economic Planning Agency, Research Division, *Asian Economy* 1996.
   Source 2:   Economic Planning Agency, *Report of National Economic Statistics*.
   Source 3:   Thirty Year History of the Economic Planning Agency, *Development of the Modern Japanese Economy*.
   [3] (*) indicates growth rate on fiscal year basis.   Otherwise in calendar year basis.
   [4] Growth rates of South Korea and Taiwan are calculated from Source 1.
   [5] Growth rate of Japan is calculated from Source 2, except for (*), which is calculated from Source 3.

Source: Japanese Economic Planning Agency, *Scenario for China in the 21st Century* (1997).

FIGURE 6. 4 Determinants of China's Economic Growth

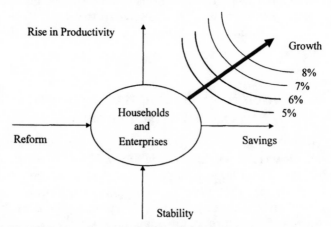

Source: The World Bank, *China 2020, Development Challenges in the New Century. 1998.*

TABLE 6. 3 Prognosis for Growth to 2050 by the Chinese Academy of Social Sciences

Economic Level	1st Phase 1996-2010	2nd Phase 2011-2030		3rd Phase 2031-2050
Average GDP growth rate	above 8.6%	c. 6.0%		4-5%
GDP	RMB 20 trillion	62 trillion		153 trillion
Per capita GDP	RMB 14,000	40,000		100,000
People's living standard	Achieving the well-off standard on an all-around basis	On average at the present level of middle-income countries; some areas at high income country levels		Reach level of the middle or upper ranks of present high-income countries
Industry structure (1995 prices)	2000	2010	2030	2050
Primary industry	17%	14%	9%	6%
Secondary industry	52%	52%	48%	42%
Tertiary industry	31%	34%	43%	52%

Notes: [1] Prices are 1995 prices.
        [2] Prognosis produced by the Volume Economics and Technological Economics Institute of the Chinese Academy of Social Sciences under commission from the State Science Commission and the Ministry of Finance.
Source: *Economic Daily*, November 3, 1997.

economic development would be undermined. The existence of this problem informs Deng Xiaoping's "development dictatorship" model for economic growth.

We can easily observe the growth in volume of the Chinese economy. However, volume-based growth merely leads easily to low-efficiency, wasteful ("extensive") growth. Facing this reality, the Chinese leadership has called for a switch to quality-based ("intensive") growth. The switch from volume-based growth to quality-based growth is a main theme of the "Outline of the Ninth Five Year Plan and Goals of the Long Term Plan for the Year 2010."

Table 6.3 presents a hopeful forecast by some Chinese economists up to the year 2050. By 2030 China becomes a "middle-income country" (in some areas equivalent to a high-income country), and by 2050 it reaches "the middle ranks" of high-income countries; thus the forecast sees China materially realizing the dream envisaged by Deng Xiaoping. The vision for the year 2050 comprises ten elements:

1. More than 50 percent of employment is in the tertiary sector;
2. Catching up with the United States in the information industry;
3. Development of a diversified consumer society;

4. High-technology industries approaching the globally advanced levels;
5. Around 2030 demand growth stops in traditional industries like steel, cement, coal, and petrochemicals; rationalization occurs in small- and medium-sized industries; both are replaced by high-technology industries;
6. The structure of employment changes; competition for employment increases as the unemployment rate remains high;
7. Reform of state-owned enterprises has been completed; modernization of agriculture is a new agenda item;
8. After 2030 the disparity between the eastern and western regions begins to narrow, but the pace is slow;
9. By 2030 industrialization is completed and thereafter pressure on the natural environment lessens; and
10. The pressure of resource shortages becomes more severe. (*Economic Daily*, November 3, 1997)

In summary, this is a vision of the postindustrial society. It is a dream of satisfying the desire to catch up with the world's advanced countries.

—*Yabuki*

7

Food Production

*Ensuring 500 Million Tons of Grain
for 1.3 Billion People*

"For the People Food Is God"

Since ancient times it has been said in China that "for the people food is god." In other words, without food there is chaos. Chinese rulers have always borne this in mind.

Figure 7.1 presents the changes in grain production from 1952 to 1996. The term *grain* includes cereals such as rice, wheat, and corn, as well as soybeans and potatoes. Looking at the composition in 1996 we see that cereals made up 90 percent of the total. Rice took slightly less than 40 percent, wheat slightly more than 20 percent, and corn 24 percent.

Looking at grain production during the Deng Xiaoping era we observe a remarkably rapid increase in the period 1982–1984. This was the result of the switch to the production responsibility system, which ignited the peasants' desire to increase production. The stagnation from 1985 to 1989 is probably a consequence of the peasants' being lured into nonfarming occupations and their leaving homes to find work elsewhere. Agricultural output increased in the period after the Tiananmen Incident until 1993, then declined in 1994 due to inclement weather. During this period prices of grain were rising as the grain distribution system became more market-driven. In the period 1995–1997 a policy of emphasizing agriculture was again affirmed. The result was harvests of 500 million tons in 1996 and 490 million tons in 1997. The Ninth Five Year Plan establishes the goal for the year 2000 of securing 500 million tons of grain to support a population of 1.3 billion. Clearly the cherished 500 million–ton goal has been reached well in advance.

We can calculate the grain holdings per capita by dividing grain production by average population during each year. The Chinese govern-

**FIGURE 7.1 Changes in Grain Production and Per Capita Grain
Holdings, 1952-1996**

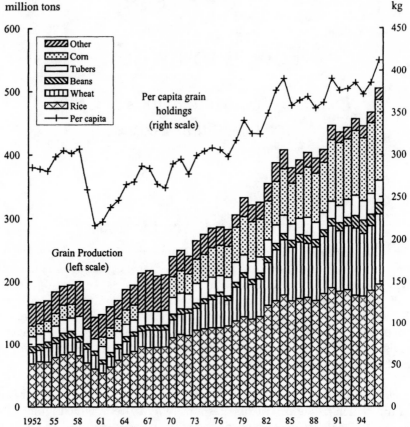

Source: Data for 1952-1992 from *China Statistical Yearbook* 1993 that for
         1993-1996 from 1996 edition.

ment has set a goal of a per capita grain holdings level of 400 kilograms.
As we can see from the line graph in Figure 7.1, the level of 393 kilograms
was attained in 1983 and 1990, and the cherished goal of 400 kilograms
was exceeded for the first time in 1996.

Why Grain Production Has Increased

Figure 7.2 presents the factors sustaining grain production. In 1979 cultivated land was 99.5 million hectares, and in 1995 it was 95.0 million. This

FIGURE 7. 2 Grain Productivity, Output, and Area Under Cultivation

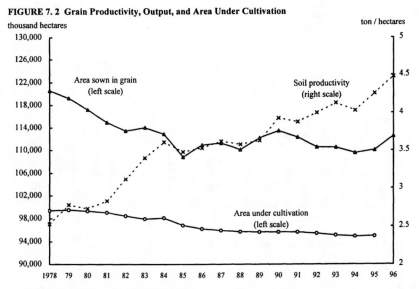

Source: *China Statistical Yearbook* (each year).

is a decrease of some 5 percent over seventeen years. More remarkable than the decline in cultivated area has been the declining trend in sown area. This is a correction of the tendency toward expanding sown area without regard to conditions during the Mao Zedong era. It reflects the peasants' own judgment as to the most productive use of land, rather than the dictates of policy.

Whereas sown area has decreased, grain production has increased. Dividing the volume of grain production by sown area, we obtain grain production volume per unit of area. This measure of land productivity is seen to have increased dramatically.

Let us look at unit productivity per hectare in 1979 and 1995. Rice increased from 4.2 tons to 6 tons (up 43 percent), wheat from 2.1 tons to 3.5 tons (67 percent), corn from 2.9 tons to 4.9 tons (69 percent), and soybeans from 1 ton to 1.6 tons (60 percent) (People's Republic of China, Ministry of Agriculture, *Report on China's Agricultural Development*, 1996 ed., pp. 187–190). During this period chemical fertilizer application increased from 1.9 tons to 3.6 tons per hectare.

Imports and Exports of Grain

Figure 7.3 takes of a view of trends in grain imports and exports. The periods 1978 through 1984, 1987 through 1991, and 1995 and 1996 were "net

FIGURE 7. 3 China's Grain Exports and Imports and Self-Sufficiency Ratio

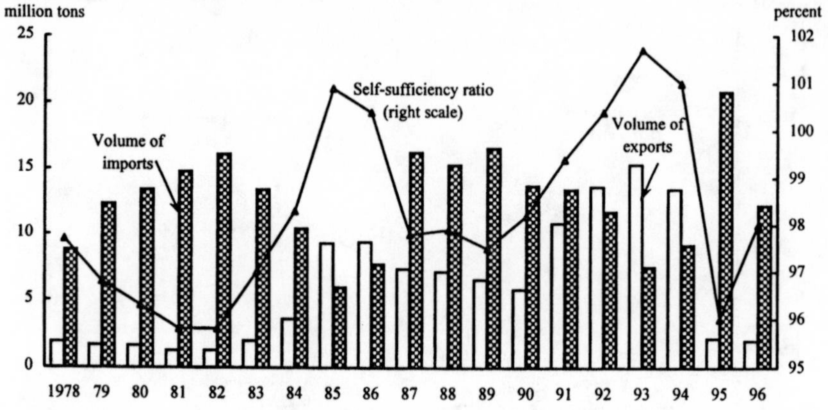

Source: *China Statistical Yearbook* (each year).

importing periods," when imports exceeded exports. The first years (1985, 1986, and 1992 through 1994) were "net exporting periods."

Dividing the volume of grain production by the volume of grain holdings [grain production + (grain imports – grain exports)] we obtain a grain self-sufficiency ratio. The line graph in Figure 7.3 traces the self-sufficiency ratio. It shows that 100 percent or greater self-sufficiency was achieved in 1985, 1986, and 1992 through 1994. Notwithstanding these figures, even during the periods of peak imports—1981, 1982, and 1995—the import ratio was less than 5 percent.

In terms of composition of imports and exports, rice was basically in balance, tending slightly toward greater exports. The main imported grain was wheat. In the period 1980–1982 the self-sufficiency ratio for wheat fell to the 80–90 percent level; in 1991, 1992, and 1995 it was slightly below 90 percent.

Outlook for Grain Supply and Demand

In October 1996 the State Council published a prognosis for grain supply and demand through the early twenty-first century in the first Chinese *Grain White Paper*.

Population begins at 1.3 billion in 2000 and increases by 100 million in each of the following three decades, peaking at 1.6 billion in 2030. Notwithstanding that China is implementing a strict one-child policy, the number of couples of childbearing age is large, and therefore the population will continue to grow to 2030.

The forecast demand for grain in 2000 is 500 million tons. This level was reached in 1996. Chinese authorities also indicate confidence that the goal of 550 million tons in 2010 will be achievable. However, authorities have a cautious view of the situation in 2030 (per capita grain demand is forecast at 400 kilograms and available supply at 640 million tons). This is because of the difficulty of forecasting some key variables.

Compare the Chinese authorities' forecast with the prognosis offered by Lester Brown of the World Watch Institute: If we calculate per capita grain consumption of 400 kilograms and a population of 1.6 billion we come up with a figure for aggregate grain demand of 640 million tons. This is also the figure in the *White Paper*. But the truth lies somewhere between the wolf call that "China will consume all the world's grain" and the Chinese authorities' rebuttal: "Who will feed China? The Chinese people themselves."

In his treatise Brown underestimates the productive capacity of China. He posits that the gap between forecast (underestimated) production volume and forecast volume demand will be made up entirely through reliance on imports. He frightened the world with figures of import volumes of 200–300 million tons. The Chinese authorities establish a maximum level of import reliance of 5 percent. They are striving to implement policies aimed at preventing the self-sufficiency ratio from falling below 95 percent under any circumstances. There are large gains to be made through expansion of unit yield. For example, they are building stable, multiple-crop farming areas that are achieving yields of 1.5 tons per hectare, reducing grain losses in the whole process from harvest to consumption.

—*Yabuki*

8

Energy

Shift to Dependency on Coal and Imported Oil

Current Energy Supply and Demand

It can be seen from Table 8.1 that in the fifteen years from 1981 through 1995 China's energy production and consumption grew at annual average rates of 4.8 percent and 5.2 percent respectively. As the real GDP average annual growth during the period was 10.2 percent, the elasticity of energy versus GDP was 0.47; versus consumption it was 0.51. At the same time, the growth rate of both production and consumption of electric power was 8.4 percent, yielding an elasticity versus GDP of 0.82 as to both production and consumption.

Observing the elasticity of energy production during the Sixth Five Year Plan period (1981–1985), the Seventh Five Year Plan period (1986–1990), and the Eighth Five Year Plan period (1991–1995), we see a decline from 0.57 to 0.37, which indicates a slowing in the rate of production increase. At the same time, consumption elasticity was 0.46, 0.66, and 0.46. The high consumption elasticity during the Seventh Five Year Plan is a reflection of the fall in production that attended the Tiananmen Incident.

Converting GDP to single output units, in the case of the Eighth Five Year Plan, per-unit energy consumption was 0.46. This indicates substantial scope for energy conservation. Compared to the Mao Zedong era, then, substantial progress has been made in energy conservation. One reason is that the economic growth during the Deng Xiaoping era tended to be driven not by high energy–consuming heavy industry but by light industry.

Looking at energy consumption by primary energy source (Figure 8.1) we see that in 1995 coal accounted for 75 percent, oil 17.3 percent, and hydropower 5.9 percent. At three-fourths of the total, coal's overwhelming

TABLE 8.1 Elasticity of Production and Consumption of Energy and Electric Power

Years	(a) Energy		(b) Electric Power		(c) GDP	(a) / (c)		(b) / (c)	
	Production Growth Rate %	Consumption Growth Rate %	Production Growth Rate %	Consumption Growth Rate %	Growth Rate %	Production Elasticity	Consumption Elasticity	Production Elasticity	Consumption Elasticity
1981-1985	6.1	4.9	6.4	6.5	10.7	0.57	0.46	0.60	0.61
1986-1990	4.0	5.2	8.6	8.6	7.9	0.51	0.66	1.09	1.09
1991-1995	4.4	5.5	10.1	10.1	12.0	0.37	0.46	0.84	0.84
1981-1995	4.8	5.2	8.4	8.4	10.2	0.47	0.51	0.82	0.82

Source: *China Statistical Yearbook 1996, 1997.*

FIGURE 8. 1 Composition of Production of China's Primary Energy

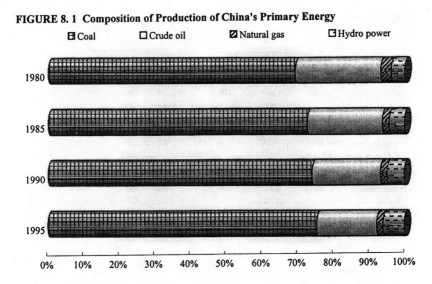

Coal   Crude oil   Natural gas   Hydro power

Source: China Statistical Yearbook 1996.

position is especially significant. The share of oil in energy production peaked in 1980 at 23.8 percent; thereafter slowing growth rates have caused a continuing decline.

The Chinese economy is now in a robust development phase. There are numerous bottlenecks, and energy insufficiency is one of the most serious.

Medium- to Long-Term Forecast for Energy Supply and Demand

A number of forecasts have been made for China's energy supply and demand. Table 8.2 is a calculation from Yan Changle's *Report on China's Energy Development* (1997). According to this forecast, net petroleum imports in 2000 will be 50 million tons, net coal exports 30 million tons. In 2010 the former will reach 100 million tons, the latter 50 million.

The figures in Table 8.2 are slightly different, but a similar outlook and basic stance inform "China's Energy Policy," released under the name of Premier Li Peng (appearing first in *Qiushi*, vol. 11, 1997). During the Ninth Five Year Plan period (1996–2000) coal production will increase at an average annual rate of 2.3 percent, by 2000 reaching 1.45 billion tons, of which 50 million tons will be exported. Elasticity of energy production should decline from 0.38 in 1997 to 0.32 in 2000, evidencing progress in energy conservation.

TABLE 8. 2 Medium and Long-Term Forecasts for China's Energy Production and Consumption

	2000		Ave. Growth Rate	2010		Ave. Growth Rate
	Forecast	Composition	(1995-2000)	Forecast	Composition	(2000-2010)
Forecast for production:		(%)	(%)		(%)	(%)
Primary energy (mil. tons)	1,464	100.0	2.6	1,955	100.0	2.9
coal (mil. tons)	1,550	75.6	2.6	1,900	69.4	2.1
petroleum (mil. tons)	160	15.6	1.3	180	13.2	1.2
natural gas (bil. m³)	25	2.3	6.9	80	5.4	12.3
hydro power (bil. kWh)	220	6.1	2.9	481	9.9	8.1
nuclear power (bil. kWh)	15	0.4		100	2.1	21.0
Forecast for consumption:		(%)	(%)		(%)	(%)
Primary energy (mil. tons)	1,514	100.0	3.3	2,063	100.0	3.1
coal (mil. tons)	1,520	71.7	2.3	1,850	64.1	2.0
petroleum (mil. tons)	210	19.8	6.1	280	19.4	2.9
natural gas (bil. m³)	25	2.2	6.9	80	5.1	12.3
hydro power (bil. kWh)	220	5.9	2.9	481	9.4	8.1
nuclear power (bil. kWh)	15	0.4	3.2	100	2.0	21.0
Net import of primary energy (mil. tons)	50			107		
net import of petroleum (mil. tons)	50			100		
net export of coal (mil. tons)	30			50		

Notes: [1]Growth rate is calculated by author.

[2]Primary energy is figured in standard coal equivalent.

Source: Yan Changle, ed., *Report on China's Energy Development*, 1997.

It is forecast that in 2000 the Daqing, Shengli, and Liaohe oil fields in the east will produce a total of 120 million tons, Kuramai and Tarim fields in Xinjiang in the west will produce a total of 20 million tons, and an additional 15 million tons will come from offshore fields, for a combined total of 155 million tons. This forecast is the basis for Table 8.2.

With regard to electric power, an electric power elasticity of 0.8 is expected during the Ninth Five Year Plan period. As a consequence, some 80 million kilowatts of new generating capacity, or an annual average of 16 million kilowatts of capacity, will be needed. In the interests of environmental protection, one goal is to change the proportion of thermal to hydropower generation from the current 75:25 percent to 70:30 percent. At present there are six regional electric power networks. It is planned to build a national electric power supply network, and thereby to take advantage of the huge electricity output of the Three Gorges dam project.

As for nuclear energy, compared with France (76 percent), Japan (33 percent), and the United States (20 percent), the three units in China at

Taishan (Zhejiang province) and Daya Bay (Guangdong) have a generating capacity of only 2.1 million kilowatts, a mere 1 percent of China's total. Currently under construction are eight units in four projects with a total generating capacity of 6.6 million kilowatts. Completion is scheduled for 2005, raising nuclear power's share of total generating capacity to 2 percent.

The Problems of Coal Transport and Environmental Pollution

Coal is the source of three-fourths of China's energy, and this proportion is not expected to change for a long time. Not only does this reality exact a high cost in terms of environmental pollution, but it also imposes a heavy burden of transporting coal from the big producing areas like Shanxi province to the consuming coastal region. In 1995 more than 50 percent of total coal shipments were by rail (*Report on China's Energy Development*). More than 30 percent of shipments were from coal-producing areas to other areas. In the future, coal might possibly be converted to electric energy or coal gas, perhaps even to coal water slurry or liquefied petroleum or another "liquid fuel" to provide cleaner energy, but so far efforts in this respect have yielded little.

During the Mao Zedong era the oft-heard saying that "the supply of coal determines the output of electric power, and the output of electric power determines industrial production" conveyed a sense of the commanding importance of coal and electric power for the entire economy. Coal supply and demand first came into balance during the Seventh Five Year Plan period. During the Eighth Five Year Plan period domestic supply slightly exceeded domestic demand, permitting exports. Thus, from the situation in which "the volume of coal production determines the volume of industrial production" we observe a change to a situation in which "the volume of coal production is determined by domestic and foreign demand." In recent years China has prided itself on being the world's largest coal producer.

Coal mines are under control of either the Central or local governments. In terms of volume of production the ratio is some 4:6, with locally controlled mines producing more. Small- and medium-sized mines predominate at the local level. These are mainly at the township and village levels and are operated as cooperate enterprises. Township and village mines produce about 610 million tons, somewhat below 50 percent of total coal output. However, their return on resources employed is low, and they pay little regard to environmental protection. Consequently the Coal Law, adopted in 1996, called for bringing the operations of these mines

TABLE 8. 3   Long-Term Forecast for China's Electric Power Supply

(unit: bil. kWh)

| | 1995 | | 2000 | | Average Growth Rate | 2010 | | Average Growth Rate |
	Actual	Compo-sition%	Fore-cast	Compo-sition %	(1995-2000)%	Fore-cast	Compo-sition %	(2000-2010)%
Output	1,008	100.0	1,400	100.0	6.8	2,500	100.0	6.0
Thermal power	804	79.8	1,165	83.2	7.7	1,919	76.8	9.1
Hydro power	191	18.9	220	15.7	2.9	481	19.2	8.1
Nuclear power	13	1.3	15	1.1	3.2	100	4.0	21.0

Note: Figures for total thermal power in 2010 calculated by author by subtracting aggregate of hydro
and nuclear power.
Source: Yan Changle, ed., *Report on China's Energy Development*, 1997.

into compliance with regulatory requirements. The Ninth Five Year Plan incorporates reform of the small- and medium-sized coal mines: A goal is to raise the operational scale of each mine to 100,000–150,000 tons. As a whole, the large- and medium-sized mines—until March 1997 under the State Council's former Ministry of Coal Industry—operate at a loss. The loss in 1992 reached RMB 5.75 billion, which was made up by state subsidies. Thereafter, efforts were made to improve operations, and in 1996 the deficit was down to RMB 400 million. A return to profitable operations is expected for 1997.

Inevitable Rise in Oil Imports

In 1996 crude-oil production was 157 million tons. China has become a net importer of crude oil (see Figure 8.2), and the volume of oil imports is expected to continue to rise during the Ninth Five Year Plan period.

China's oil-industry policy is to "stabilize the eastern region and develop the western region." In 1996 the aggregate production volume of fields in the east such as Daqing, Shengli, and Liaohe was 120 million tons, whereas that for the western fields such as Kuramai and Tarim (Xinjiang province) was 20 million tons, and that for offshore fields was 15 million tons. Daqing is China's largest oil field, steadily supplying crude oil at an annual volume of more than 50 million tons since 1976. In recent years it has become clear that the field's output will not rise. The target now is to maintain production at a level of 50 million tons for another fifteen years.

Outlook for Electric Power Development

Table 8.3 offers a medium-to-long–term prognosis for the supply of electric power. In 1995 thermal power stations contributed just less than 80

FIGURE 8. 2 Trends in Balance of China's Petroleum Exports and Imports

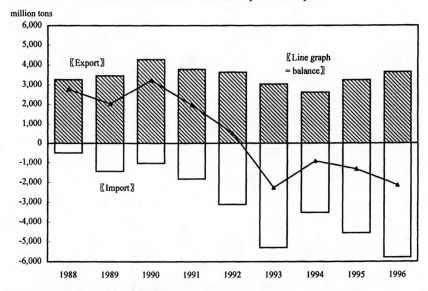

Source: *Customs Statistics of China Yearbook* (each year).

FIGURE 8. 3 Position of Daqing Oil Field in China's Petroleum Production
million tons

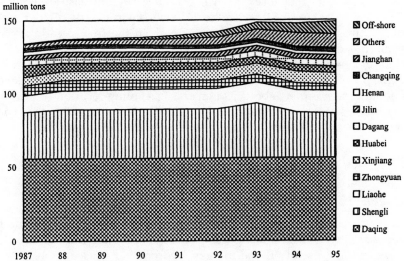

Source: *China's Petroleum Production and Petrochemical Industry,* p. 39.

TABLE 8. 4   Balance of Demand and Supply for Coal

(unit: mil. tons)

	1980	*1985*	*1990*	*1995*
Aggregate supply	626	828	1,022	1,335
production	320	872	1,080	1,361
import	1.9	2.3	2.0	1.6
export (minus)	6	8	17	29
stock changes				
in the year	10	-39	-42	0.9
Consumption	610	816	1,055	1,377
of which				
five sectors including				
industry, agriculture	483	644	868	1,222
residential consumption	116	156	167	135
Difference between				
demand and supply	16	12	-33	-42

Source: China Statistical Yearbook 1997.

percent, and hydropower stations contributed just less than 20 percent of total supply. Hydropower is expected to decline to 15.7 percent in 2000 and to recover to the 20 percent level in 2010. Nuclear power should reach 4 percent by 2010. Total electric power output should increase annually at 6.8 percent to 2000 and 6.0 percent to 2010, not a particularly high growth rate. Showing the most remarkable growth in the first decade of the twenty-first century will be nuclear power.

In order to meet the needs of a more developed economy, the share of electric power in total final energy consumption should approach the level of advanced countries, about 20 percent. Promoting location of electric power plants at coal mines and transporting electric power rather than coal should substantially alleviate the current transportation bottleneck.

Approaches to Solving the Energy Problem

Structural Problems in Energy Production and Consumption

The proportion of coal in China's energy production and consumption is overwhelming. Thus, reducing this proportionate share through the development and use of oil, natural gas, hydropower, nuclear power, and other new energy sources is an urgent task. However, because no substantial change is foreseen in the coal-based structure in the longer term, a policy to deal with the overdependency on coal is most important. Because the efficiency of energy consumption is low in China, efforts must be made to raise it.

To relieve the stress placed on the transportation system from shipping coal, it is necessary to pursue—in addition to continuing the expansion of railway, canal, and road transport systems—the possibility of adding coal slurry transport systems.

Energy Conservation

Energy conservation since the late 1980s has achieved average annual results of 3.9 percent. It is hoped that efforts will be made to conserve energy at a rate of 4 percent or higher in the future. To this end, market mechanisms should be more vigorously applied, and energy conservation laws should be more strictly and vigorously enforced. In addition, incentives for energy conservation and punishments for waste should be implemented. To facilitate the scrapping of obsolete, energy-wasting equipment and the introduction of new equipment, replacement of old technology should be encouraged by raising depreciation rates, thereby shortening depreciation periods.

Environmental Protection

The use of coal by people in their daily living should be avoided. Efforts should be made in cities to convert to other energy sources such as gas. The use of coal in medium- and small-sized boilers should be reduced as far as possible. Although there is no alternative to using coal in larger boilers (including electric power plants) and in large-scale industrial ovens (e.g., in steel production coal is necessary for the reduction process), scrubbing and other antipollution equipment should be installed.

For Humanity in the Twenty-First Century

There would be a huge increase in energy consumption if per capita energy consumption for China's 1.2 billion people is ever raised to the level of advanced countries. This implies a potential challenge to the limits of world energy resources. Economically advanced countries, where awareness of the ecology has been deepening, are searching for an economic growth model that can substitute for the "big growth, big consumption, big pollution" model of the past. This search should also be an extremely important issue for the developing world, whose best representative may be China.

—*Yabuki*

9

Environmental Destruction

The Status of Air Pollution and Policies to Improve Air Quality

The Principal Pollutants in China

In the context of environmental pollution in China, the most important elements are sulfur dioxide, which manifests as acid rain, and industrial wastewater, which pollutes water resources. Table 9.1 shows the how the volume of three elements—sulfur dioxide, coal dust, and industrial wastewater—has increased and decreased during the ten-year period 1985–1995. During the mid-1980s the volume of sulfur dioxide emissions was in the range of 12–13 million tons. By 1995 it was approaching 20 million tons, an increase of 40 percent. Coal dust increased about 10 percent. Industrial wastewater decreased somewhat more than 10 percent.

The moderate increase in coal dust and the decrease in industrial wastewater are the result of remedial efforts. This is seen in the declining trend of industrial pollution incidents and the value of recompense awards, which peaked around 1990. The problem, then, is the increase in sulfur dioxide. This is the major cause of air pollution and of acid rain, which can cross borders into other countries.

Table 9.2 presents the findings of a survey by the Japanese Office of Science and Technology on sulfur dioxides emissions volume in the Asian region. From this table we see that the volume of emissions emanating from individual Chinese provinces is on par with individual Asian countries. The survey forecasts Chinese sulfur dioxide emissions in 2010 at 37.24 million tons. This assumes an average annual GNP growth rate of 4 percent. Since China is actually expected to grow at faster than twice that rate, we must also expect sulfur dioxide emissions to far exceed the forecast unless effective countermeasures are taken.

China relies upon coal for three-fourths of its primary energy. Compared to other energy sources, desulfurizing coal is technically difficult.

TABLE 9. 1 Environmental Pollutants and Environmental Recompensations and Fines, 1985-1995

Year	Sulfur Dioxide (mil. ton)	Coal Dust (mil. ton)	Industrial Wastewater (mil. ton)	Pollution Incidents (no.)	Pollution Recompensation (mil. RMB)	Pollution Fines (mil. RMB)
1985	13.25	12.95	257.4	2,716	506.9	9
1990	14.94	13.24	248.7	3,462	974.3	16
1995	18.91	18.91	221.9	1,966	385.4	4
1995/1985	1.4	1.1	0.9	0.7	0.8	0.4

Source: China Statistical Yearbook (each year).

Moreover, the coal produced in certain regions of China has a particularly high sulfur content. This places an increasingly heavy burden on the global environment.

Where Acid Rain Is Falling

Figure 9.1 illustrates the density level of sulfur dioxide in the air of major cities in China. The five worst areas in the south are Guiyang (Guizhou province), Chongqing (a directly administered municipality since 1997), Yichang (Hubei province, the city nearest the Three Gorges dam), Yibin (at the lower reaches of the Yangtze River in Sichuan province), and Wuzhou (Guang Zhuang Autonomous Region). What these five cities have in common is that they were developed as bases for heavy industry under the so-called Third Front policy for national defense (the third front was the most-interior line of defense, assuming a foreign attack came from the coastal region). China continues to suffer various damaging consequences of the Third Front policy. One is massive air pollution.

Including the five worst cities just mentioned, twenty-two cities—up to Leshan (Sichuan province)—have pollution levels exceeding China's second-level national standard. China's "atmospheric environment quality standard" establishes three levels: the first standard is for protected natural areas; the second is for urban residential and commercial areas and broad rural areas; the third is for industrial areas with severe air pollution. The standards are measured by three numerical values: (a) daily average numerical values over a one-year period (annual daily average); (b) daily numerical values that should never be exceeded (daily average);

TABLE 9. 2 Trends in Sulfur Oxides Emissions in the Asian Region

(unit: thousand tons / year)

Rank	Country/Region/ Province of China	2010 Forecast	Composition (a) (%)	1987 Actual	Composition (b) (%)	(a)/(b)
1	China	37,240	60.1	19,950	68.6	1.87
2	India	8,170	13.2	3,060	10.6	2.66
3	Sichuan	4,760	7.7	2,570	8.8	1.85
4	South Korea	3,880	6.3	1,290	4.4	3.00
5	Jiangsu	3,830	6.2	1,600	5.5	2.39
6	Taiwan	3,650	5.9	600	2.1	6.06
7	Shandong	3,310	5.3	1,970	6.8	1.68
8	Shaanxi	1,940	3.1	1,010	3.5	1.91
9	Shanghai	1,900	3.1	650	2.2	2.92
10	Liaoning	1,830	3.0	990	3.4	1.84
11	Thailand	1,800	2.9	610	2.1	2.96
12	Hebei	1,780	2.9	1,060	3.7	1.68
13	Henan	1,700	2.7	980	3.4	1.73
14	Japan	1,490	2.4	1,140	3.9	1.31
15	Indonesia	1,450	2.3	480	1.7	3.00
16	Guangdong	1,400	2.3	520	1.8	2.68
17	Shanxi	1,310	2.1	830	2.9	1.58
18	Yunnan	1,250	2.0	740	2.6	1.67
19	Guizhou	1,170	1.9	750	2.6	1.56
20	Zhejiang	1,150	1.9	410	1.4	2.79
21	Hubei	1,130	1.8	570	2.0	1.98
22	Pakistan	740	1.2	380	1.3	1.94
23	Malaysia	730	1.2	260	0.9	2.81
24	Philippines	730	1.2	370	1.3	1.98
25	Singapore	650	1.1	150	0.5	4.23
26	North Korea	520	0.8	330	1.1	1.59
27	Hong Kong	460	0.7	150	0.5	3.07
13 Asian regions		61,550	99.3	28,800	99.0	2.14
14 Provinces of China		28,500	46.0	14,690	50.6	1.94
Total in Asia		61,970	100.0	29,080	100.0	2.13

Source: Office of Science and Technology, Science and Technology Policy Research Institute, *"Energy Use and Volume of Emissions of Materials Affecting the Earth's Environment in the Asian Region,"* (April 1993), pp. 82-85.

76

FIGURE 9. 1 Sulfur Dioxide Density in the Air of Main Cities of China, 1995

unit: micrograms / m³ annual daily average

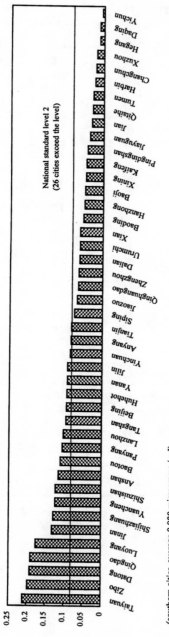

(northern cities, average 0.081 micrograms / m³)

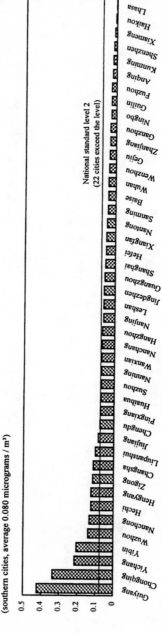

(southern cities, average 0.080 micrograms / m³)

Notes: ¹Annual daily average is the average of daily average densities throughout one year.

²National standard level 2 is 0.06 micrograms / m³.

Source: China Environment Yearbook 1996.

MAP 9.1 Areas with High Frequency of Acid Rain

Source: *China Environment Yearbook*, p.89.

and (c) numerical values that should not be exceeded even one time. Air pollution is elusive, but it can be captured using these three indicators. For example, the number-two standard for sulfur dioxide pollution (i.e., for urban residential and commercial areas and broad rural areas) is an average density of 0.06 micrograms per cubic meter and above for the annual daily average value; 0.15 micrograms and above for the daily average value; and 0.5 micrograms and above for the one-time value (Wang Hanmin, *China's Air Pollution and Its Countermeasures*, p. 67).

The five worst cities in the north are Taiyuan (Shanxi province), Zibo (Shandong province), Datong (Shanxi), Qingdao (Shandong), and Luoyang (Henan province). Shanxi province is China's largest coal-producing area. The pollution may be attributed to the brisk activity of township and village enterprises (TVEs) in the three cities. Including the worst five, twenty-six cities exceed the number-two standard of air pollution in the north, four more than in the south.

When it combines with rain, airborne sulfur dioxide produces acid rain. Maps 9.1 and 9.2 and Table 9.3 describe the scope of acid rain in China. Acid rain is prevalent in the southwest (Xinan), south (Huanan), central (Huazhong), and east (Huadong) regions. Some cities where the incidence of acid rain is high are Changsha, Ganzhou, Yibin, Huaihua, Leshan, Nanchang, Hengyang, Xiamen, and Nanchong.

MAP 9.2 Cities with High Frequency of Acid Rain

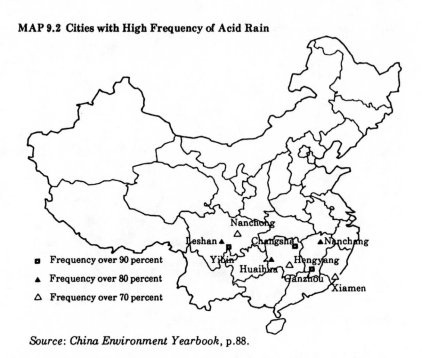

- ▣ Frequency over 90 percent
- ▲ Frequency over 80 percent
- △ Frequency over 70 percent

Source: *China Environment Yearbook*, p.88.

TABLE 9.3 Regions with High Incidence of Acid Rain, 1995

Region	Situation of Acid Rain
Central China	The most polluted. Acidic degree below 4 PH in the most impacted areas. Occurrence of acid rain over 80 percent.
Southwest China (main areas: Nanchong, Yibin, Chongqing, Zunyi)	Declining in recent years, but acidic degree below 5 PH in main areas. Occurrence of acid rain over 80 percent.
East China (the area south of the lower Yangtze to Xiamen)	Less severe than in the central China and southwest China regions. Widely spread over southern Jiangsu province, southern Anhui province, and most parts of Zhejiang province and the coastal section of Fujian.
South China (Pearl River delta and eastern Guangxi region)	Average annual 4.5-5.0 PH in heavily polluted cities. Frequency of acid rain in central areas 60-70 percent. Acid rain frequency in Guangxi above 30 percent.

Notes: [1]Acid rain in China occurs mainly south of the Yangtze River, east of the Qinghai-Tibet Highland, and in the Sichuan Basin.

[2]Among northeastern cities, Qingdao, Cumen, Taiyuan, and Shijiazhuang have below 5.6 PH.

Source: *China Environment Yearbook* 1996.

Where Black Rain Is Falling

According to observations made in eighty-seven key cities, the annual daily average value of total floating dust level in the atmosphere is 55–732 micrograms per cubic meter. The average is 392 micrograms per cubic meter for northern cities, 242 for southern cities. The annual daily average value in forty-five cities exceeds the second-level standard (51.7 percent of the observed cities; see Figure 9.2).

The five worst northern cities are Lanzhou, Jilin, Taiyuan, Jiaozuo, and Urumchi. Of the observed cities, thirty-four exceeded the national second-level standard. One cause is the use of coal as energy; another cause is loess dust. The five worst southern cities are Wanxian, Yichang, Liupanshui, Chengdu, and Guiyang. Only eleven of the observed cities exceeded the national second-level standard, however. This may be attributed to the south's avoidance of the damage done by loess dust as well as to its relatively greater rainfall, which naturally cleanses the atmosphere. According to observations made in eighty-four key cities, the annual daily average value of fallen coal dust was 3.7–60.13 tons per square kilometer per month, and the daily average was 17.7 tons per square kilometer per month. For southern cities the daily average was 10.16 tons per square kilometer per month, for northern cities 24.73 tons per square kilometer per month.

Japanese Environmental Aid to China

Table 9.4 presents a summary of environmental projects included in the first-half three-year period of the Japanese government's fourth yen loan program for China. Environment-related projects have been one of the main components of the Japanese yen loan program, and there are many projects. Environmental projects fall into three categories: water and sewer systems, antiatmospheric pollution measures, and water quality and pollution treatment. In short, air and water. In these areas, measures to address sources that generate pollution are important. In cities it is possible to centralize management of such sources by converting to town gas and by reducing the generation of sulfuric emissions from individual boilers.

With respect to protecting water quality, untreated or inadequately treated industrial wastewater-flows into streams and rivers are a problem. An effort is being made to offer a model for the hardware necessary to adequately treat sewage and wastewater.

FIGURE 9. 2. Total Volume of Suspended Particulates in the Air of Main Cities of China, 1995

(northern cities, average 392 micrograms / m³)   unit: micrograms / m³ annual daily average

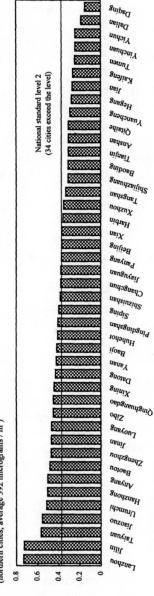

(southern cities, average 242 micrograms / m³)

Notes: [1] Annual daily average is the average of daily average densities throughout one year.

[2] National standard level 2 is 0.30 micrograms / m³ which is used in cities.

Source: China Environment Yearbook 1996.

MAP 9.3 Cities with High Total Suspended Particulates

(0.3 micrograms/cubic meter annual daily average value and above)

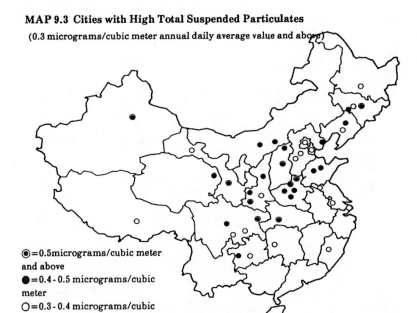

⊙ =0.5micrograms/cubic meter
and above
● =0.4 - 0.5 micrograms/cubic
meter
○ =0.3 - 0.4 micrograms/cubic
meter

Source: China Environment Yearbook.

At the December 1997 Global Warming Policy Conference in Kyoto, a great amount of time and effort was expended in "environmental diplomacy" (i.e., trying to accommodate conflicting interests between developed countries and between developed countries and developing countries). Such efforts were indicative of the difficulty of this issue. If the environmental cooperation between Japan and China can serve as a model, this will be much to the good.

—Yabuki

TABLE 9.4 Some Environmental Projects in the Fourth Yen Loans to China, first three years

Project	Project Summary	Cost
Waterworks		
Huhehot waterworks	To meet the needs of Huhenot city in Inner Mongolia. Construct a waterworks with 400,000 cubic meters/day capacity.	Yen 6 billion
Guiyang Western suburbs clean water plant	To remedy inadequate water supply situation, and meet future needs. Construct a waterworks with 400,000 cubic meters/day capacity.	Yen 5.8 billion
3rd Phase of Beijing No. 9 water plant	To deal with increased demand for water in Beijing city, construct a waterworks with 500,000 cubic meters/day capacity.	Yen 7.8 billion
"Yinghe Jiyan"	To increase water supply and to relieve intrusion of sea water due to excessive pumping of underground water, take water from a mid-point in Huanghe-Qingdao canal, channel the water to Yantai in Shandong province and build a water plant.	Yen 8.8 billion
Atmospheric Pollution		
Counteracting acid rain in Liuzhou	To counteract acid rain from coal burning, promoting gasification in the city, and constructing a waste treatment plant to deal with solid wastes.	Yen 10.5 billion
Counteracting air pollution in Benxi	To ameliorate air and water pollution from use of coal, construct facilities to treat emissions and waste water in Benxi in Liaoning province.	Yen 10.3 billion
Counteracting air pollution in Huhehot and Baotou	To comprehensively improve the environment in Inner Mongolia, supply concentrated heat and gas in the main cities of Huhehot and Baotou.	Yen 15.0 billion
Comprehensive environmental improvement in Lanzhou	To improve the environment in Lanzhou in Gansu province, construct gas pipelines and heat transporting pipelines. Also construct waterworks.	Yen 7.7 billion
Water Quality		
Comprehensive treatment of pollution of the Huaihe	To improve water quality in the Huaihe, construct industrial waste water and downstream treatment facilities in Henan province.	Yen 0.1 billion
Counteracting pollution in the Xiangjiang basin of Hunan	To ameliorate deteriorating water quality in the Xiangjiang due to city waste water, construct waste water treatment facilities.	Yen 0.2 billion

Source: Japanese Ministry of Foreign Affairs, Economic Cooperation Bureau.

10

Income Disparity

Can Economic Growth Close the Gap?

The Expanded Income Gap Between
Urban and Rural Residents

The Ninth Five Year Plan began in 1996. When drafting began in 1994–1995, regional disparity and income disparity were the subjects of loud and active debate. A then-recent World Bank report, *The East Asian Miracle* (1994), did not cover China, but its analysis of how the region had achieved a narrowing of income inequality while experiencing high economic growth was widely noted.

What about China?

Figure 10.1 and Table 10.1 present changes in per capita income of farm residents and city residents for the period 1985–1996. Per capita income for farm residents increased nearly fivefold, from RMB 398 in 1985 to RMB 1,926 in 1996. Adjusting for inflation, the increase in real terms would be 1.6 times greater. Per capita income for city residents increased 6.4 times from RMB 685 in 1985 to RMB 4,377 in 1996. Adjusting for inflation, the increase was 1.8 times greater in real terms.

Because the increase in income for farm residents increased only 1.6 times during this ten-year period, whereas that for city residents increased 1.8 times, the income disparity between the countryside and city widened. In 1985, if farm residents' income was given a value of one, then the value of city residents' income was 1.7 times. In 1994 it was 2.6 times, in 1995 2.5 times, and in 1996 2.3 times. Thus, until 1994 the trend was a widening disparity between the cities and farms, but in 1995–1996 the disparity actually narrowed. We can conceive of many reasons for this. In 1994 the farming areas took advantage of the commotion, prompted by a grain shortage, to raise prices for agricultural products. At the same time, many policies favoring agriculture were implemented, which fostered increased production. Also, the weather was good. Yet cities were feeling

FIGURE 10. 1 Trends in Income Per Capita of Urban and Rural Residents

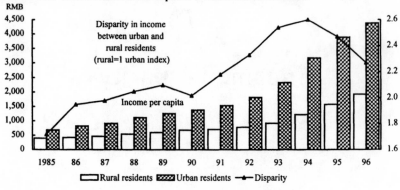

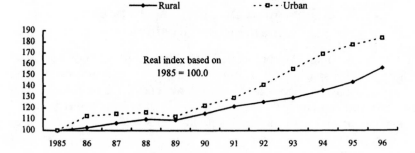

Source: Table 10. 1.

TABLE 10. 1 Trends in Income Per Capita of Urban and Rural Residents

(1985=100, growth rate is YoY %)

Year	Net Income Per Capita for Rural Residents				Disposable Income Per Capita for Urban Residents				Disparity
	RMB (A)	Nominal Growth Rate	Real Index	Actual Growth Rate	RMB (B)	Nominal Growth Rate	Real Index	Actual Growth Rate	(A) : (B)
1985	398	12.5	100.0		685	12.8	100.0		1 : 1.72
1986	424	6.6	102.6	2.6	828	20.8	112.9	12.9	1 : 1.95
1987	463	9.2	106.6	3.9	916	10.6	114.9	1.7	1 : 1.98
1988	545	17.8	110.1	4.0	1,119	22.2	116.3	1.2	1 : 2.05
1989	602	10.4	109.4	-1.3	1,261	12.6	112.4	-3.2	1 : 2.10
1990	686	14.1	115.1	5.2	1,387	10.0	122.4	8.9	1 : 2.02
1991	709	3.2	121.7	5.7	1,544	11.3	129.6	5.9	1 : 2.18
1992	784	10.6	125.6	3.2	1,826	18.2	141.3	9.0	1 : 2.33
1993	922	17.6	129.6	3.2	2,337	28.0	155.7	10.2	1 : 2.54
1994	1,221	32.5	136.1	5.0	3,179	36.1	169.4	8.8	1 : 2.60
1995	1,578	29.0	143.7	5.6	3,893	22.5	177.7	4.9	1 : 2.47
1996	1,926	22.1	156.6	9.0	4,377	12.4	183.6	3.3	1 : 2.27

Source: *China Statistical Yearbook* 1988, 1993-1997.

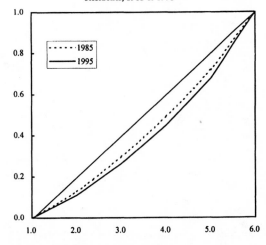

FIGURE 10. 2 Lorenze Curve for Per Capita Income of Urban
Residents, 1985 & 1995

Source: China Statistical Yearbook 1986, 1996.

the effects of a tightening of money and credit, and the consumer boom
was ending.

Lorenze Curve Illustration of Urban Residents' Income Inequality

The Lorenze curve is a graphic depiction of equality of income distribution. A graph is plotted against a horizontal axis measuring the proportion of the total population of income earners (cumulative percentage of
persons) and a vertical axis measuring the proportion of the total income
earned by persons (cumulative percentage of income). If income is dis-
tributed completely equally, the plotted line is a diagonal line. The curve
plotted below the diagonal line indicates inequality, and the area between
the curve and the diagonal line indicates the degree of inequality.

Figure 10.2 presents the Lorenze curve using per capita income for city
residents in 1985 and 1995. It shows that there has been a widening of income inequality.

Gini Coefficient Illustration of Urban Residents' Income Inequality

The Gini coefficient is a measure of the correlation between the Lorenze
curve (the inequality line) and the diagonal line (equality line). If the
Lorenze curve line tracks the diagonal line exactly, indicating complete

FIGURE 10. 3 Trends of Disparity in Per Capita Income for Urban Residents

Source: China Statistical Yearbook (each year).

FIGURE 10. 4 Trends of Disparity in Per Capita Income for Rural Residents

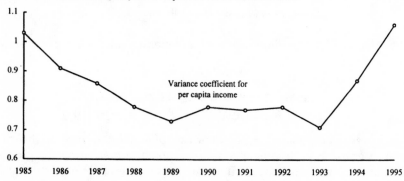

Source: China Statistical Yearbook (each year).

equality, then the value of the coefficient would be zero. If all income is in the hands of the ruler individually, then the value is one. Thus, the values of the Gini coefficient are from zero to one: the closer to one, the greater the inequality. Figure 10.3 presents changes in the disparity in per capita income for city residents. In 1985 the coefficient was 0.07. By 1995 it had increased to 0.10, indicating an increase in income disparity.

Variance Coefficient Illustration of Rural Residents' Income Inequality

Figure 10.4 presents the variance coefficient of per capita gross income in order to illustrate the changes in per capita income disparity for farm residents. From 1985 through 1989 the variance coefficient was consistently trending downward, indicating a narrowing of income disparities. The period 1990–1993 saw little change, as farming life reflected the slow-down in reform following the Tiananmen Incident. In summary, the trend was positive through 1993. However, 1994 and 1995 witnessed a rapid widening in income disparity.

Ranking of Personal Income by Province

The Gini coefficient and change coefficient are somewhat abstract concepts. Let us now consider more concrete evidence.

Figure 10.5 presents the province-level ranking of gross per capita income for farm residents (the category includes the income of "farmers" and the income of "workers" in township and village enterprises as well as "laborers" working outside the farm). The left axis plots money value at 1995 prices. The right axis is an index plotting China's province level units with the poorest, Gansu province, at a value of one, the others being at a multiple of this value. The richest "farm residents," in Shanghai's suburbs, had a per capita income of RMB 4,245, 4.8 times the RMB 880 in Gansu. The national average was RMB 1,578, about the level of Jilin and Jiangxi provinces.

Figure 10.6 presents the province-level ranking of gross per capita income of city residents. The parameters are the same as for the previous graph: The left axis is value in money at 1995 prices. The right axis is an index plotting China's provinces, with the poorest, the Inner Mongolia Autonomous Region, at one, and the other provinces at some multiple of this. The richest "city residents," in Guangdong province, had a per capita income of RMB 6,822, 2.6 times the RMB 2,587 of city residents in Inner Mongolia. The national average was RMB 3,893, roughly the levels in Shandong province and the Xinjiang Autonomous Region.

For city residents, the widest disparity is 2.6 times, compared with 4.8 times for farm residents. Generally speaking, this is because farmers near bigger cities can earn cash income by providing vegetables and other cash crops (e.g., flowers) to city residents and because they can receive wage income from work in township and village enterprises. In terms of wealth, they are better off than average workers in the cities.

Figure 10.7 compares the income disparity between cities and farms at the province level using 1995 prices. The smallest disparity is seen in Shanghai, the largest in Gansu province. How should we read this right-upsloping graph? It is interesting to contrast it to the right-downsloping graph in Figure 10.5. What can be understood is that the farther down the scale of rural poverty, the greater the disparity between city and farm incomes in the particular province.

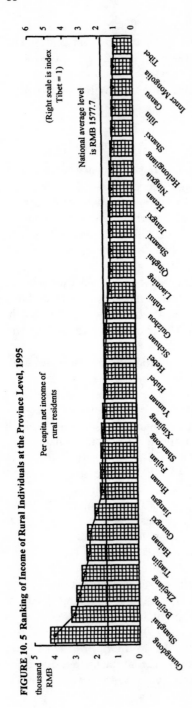

FIGURE 10. 5 Ranking of Income of Rural Individuals at the Province Level, 1995

Per capita net income of
rural residents

National average level
is RMB 1577.7

(Right scale is index
Tibet = 1)

Source: China Statistical Yearbook 1996.

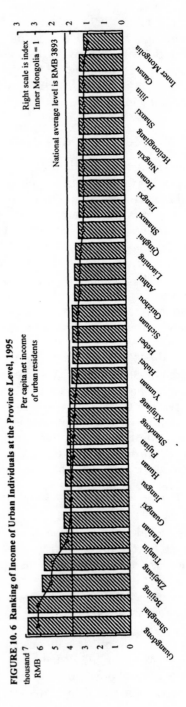

FIGURE 10. 6 Ranking of Income of Urban Individuals at the Province Level, 1995

Per capita net income
of urban residents

National average level is RMB 3893

Right scale is index
Inner Mongolia = 1

Source: China Statistical Yearbook 1996.

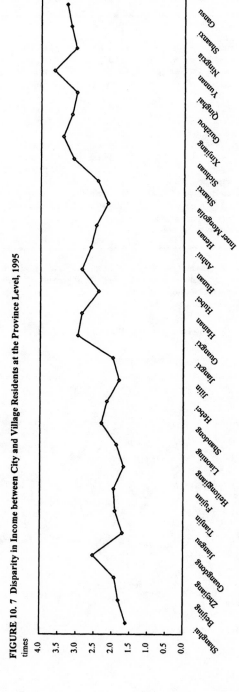

FIGURE 10. 7 Disparity in Income between City and Village Residents at the Province Level, 1995

Source: China Statistical Yearbook 1996.

90

TABLE 10. 2 Degree of Achievement of the "Well-Off" Standard

"Well-Off" Measurement Standard	"Well-Off" Standard	1995	Achievement Rate (percent)
Per capita GNP (1980 prices)	RMB 2,500	RMB 2,667	106.68
Income of urban residents (1980 prices)	RMB 2,400	RMB 1,787	74.44
Net income of rural residents (1980 prices)	RMB 1,200	RMB 734	61.13
Per capita living area in cities	8.0 sq. m.	8.1 sq. m.	101.25
Per capita living area in villages	15.0 sq. m.	15.0 sq. m.	100.00
Per capita protein consumption	114.3 grams	64.0 grams	56.00
Paved road area per capita in the cities	8.4 sq. m.	7.3 sq. m.	86.54
Proportion of village administrative areas reachable by motor vehicle roads	92 percent	88 percent	95.94
Adult literacy rate	91 percent	83.5 percent	91.00
Infant mortality rate	15.1 percent	33 percent	45.90
Proportion of consumer expenditures on education, culture, and entertainment	12.7 percent	8.1 percent	63.88
Forest coverage ratio	28.7 percent	8.1 percent	46.67
Ratio of elementary health protection services meeting basic standards in county level rural districts	100 percent	64.1 percent	64.10

Note: Figures from compilations in "China's Well Off Research," State Statistics Bureau. According to these compilations, at the end of 1995, 75.61 percent of the Chinese people were living at the "well-off" standard.
Source: Xinhua News Bulletin, October 1, 1997.

FIGURE 10.8 Level of Attainment of the "Well - Off" Standard, 1995

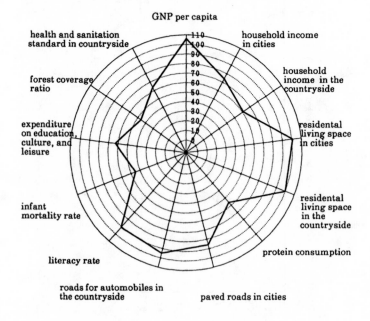

Source: Table 10.2.

TABLE 10.3   The Rural Poor and Their Distribution

Year	Poor Population	Ratio to Total Population	Ratio to Farm Population
1978	250 million persons	26.0%	31.6%
1995	65 million persons	5.4%	7.6%

Notes: [1]Annual net income per capita for half of the poor population is RMB 300 (at 1995 prices) or below, which is barely subsistence level.
[2]Those at subsistence level are living primarily in the deep mountain, desert, loess, plateau, and border areas of the central and western regions.

Source: "Decision by Party Central and State Council in Solving the Problem of the Poor Rural Population," October 23, 1996.

China's "Well-Off Standard" and Poverty Alleviation Plan

Table 10.2 and Figure 10.8 present data on China's "well-off standard" as of the end of 1995. The standard was met in such categories as GNP, housing, and living space. However, achievement was at only about 50 percent of the standard's objective in such categories as forest coverage area, infant mortality, and per capita protein intake.

Table 10.3 presents the number and regional distribution of persons in poverty in the countryside. In accordance with the so-called National 8 7 Anti-Poverty Campaign Plan (a policy adopted in 1994), China should strive to alleviate rural poverty before the beginning of the twenty-first century. The "8 7" refers to the goal of lifting 80 million persons in the countryside out of poverty in seven years' time (1993 to 2000) by solving the most basic needs of "warmth and adequate food" as the first step in meeting the "well-off standard."

The specific standard for "warmth and adequate food" (Chinese: *wen-bao*) is per capita gross income of RMB 300 per year (at 1995 prices). The number of people falling below this "poverty line" in 1995 had already been reduced to 65 million, or 5.4 percent of the total population (7.6 percent of the rural population). These were principally in the mountainous areas of the west-central region, in other mountainous regions, in desert areas, in colder high-elevation areas, and in loess plateau regions ("Decisions by Party Central and the State Council on Solving the Problems of the Poor Rural Population," October 23, 1996).

—Yabuki

11
Regional Disparity

Disparities Between East and West and Among the Coastal Provinces

Province-Level Results of the GDP Quadrupling Plan

We learned in Chapter 1 that the dream-plan of quadrupling GNP was realized on a national level. Let us investigate its achievement at the provincial level.

Table 11.1 presents the average (real) GDP growth rate at the province level for each five-year period after 1980, and the economic-plan targets up to 2000, and for some provinces to 2010. Figure 11.1 provides a test of the status of realization of the GDP quadrupling plan in 1995 by presenting an index of province-level GDP (in real terms) for each five years from 1980, with the 1980 baseline equaling 100.

The upper panel of Figure 11.1 is the GDP index. The index for Beijing municipality and Shaanxi province is 400. The regions to the right of Beijing all exceeded the quadrupling target. Taking the top provinces in order of highest achievement, the best six are Guangdong, Fujian, Zhejiang, Hainan, Jiangsu, and Shandong. All are located along the coast. In contrast, the worst six are Heilongjiang province, Qinghai province, Tibet Autonomous Region, Tianjin municipality, Hunan province, and Liaoning province. If we take Beijing and Shanghai together with Tianjin and Liaoning, we realize that there was a slowing in the growth of some coastal areas that had enjoyed relatively early starts at economic development. As a result, we may speculate that the disparity in economic levels between the coastal area and the interior have begun to show a narrowing trend during these fifteen years.

The regions where the GDP quadrupling plan was realized late or not realized at all were all located in central and western parts of China. As a consequence, we can easily speculate that the gap between the coastal

94

TABLE 11. 1   Economic Development Results and Plan at the Province Level

Region	GDP (real) Growth Rate			GDP Growth Rate Plan		GDP Quadrupling Realization Year	GDP Per Capita Quadrupling Realization Year
	80-85	85-90	90-95	1995-2000	2000-2010		
Coastal Region							
Beijing	9.2	8.2	11.8	9.0	9.0	1995	2000
Tianjin	9.3	5.2	11.8	10.0	8.4	1996	1998
Hebei	10.1	8.4	14.6	11.0		1994	
Liaoning	9.2	7.5	10.2	9.0-10.0	8.0-9.0		
Shandong	11.9	8.3	16.7	10.0	8.0-9.0	1993	1994
Shanghai	9.1	5.7	13.0	10.0	8.0	1996	1998
Jiangsu	13.2	10.0	17.0	12.0	12.0	1992	1993
Zhejiang	14.7	7.6	19.1	10.0		1992	
Fujian	13.2	9.8	19.3	13.0	11.5	1993	
Guangdong	12.2	13.3	19.1	about 11.0		1992	1993
Guangxi	8.3	6.1	16.7	17.6	15.0	1995	
Hainan	14.8	n. a.	17.9	about 15.0		1992	
Central Region							
Shanxi	10.0	6.4	10.1	12.0	11.8	1996	
Inner Mongolia	12.7	6.9	9.7	10.0	9.0	1995	
Jilin	10.7	7.7	10.9	10.0	9.5	1995	2000
Heilongjiang	7.2	5.2	7.9	11.6	7.2	1999	2000
Anhui	14.2	5.8	14.1	12.5	11.0	1994	1995
Jiangxi	10.3	7.4	13.8	10.0-12.0	8.0-10.0	1994	
Henan	11.7	7.6	13.0	10.0-12.0		1994	
Hubei	12.2	6.2	12.9	12.0	10.0	1995	2000
Hunan	9.1	6.6	11.1	10.0		1996	1998
Western Region							
Sichuan	9.7	6.4	11.5	10.0	8.0	2000	2000
Guizhou	12.4	6.7	8.7	9.0	10.0	1996	
Yunnan	11.8	9.3	10.2	10.0	about 8.0	1995	
Tibet	10.6	2.3	9.7	10.0	10.0-13.0		
Shaanxi	10.9	8.7	9.4	10.5		1995	
Gansu	8.1	9.6	9.7	8.0	8.0	2000	
Qinghai	9.0	5.3	7.6	9.0	9.0	1999	
Ningxia	11.4	7.9	8.1	9.0		1996	
Xinjiang	12.5	9.7	11.8	10.5	9.0	1994	
Total	10.7	7.9	12.0	8.0		1995	2000

Sources: *China's Regional Economy Through Seventeen Years of Reform and Opening-Up.*
Plan values from Overseas Economic Cooperation Fund, *China's Regional Development
Strategy: Status and Issues,* Ninth Five Year Plan for each province, Long Term Plan for 2010
(Excerpts), and government work reports.

95

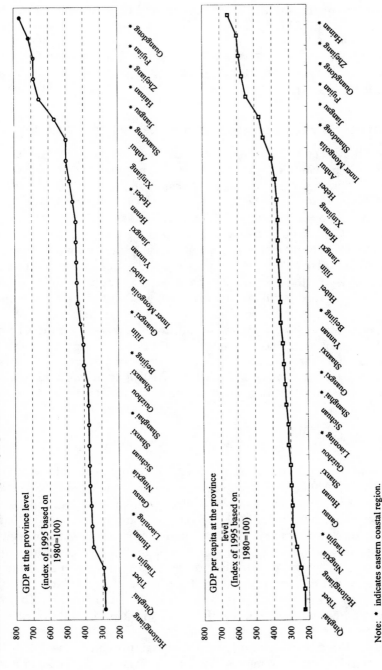

FIGURE 11.1 Realization of the GDP Quadrupling Plan at the Province Level

Note: * indicates eastern coastal region.

Source: Table 11.1.

and eastern region and the interior central and western regions probably expanded from 1980 to 1995.

The lower panel of Figure 11.1 is an index of per capita GDP at the province level. As at 1995, Anhui province had just achieved the target. The seven provinces to the right side of Anhui had all previously achieved the target.

Province-Level Changes in Shares of Economic Power

How did the relative balance of economic power, as measured by share of GDP at the province level, change during the process of economic growth from 1980 through 1995? Taking provincial GDP shares in 1980 as the horizontal axis and shares in 1995 as the vertical axis, we create Figure 11.2.

Provinces appearing above the diagonal line have achieved an increase in relative GDP share. They include: Guangdong, Jiangsu, Shandong, Fujian, and Hainan. By ranking, Guangdong catapulted from sixth place in 1980 to first place in 1995, Jiangsu from twelfth place to fifth. In contrast, provinces below the diagonal line have seen their relative shares diminish. They include Sichuan province, Shanghai municipality, Liaoning province, Tianjin municipality, and Beijing municipality. Sichuan province, first in 1980, declined to fourth place in 1995, Shanghai from third place to ninth, and Liaoning from fifth place to eighth. Almost all provinces and autonomous regions in the interior's central and western regions saw their relative shares diminish. This indicates a general decline in the share of the national economy of the central and western regions.

Province-Level Changes in Per Capita GDP

Let us look at changes in per capita GDP rankings at the province level (Table 11.2). Although their advantage versus the national GDP average narrowed in the fifteen years (1980–1995), Shanghai, Beijing, and Tianjin municipalities maintained their top rankings on a per capita GDP basis. Due to the slowdown in GDP growth of the three northeastern provinces, the position of Liaoning province declined from fourth place to eighth, Heilongjiang fell from fifth place to tenth, and Jilin province dropped from eleventh to fourteenth. By contrast, the frenetic growth of Guangdong province propelled it from seventh place to fifth, and Zhejiang province jumped from tenth to fourth. Other significantly advancing provinces were Shandong, Fujian, Hainan, and the Guangxi Autonomous Region. Notably stagnating were Qinghai province, the Tibet Autonomous Region, the Ningxia Autonomous Region, and Gansu province in the western region.

FIGURE 11.2 Change in GDP Share at the Province Level, 1980-1995

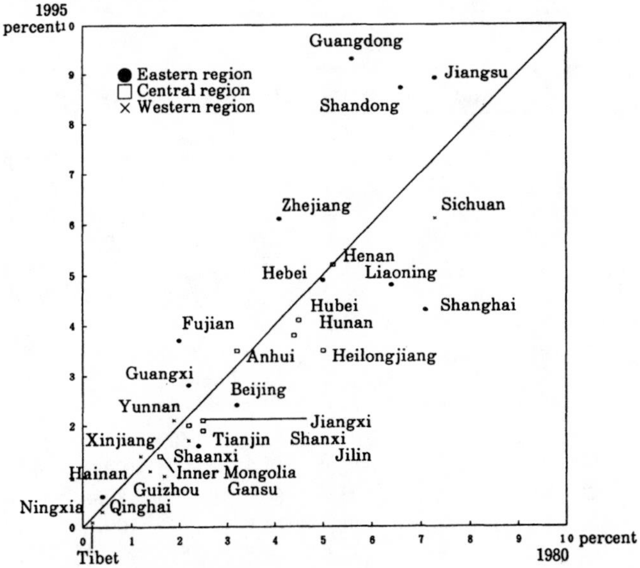

Source: *China's Regional Economy Through Seventeen Years*
         of Reform and Opening-Up, p.165.

How Should We View
Regional Income Disparities?

There has been much debate about China's regional disparities based on various indicators. One particularly interesting article that brings together the strands of the debate is "An Analysis of China's Regional Income Disparities" (*Economic Research*, November 1996), by Wei Houkai of the Industrial Economy Research Institute of the Chinese Academy of Social Sciences. Wei Houkai uses the Shollock's coefficient to test the relationship of the disparities. Let us look at his findings.

The main disparities in regional income in China are disparities at the province level among the provinces in the eastern region and disparities among the three great regions of the East, Center, and West.

At the province level in the East, the greatest disparities are the gaps between the income levels of Shanghai, Beijing, and Tianjin and the provinces of Guangxi, Hebei, and Hainan. The 1990s income levels in Guangdong, Fujian, Zhejiang, and Hainan have risen rapidly. This is seen in a narrowing of the province-level disparities in the eastern region from 1985 to 1995.

In contrast to the narrowing of the disparities at the province level in the eastern region, the disparities among the three great regions of the

TABLE 11. 2 Province Level Per Capita GDP, 1980-1995

Region	1980		1985		1990		1995	
	RMB	index	RMB	index	RMB	index	RMB	index
Shanghai	2,738	595.2	3855	450.9	5910	360.8	18943	398.5
Beijing	1,582	343.9	2704	316.3	3224	196.8	13073	275.0
Tianjin	1,392	302.6	2198	257.1	3621	221.1	10308	216.8
Zhejiang	470	102.2	1063	124.3	2122	129.5	8074	169.8
Guangdong	473	102.8	982	114.9	2395	146.2	7973	167.7
Jiangsu	541	117.6	1053	123.2	2103	128.4	7299	153.5
Fujian	350	76.1	741	86.7	1788	109.2	6965	146.5
Liaoning	811	176.3	1413	165.3	2698	164.7	6880	144.7
Shandong	402	87.4	887	103.7	1815	110.8	5758	121.1
Heilongjiang	694	150.9	1062	124.2	2028	123.8	5465	115.0
Hainan	354	77.0	729	85.3	1589	97.0	5225	109.9
Xinjiang	410	89.1	820	95.9	1799	109.8	4819	101.4
Hebei	427	92.8	719	84.1	1465	89.4	4444	93.5
Jilin	445	96.7	868	101.5	1746	106.6	4414	92.8
Hubei	428	93.0	808	94.5	1556	95.0	4162	87.5
Inner Mongolia	361	78.5	809	94.6	1478	90.2	3639	76.5
Shanxi	442	96.1	838	98.0	1528	93.3	3569	75.1
Guangxi	278	60.4	471	55.1	1066	65.1	3543	74.5
Hunan	365	79.3	626	73.2	1228	75.0	3470	73.0
Qinghai	473	102.8	808	94.5	1558	95.1	3430	72.1
Anhui	291	63.3	646	75.6	1182	72.2	3357	70.6
Ningxia	433	94.1	737	86.2	1393	85.0	3328	70.0
Henan	317	68.9	580	67.8	1091	66.6	3313	69.7
Sichuan	329	71.5	599	70.1	1105	67.5	3201	67.3
Jiangxi	342	74.3	597	69.8	1128	68.9	3080	64.8
Yunnan	267	58.0	486	56.8	1224	74.7	3044	64.0
Shaanxi	338	73.5	608	71.1	1244	75.9	2843	59.8
Tibet	471	102.4	894	104.6	1276	77.9	2392	50.3
Gansu	388	84.3	608	71.1	1099	67.1	2288	48.1
Guizhou	219	47.6	420	49.1	810	49.5	1853	39.0
Total	460	100.0	855	100.0	1638	100.0	4754	100.0

Note: Index calculated as national average equals 100.

Source: *China's Regional Economy Through Seventeen Years of Reform and Opening-Up.*

East, Center, and West widened from 1985 to 1995 so that the disparities are greater than in the East. However, improvement in both was observed in 1994 and 1995. In short, the strategy of developing the coastal region was effective, and as a consequence of development of the coastal region the gap between that region and the central and western regions of the country widened.

In view of this situation Chinese authorities have resolved to develop the central and western regions by, among other things, improving infrastructure in those areas within the regions where development potential is greatest. Also, through adjustments in liberalization policies, the goal is to shift a portion of foreign investment from the East to the Center and West. However, China has been, from the start, a country with huge regional disparities. And in a country with such diversity, the notion of equal regional development is highly unrealistic. In reality, the widening of regional disparities, that is, wage disparities, has given rise to movement of large numbers of laborers to higher-wage areas. We can view this as one of the factors that has been underpinning China's rapid growth. In short, although the authorities seek to eliminate regional disparities, realistically there are limits to what can be done, and we should not be too optimistic. It is probably enough to hope that regional disparities can be contained within limits in a way that poses no serious threat to political stability.

Correlation Between GDP Growth Rate and the Non–State-Owned Industrial Sector

The first half of the 1990s was a period of spectacular growth for the Chinese economy. From 1990 through 1995 the average annual growth rate reached 11.6 percent. Especially remarkable were provinces that achieved growth rates close to 20 percent, like Fujian at 19.3 percent, Guangdong at 19.1 percent, and Zhejiang at 19.1 percent. Some provinces' performances were less spectacular, however, with the worst three being Qinghai at 7.6 percent, Heilongjiang at 7.9 percent, and the Ningxia Autonomous Region at 8.1 percent. Still, in a today's global slow-growth era, 7–8 percent growth is exceptional.

China is a huge country with great disparities in resources. The conditions underpinning development in each locality are different, and results vary greatly. We can, however, identify some common factors that contribute to high growth as well as those that inhibit growth.

We have seen many reports of the dynamism of foreign-invested enterprises and township and village enterprises and of the declining status of state-owned enterprises. There is a clear tendency toward higher GDP growth rates as the proportion of non–state-owned enterprise increases. In Fujian, Guangdong, and Zhejiang provinces the non–state-owned sector accounts for more than 70 percent of industrial output. By contrast, in the low GDP growth rate provinces of Qinghai, Heilongjiang, and the Ningxia Autonomous Region the non–state-owned output share rests at 12.4 percent, 25 percent, and 25.5 percent respectively.

Differences in Ownership, Enterprise Scale, and Heavy and Light Classifications in Industry for Key Provinces and Cities

The category of non–state-owned industry used in the previous section is not a rigorous one, so let us try to be more specific. Figure 11.3 presents a breakdown of share of gross output value at the province level of enterprises according to ownership, enterprise scale, and heavy or light industrial structure. In the case of two provinces that leaped forward during the period 1980–1995, Guangdong and Fujian, FIEs were contributing almost 50 percent of industrial output value by 1995, whereas the state-owned industry's share was less than 30 percent. Looking at the chart, it is obvious which sector has been the driver of industrial development in Guangdong and Fujian provinces.

A second model is observed in analyzing Jiangsu and Zhejiang provinces. Here, state-owned industry has declined to less than 30 percent of output, whereas collectively owned industry accounts for more than 50 percent. FIEs constitute between 10 and 20 percent. Thus, we see that TVEs have been a large contributing factor in these provinces. We can point to a third type, a region where SOEs still contribute more than 50 percent of industrial output. This is the case in the interior provinces of Heilongjiang, Hunan, and Sichuan. At the same time, FIEs make up less than 5 percent of output value. And whereas Liaoning province resembles the interior provinces in terms of the large share of SOEs, by virtue of having the open city of Dalian its FIEs contribute 10 percent of production. The relatively good infrastructure of the directly administered municipalities of Beijing, Tianjin, and Shanghai creates conditions that appeal to FIEs, and the share of such enterprises is high. However, the share of SOEs reaches 40–50 percent, presenting yet another model.

It gets more complicated still. In the 1990s many SOEs incorporated and reorganized as limited liability stock companies. By the end of 1997 more than 700 erstwhile SOEs had issued shares to the public and were being traded on stock exchanges. The Fifteenth Party Congress in fall

FIGURE 11. 3 Composition of Industrial Enterprises by Ownership in Main Provinces and Cities

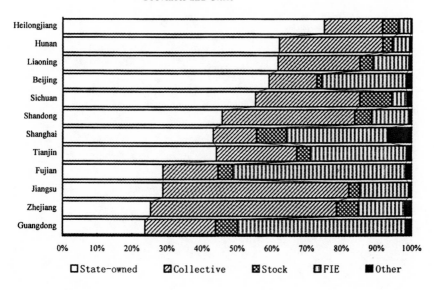

Source: Table 6.6.

1997 officially endorsed the process of corporatization and transformation to limited liability stock companies. Thus, what is happening is not simply a change in name but also a transformation of China's state-owned sector into real companies.

—Yabuki

12

The Consumption Revolution

The Chinese Market— Toward Multistrata Development

The Consumption Revolution in China

One can point to a number of major differences between the Mao Zedong and Deng Xiaoping eras, but particularly striking is the emergence of what might be called a consumer culture. During the Mao Zedong era the "four precious items" were a bicycle, a sewing machine, a radio, and a wristwatch. One of the most remarkable developments of the Deng Xiaoping era has been how in the minds of many Chinese consumers a color television has gradually replaced a radio, an automobile replaced a bicycle, a mobile telephone replaced a wristwatch, and buying name-brand fashions in boutiques replaced making clothes on a home sewing machine.

During the Mao Zedong era, still under the Cold War system, Chinese people were required to restrict consumption to the bare necessities. To the extent practicable, "forced savings" was enforced. There was a rush to industrialize and to strengthen military power. The official line was *fumin qiangguo*, or "a powerful nation and a rich people," but by the end of the period the people had become deeply dissatisfied with the meager consumption level. This was particularly true of domestic (mainland) Chinese, who observed the relative opulence of Chinese from Taiwan, Hong Kong, or Southeast Asia when those overseas citizens returned for visits to the mainland.

Deng Xiaoping, observing the stagnation brought about by the planned economy system, particularly the detrimental effects on agricultural production of the collectivization, implemented agricultural reform during the first half of the 1980s. This led to a substantial rise in farm incomes, but the purchasing power of farmers tended to go first into building new houses, then into acquiring the old "four precious items." From the second half of the 1980s through the 1990s, foreign-invested joint-venture companies built large-volume production lines for consumer durable products, of which the color TV is a symbol. These new products have found some overseas markets and become a source of foreign exchange earnings while also finding an expanding domestic market.

Now consumption has become a major driver of economic development. The structure of the Chinese economy has changed from "forced savings, low consumption, and low growth" to "forced consumption, high growth."

Differences in Consumption Levels Between Cities and Villages

Figure 12.1 presents trends in the consumption levels of farmers and nonfarmers. During the Deng Xiaoping era consumption as measured in nominal prices increased dramatically, that is, the absolute value of consumption for farmers increased from RMB 138 per year in 1978 to RMB 1,756 in 1996. For nonfarmers (including rural residents not classified as farmers) the figure increased from RMB 405 to RMB 5,626. In each case this was more than a tenfold increase. However, with the abandonment of the policy of frozen prices during the Mao Zedong era, prices were allowed to rise, and this "catch-up" process appeared as general inflation. Thus, to measure real effects we should apply a "deflator." If we take the price level in 1978 as a value of 100 and apply a real index, we calculate farmers' annual consumption in 1996 at 350. For nonfarmers the index was 308. In other words, in each case there was a roughly threefold increase. Also apparent is the fact that the countryside has taken the lead in reform, whereas cities and industrial reforms have been trailing.

If we assign a farmer's consumption a value of one, then compare the consumption of a nonfarmer, we find that in 1978 the index was 2.9, whereas in 1985 it had declined to 2.3. This was the period of rapid advances in rural reform. Afterward, development in villages moderated while reform momentum grew in cities, so that by 1994 the nonfarm figure had widened to 3.5, declining slightly to 3.4 in 1995 and to 3.2 in 1996.

The Chinese People's Changing Diet

Figure 12.2 shows the items that Chinese people have begun to eat more of and less of during this process of development. In cities and the countryside, the item topping consumption growth is alcoholic beverages

FIGURE 12. 1 Trends in Consumption Level for Farmers and Nonfarmers

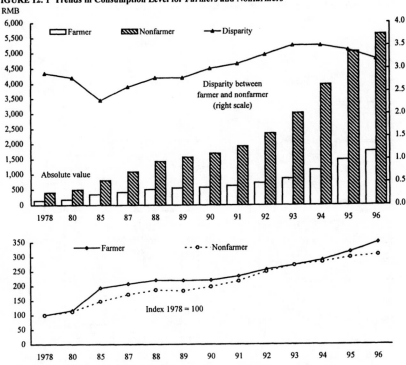

Source: China Statistical Yearbook 1997, p. 292.

(beer, wine, and spirits). Does this reflect the many banquets that were held to celebrate higher living standards arising from reform and liberalization?

Next is poultry, meat, and eggs. It is interesting to note this growth in contrast to the stagnation of pork consumption. In the cities, pork consumption changed hardly at all. During the recession of 1990, an aftereffect of the Tiananmen Incident, consumption of poultry, meat, and eggs stagnated while pork consumption increased. This phenomenon is attributable to the abundant supply of pork in cities and the tendency of people to turn toward this cheaper meat during times of recession. The situation is basically the same in the countryside. Taking 1980 as a base-level year, consumption of pork has been stable since rising by 40 percent to 1985.

Consumption of vegetable oil has been rising, but this is related to the decline in pork consumption. Poor people use lard in wok-style fry cooking. When cooled, lard becomes like wax and is foul-smelling. When people become more affluent, they tend to use vegetable oil. Pork has held a preeminent position in Chinese cuisine for millennia, but as the Chinese

106

FIGURE 12.2 Change in Volume of Items Purchased by Urban and Rural
Households

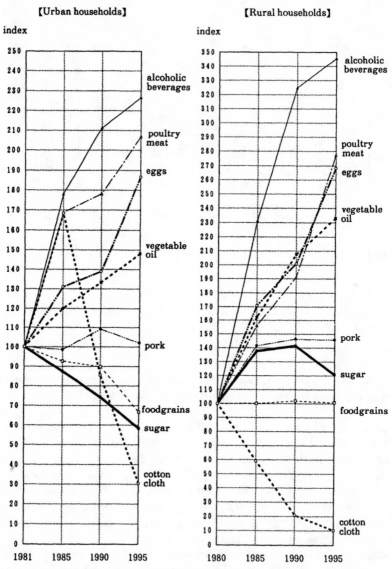

[Urban households]　　　　　　　[Rural households]

Source: China Statistical Yearbook, 1988, pp. 808, 825; 1996, pp. 283, 309.

prosper they want something different. Now the most desired menu is seafood prepared Hong Kong–style.

What, then, has been decreasing in the Chinese menu? In the cities, food grains (rice and wheat) and sugar have registered continuous declines. This shows that the main dish is now something more substantial than rice, noodles, or buns. The graph shows that consumption of starchy foods is declining while that of higher-quality foods is rising at a rapid rate.

In the countryside, in contrast, consumption of food grains has been basically stable, or at least has not entered a period of sustained decline. After rising until 1990, sugar consumption is trending down. This hints that the patterns observed today in the cities will begin to prevail in the countryside tomorrow. When synthetic fibers and fabrics became widely available after 1985, consumption of cotton cloth declined steadily. This trend was the same in cities and the countryside.

Changes in Ownership Levels of Consumer Durables

How widespread have consumer durable goods become? Let us look at holdings per 100 households over a number of five-year periods (Figure 12.3).

In the cities the most widely held goods are color TVs and washing machines, already in more than 90 percent of households. Refrigerators are found in somewhat less than 70 percent of households, cameras in 30–40 percent. Showing declines are sewing machines and black-and-white TVs.

Looking at farm households, we see a slightly different situation. The most widely held durable is still the sewing machine, and the ownership level of this durable good continues to rise. From this we can understand that farms remain distant from city boutiques and department stores. And although black-and-white TVs are rapidly being replaced by color TVs in cities, the older technology is still found in more than 60 percent of farm households—and the figure continues to rise.

This suggests that the growth potential for color TVs and washing machines, among other consumer durables, may be greater in the countryside than in the nearly saturated cities. This will require, on the one hand, larger-scale production and resulting lower sales prices, and, on the other hand, increases in purchasing power in the countryside. Both these trends are clearly evident. At the same time, manufacturers believe that saturation in the cities is more apparent than real. The TVs and washing machines of many city residents were purchased during the late 1980s or early 1990s, meaning that they are already five to ten years old and ready for replacement by newer, more technologically advanced models.

FIGURE 12.3 Trends in Holdings of Durable Consumer Goods Per 100 Urban and Rural Households

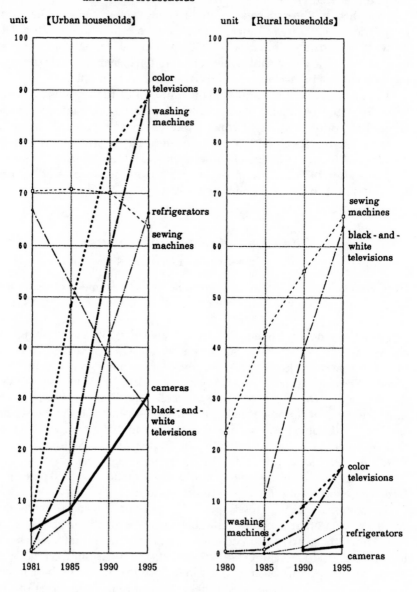

Source: China Statistical Yearbook 1996, pp. 283, 309.

Consumption Patterns of City Residents by Income Levels

Figure 12.4 divides urban household incomes into seven levels and shows for each level the volume of purchases of various goods. An index is provided whereby purchase volumes of the lowest-income households are given a value of one. Looking first at foodstuffs, the largest income-associated gap—three times—is seen in dairy products. Furthermore, the gap up to the higher-middle–income rank is only two times. Thus we see that dairy-product consumption rises rapidly in the high-income range. Following are beer and fruits, which show a sharply rising consumption trend as income rises. This is in contrast to pork, eggs, and sugar, consumption of which does not increase at the same pace as income grows, indicating a situation of saturation. This is particularly evident with starch and tubers.

Looking at clothing, we see an order of women's clothing, men's clothing, and children's clothing. This is the age of treating the only child as a "little emperor." Up to the middle income level, purchases of children's clothes rise with income, but it appears that at this level everything that might be desired has already been purchased, so there is no further increase up the income scale. The good that most reflects income levels is women's clothing. Chinese cities are no exception when in comes to providing an environment in which women pursue fashion.

FIGURE 12. 4 Volume of Goods Purchased Per 100 Urban Households Viewed by Income Level

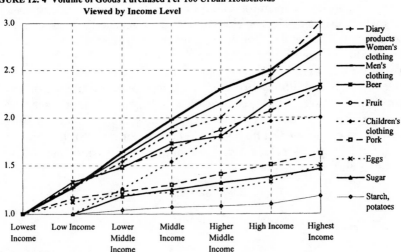

Source: *China Statistical Yearbook* 1996, p. 295.

FIGURE 12. 5 Holdings of Durable Consumer Goods per 100 Urban Households
units   Viewed by Income Level

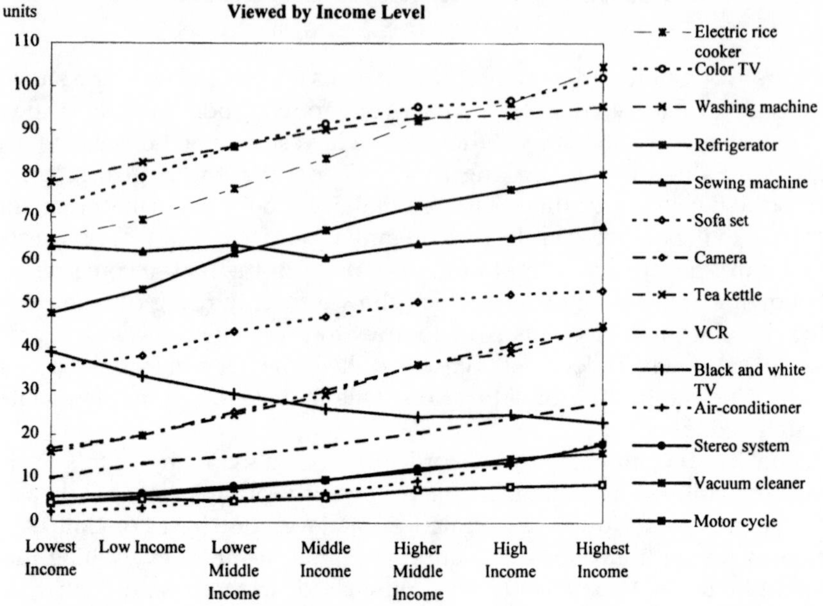

Source: *China Statistical Yearbook* 1996, p. 295.

Holdings of consumer durables per 100 urban households are presented in Figure 12.5. Color TVs are found in nearly 80 percent of even the poorest households, meaning that they are close to the next stage: two TV sets per household. Electric rice-cookers have reached a peak of market penetration. The gentle slope of the line for washing machines shows that there is little variance among income levels. The association between rising income and possession is notable for refrigerators. There is considerable regional variation, with much greater demand in the south. In the north, and in much of the countryside, a refrigerator is not considered a necessity, and is not in fact a necessity, for most Chinese families. Food is purchased or grown and then prepared daily. For much of the year, food keeps in the open for days without spoiling. Beer is consumed warm in summer and cold in winter.

—*Yabuki*

13

Industry Structure

Structural Adjustment Occurring Alongside Growth

The Relative Contraction of Primary Industry and the Expansion of Tertiary Industry

The upper panel of Figure 13.1 shows changes in contributions to GDP by different industrial sectors from 1980 through 1996. Looking at the structure in 1980 we see that primary industry accounted for 30.0 percent of GDP, secondary industry 48.6 percent, and tertiary industry 21.4 percent. Looking at the structure in 1996 we find primary industry at 20.2 percent, secondary industry 49.0 percent, and tertiary industry 30.8 percent. During this sixteen-year period the proportion of primary industry declined by 10 percentage points, that of tertiary industry increased by 10 points, with that of secondary industry remaining roughly unchanged.

What, then, was the sectoral composition of employment? As we see in the lower panel, 68.7 percent of employment in 1980 was in primary industry, 18.3 percent in secondary industry, and 13.0 percent in tertiary industry. By 1996 the proportion of employment in primary industry was 50.5 percent, secondary industry 23.5 percent, and tertiary industry 26.0 percent. Employment in primary industry declined 18.2 percentage points, that of secondary industry increased 5.2 points, and that of tertiary industry increased 13.0 points. Thus, the decline of relative employment in the primary sector was made up by employment in the secondary and tertiary sectors at a ratio of 1:2.5.

Figure 13.2 presents a ranking by primary industry of the proportion of primary, secondary, and tertiary industry in GDP at the province level. Primary industry makes up the greatest proportion of GDP in Tibet, whereas it makes up the smallest in Shanghai. The relative shares in

112

FIGURE 13. 1 Trends in Composition of GDP and Number of Employees, 1980-1996
〖Composition of GDP〗

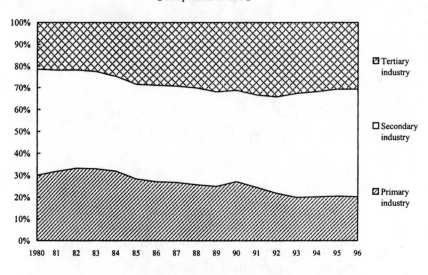

〖Composition of number of employees〗

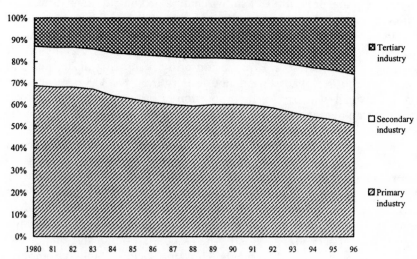

Source: *China Statistical Yearbook* 1997, pp. 42, 94.

113

FIGURE 13. 2 Industry Composition of GDP at the Province Level, 1995

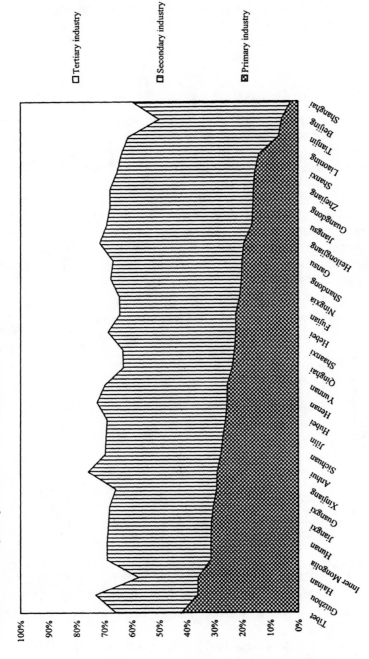

Source : China Statistical Yearbook 1997, p. 44.

Shandong province approximate the situation for the country as a whole. The shares of tertiary industry in Beijing and Hainan are extraordinary. In Anhui, Henan, Heilongjiang, and Shanghai, secondary industry occupies a relatively large share.

A View of Industrial Structure by Ownership

Secondary industry comprises manufacturing and construction. The construction sector constitutes some 12–13 percent of secondary industry. The share of state-owned companies, which had been slightly less than 80 percent at the beginning of the reform period, had fallen to less than 30 percent by 1996.

Figures 13.3 and 13.4 suggest that the reason for the rapid development of foreign-invested industrial enterprises and private industrial enterprises, and the stagnation of state-owned industrial enterprises, is the great disparity in labor productivity. The productivity of SOEs as measured by output per worker shows essentially no increase. There appears to be some improvement after 1990, but this is only the result of restating

FIGURE 13. 3 Trends in Labor Productivity of Industrial Enterprises by Ownership

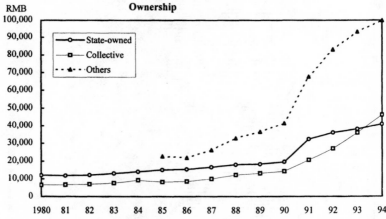

Notes: [1]Figures are for nation-wide independent accounting enterprises at or above village level.

[2]Labor productivity = industrial production value added / average number of employees.

[3]Figures before 1990 are based on 1980 prices, whereas those after 1991 are based on 1990 prices.

[4]Figures for collective industry are figures for city collective industries before 1984. After 1985 the figures are for industries at or above village level.

Source: *Almanac of China's Economy 1995.*

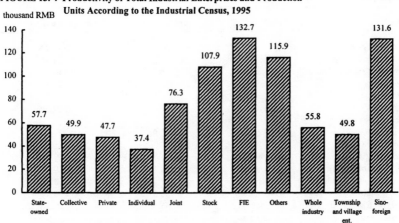

FIGURE 13. 4 **Productivity of Total Industrial Enterprises and Production Units According to the Industrial Census, 1995**

Note: Productivity = total industrial production / year-end employees.

Source: *The Data of the Third National Industrial Census of the People's Republic of China in 1995.*

1980 prices at a new standard introduced for 1990 prices. The character of collective industry is close to that of private industry. Combining with state-owned industry forms that are close to it, we have two major and separate categories. If we consider the average of the former and the latter, we get figures that are close to those for state-owned industry, but we can also see the strong development trend in recent years of private industry and foreign-invested industry.

Growth of Key Industrial Products

What industrial products have registered the fastest growth in the ten years between 1985 and 1995? Table 13.1 shows that the highest growth rate is in personal computers. We may view this as ample evidence that China is actively pursuing the goal of creating an information society. The second fastest growth rate is in home air-conditioners. As in the case of personal computers, the immense increase (fifty-five–fold) is a result of development from zero ten years before. In third place is household refrigerators. The annual production of close to 10 million units is six times greater than ten years before.

Such basic industrial materials and infrastructure-related products as cement, flat glass, nonferrous metals, and electric power–generating equipment registered some threefold growth. In 1995 automobile production was 1.45 million vehicles. Of this, less than 20 percent were passenger cars, the rest being trucks.

TABLE 13. 1 Output and Growth Rates of Important Industrial Products, 1985-1995

Product	Unit	Output in 1995	Growth Rate versus 1985
Personal computers	thousand	836.0	6964.0 %
Room airconditioners	million	6.8	5530.0 %
Refrigerators (family use)	million	9.2	630.0 %
Cement	million tons	475.6	330.0 %
Automobiles	million	1.5	330.0 %
Flat glass	million	157.3	320.0 %
Ten types of non-ferrous metals	million tons	5.0	320.0 %
Electric power generating equipment	million kw	16.7	300.0 %
Paper and paper board	million tons	28.1	310.0 %
Electric power (volume)	billion kwh	1,007.0	250.0 %
Diesel engines	million kw	158.2	250.0 %
Television sets	million	35.0	210.0 %
Crude steel	million tons	95.4	200.0 %
Agricultural chemical fertilizer	million tons	25.5	92.7 %
Cloth	billion meter	26.0	77.4 %
Coal	billion tons	1.4	56.1 %
Sugar	million tons	5.6	23.8 %
Metal working machine tools	thousand	203.0	21.7 %
Natural gas	million tons	150.0	20.4 %
Wood products	million m^3	67.7	7.0 %
Washing machines (family use)	million	9.5	6.9 %

Source: *The Data of the Third National Industrial Census of the People's Republic of China in 1995.*

The low growth rate of energy resources such as coal and natural gas is a reflection of the severe difficulties China is facing in energy supply. The shortage in timber is acute.

Pillar Industries in the Ninth Five Year Plan

The Ninth Five Year Plan (1996–2000) and key elements of the Long Term Goals for 2010 were announced at the National People's Congress in March 1996. What are termed "leading industries" in the West are called "pillar industries" in China. Pillar industries comprise six separate industries: machinery, electronics, petrochemicals, automotive, construction and building materials, and light industry and textiles.

Province-level authorities eagerly have incorporated development of pillar industries into provincial plans. This reflects the desire of every province to stand on an equal footing with every other province in terms of development, although to a large degree that contravenes the intent of the Central government's policy. A symbol of this "one-set" mentality is the automotive industry, which was universally targeted for development.

The director of the (former) State Planning Commission (SPC), Chen Jinhua, had this to say about the difficulty of overcoming duplicate investment:

> Looking at the Ninth Five Year Plan drafted by the localities, we can say that we still have not avoided the pitfalls of duplicate investment. Of the 30 planning level units, 22 have designated automobiles as a pillar industry, and all propose final automobile assembly plants. If we aggregate the plans of the localities, we will have production volume of 5.7 million vehicles in the year 2000. This is 2.1 times the 2.7 million vehicle target for 2000 in the Ninth Five Year Plan. We see similar phenomena in the electronics, petrochemical, and petroleum refining sectors. On the other hand, when we look at demand and sales ratios, we see a decline. The situation is changing from a "seller's market" to a "'buyer's market." (*People's Daily*, December 17, 1997)

Restructuring Industry to Enhance International Competitiveness

Table 13.2 is an excerpt of an article that appeared in the March 5, 1997, *Economic Daily* that provided an analysis, from an international perspective, of the extent of backwardness in Chinese enterprises. Table 13.3 is a summary based on data collected in China's industrial census, showing how duplicate investment has led to low rates of capacity utilization.

What is termed "structural adjustment" in Japan (Chinese: *jiegou tiaozheng*) is now a dominant theme in China. The phrase means change in the structure of enterprise organizations and industries, of geographic regional relationships, and of products produced. Everything is now the target of structural adjustment. We can analyze generally structural reform in the national economy.

Today, particular focus is placed on sectoral adjustment in such "basic industries" as energy and transport. The aim is to elicit active involvement of commercial and government entities at the local and Central levels by permitting to exist or by creating multiple investment vehicles or entities (as opposed to the previous system of a single, monopolistic state investment entity). Among the forms in which structural adjustment is proceeding are the following:

- In such "leading industries" of the national economy as construction, electrical machinery, and auto manufacturing, a system of organizing operations under a "parent company" based on share ownership is being instituted.
- In high-technology and highly specialized industries related to national defense (and having importance for raising the overall level

TABLE 13. 2 The Level of Backwardness of Chinese Enterprises

According to a 1995 survey of the State-Owned Assets Administration Bureau, the aggregate assets value and total sales volume of China's largest 500 state-owned enterprises would be matched by two of the companies in America's top-500 corporations. Total profits of China's top enterprises would be match by three big U.S. corporations.

According to the third Chinese industrial census, the average operating rate of equipment of the 900 surveyed enterprises was less than 50 percent.

In the case of the automotive industry, in 1995 China produced 1.45 million vehicles, but there were over 120 automobile manufacturers. In the United States three companies produced 9.87 million vehicles. In Japan seven companies produced 10.11 million vehicles. In Germany three companies produced 4.27 million vehicles, and in Italy one company produced 1.5 million vehicles.

In terms of scale, China's machine tool industry has 19 enterprises that each employ over 3,000 workers and undertake the full process from forging, to machining, to final assembly. In 1994 for 239 enterprises the per capita value of output was only US$4,000. In Japan in 1988 the same measure was US$230,000. In France the same type of enterprise had per capita output of US$145,000.

There are over 6,000 paper-making factories nationwide, and the average production scale is 4,000 tons. This is far below the world average of 50,000 tons.

Source: *Economic Daily*, March 5, 1997.

TABLE 13. 3 Operating Rates of Production Equipment in Chinese Industry

Operating Rates (percent)	Industry Sectors
100	Natural gas, industrial wood, veneer panels, synthetic rubber, spirits
Over 90	Paper pulp, crude oil, stereo systems, pig iron, plywood, fans
85-90	Dyes, acetic acid, ethylene, soda, caustic soda, synthetic ammonia, benzene, flat glass
80-85	Sulfuric acid, railway engines, magnetic tape, railway passenger cars, fabricated steel, cigarettes, art paper, cement
Over 80	Coal, building materials, daily-use porcelain, daily-use glass products
70-79.9	Copper, hydrochloric acid, steel alloys, veneer, fiberboard, integrated circuits, chemical fertilizer, radios, sewing machines, wristwatches, alcohol
60-69.9	Beer, nitric acid, railway freight cars, tractors, mining equipment, sweepers, synthetic detergent
50-59.9	Refrigerators, herbal medicine, telephone sets, edible oil, tires, bicycles, motorcycles, sugar, cameras, methyl alcohol
Under 50	VCRs, washing machines, diesel engines, automobiles, color televisions, machine tools, paint
31-38.5	Aluminum daily-use products, air conditioners, copiers, pesticides, chemical-based medicines, microwave ovens
Under 25.5	Electric power generating equipment, micro computers, photo film, movie film
Under 3.5	Small calculators

Source: *Economic Daily*, March 5, 1997.

FIGURE 13. 5 Composition of Total Industrial Production Value by Ownership, 1980-1996

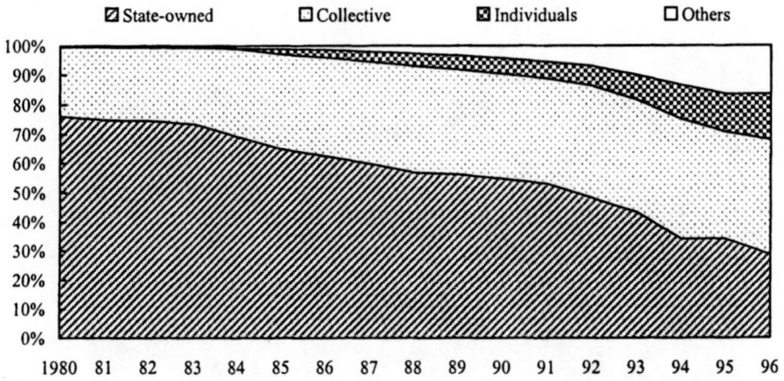

Note: Figures for 1991-1994 are adjusted according to the results of 1995 industrial census.
Sources: 1980-1989, *China Statistical Yearbook* 1993; 1990-1995, *China Statistical Yearbook* 1997.

of industry) such as information, electronics, and aeronautics and aerospace, the state is raising its investment.

- In such highly competitive industries as petroleum and chemicals that are integrated with international markets, a system of "state assets management group companies" has been instituted. Two examples are China National Petroleum Corporation (CNPC) and China Petrochemical Corporation (Sinopec). These huge groups are being merged pursuant to a decision ratified by the National People's Congress in March 1998.
- In such traditional sectors as light industry, textiles, and machinery, where efficiency is especially low, an effort is under way to rationalize organization structure. In the case of cotton-spinning, it means ordering the closing of more than one-third of all spinning mills to reduce overcapacity.

The Chinese government authorities' push for structural adjustment is a response to the need to strengthen international competitiveness. Not only is entry into the World Trade Organization (WTO) merely a matter of time, but it is inevitable that the Chinese economy will find itself buffeted by the winds of international competition and the world economy. Although China possesses some industries that are competitive from an international perspective, a major challenge in moving forward will be to strengthen competitiveness in new and high-tech industries.

—*Yabuki*

14

State-Owned Enterprises

The Difficulty of Letting "Socialism" Die Naturally

The Position of State-Owned Enterprises in China's Industry

Figure 14.1 and Table 14.1 present the position occupied by state-owned enterprises among all of China's enterprises. According to a 1995 census, in terms of numbers of enterprises, SOEs accounted for only 1.6 percent; in terms of employment and output value they constituted something more than 30 percent. Figure 14.2 displays SOEs according to size. Figure 14.3 distinguishes them according to whether they are subordinate to local or Central authority.

It is now widely known that the position of SOEs in Chinese industry has declined to some one-third; the remaining two-thirds comprises constituents of the market economy. However, it is widely believed that in terms of industrial employment SOEs still provide more than 50 percent of jobs and that it is extremely difficult for SOEs to reduce workers (the latter belief is actually a misconception, as we illustrate below). Let us look carefully at the analysis of 1995 industrial census data presented in Table 14.2. In the left column, showing all industrial enterprises at the national level, we see that SOEs' share of output volume has declined to 32.6 percent, their share of employees declining to 31.6 percent. In other words, SOEs have been steadily reducing workers in line with their declining share of output.

Why, then, has the misconception that SOEs cannot reduce workers become so widespread? The reason is the mistake (even by Chinese statisticians) of confusing two different relational databases: The employment figure has been not of SOEs constituting 31.6 percent of all industrial enterprises but rather of SOEs constituting 52.1 percent of the "independent accounting unit industrial enterprises at or above the county level" (i.e., the

122

FIGURE 14. 1 Position of SOEs within China's Total Industrial Enterprises

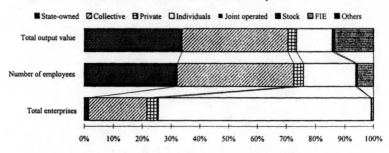

Source: Table 14. 1.

FIGURE 14. 2 State-Owned Industrial Enterprises by Scale

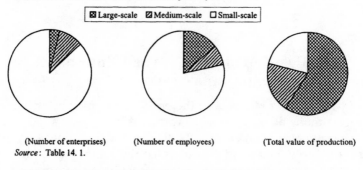

(Number of enterprises) (Number of employees) (Total value of production)

Source: Table 14. 1.

FIGURE 14. 3 State-Owned Industrial Enterprises by Administrative Level

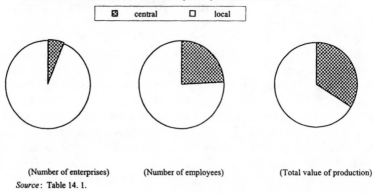

(Number of enterprises) (Number of employees) (Total value of production)

Source: Table 14. 1.

TABLE 14.1 Position of SOEs Within China's Total Industrial Enterprises and Production Units

Ownership	Total Enterprises (Units)	(%)	Year-End Employees (million persons)	(%)	Total Output Value (billion RMB)	(%)
Total	7,341,517	100.0	147.4	100.0	8,229.7	100.0
State-owned	118,000	1.6	46.5	31.6	2,684.1	32.6
of which:						
central	7,275	6.2	11.2	24.1	913.1	34.0
local	110,725	93.8	35.3	75.9	1,770.9	66.0
of which:						
county	67,686	57.4	112	25.8	559.2	20.8
of which:						
light industry	62,862	53.3			884.7	33.0
heavy industry	55,138	46.7			1,799.3	67.0
of which:						
large scale	4,685	4.0	20.9	14.2	1,590.7	59.3
medium scale	10,983	9.3	10.9	7.4	530.2	19.8
small scale	102,332	86.7	115.5	78.4	563.1	21.0
Collective	1,465,628	20.0	58.6	39.8	2,925.3	35.5
Private	287,483	3.9	4.9	3.3	233.9	2.8
Individuals	5,403,643	73.6	25.8	17.5	963.3	11.7
Joint operated	2,903	0.1	0.9	0.6	66.7	0.8
Stock	5,873	0.1	2.5	1.7	275.0	3.3
FIE *	54,045	0.7	8.1	5.5	1,072.2	13.0
Others	942	0.0	0.08	0.1	9.2	0.1
Township	6,517,818	88.8	73.1	49.6	3,638.4	44.2
"Three capital" **	59,311	0.8	9	6.1	1,182.4	14.4
Light industry	5,101,409	69.5	68.5	46.5	3,890.3	47.3
Heavy industry	2,240,108	30.5	78.8	53.5	4,339.4	52.7
Large-scale	6,416	0.1	24.1	16.4	2,182.8	26.5
Medium-scale	16,591	0.2	14.8	10.1	907.8	11.0
Small-scale	7,318,510	99.7	108.4	73.6	5,139.1	62.4

Notes: [1] Figures for all industrial enterprises and production units.

[2] (%) is ratio of state-owned enterprises.

[3] FIE * indicates foreign companies and companies invested from Hong Kong, Macao, and Taiwan.

[4] "Three capital" ** includes: (a) 100% foreign investment, (b) Sino-foreign equity joint ventures, and (c) Sino-foreign cooperative joint ventures.

Source : *The Data of the Third National Industrial Census of the People's Republic of China in 1995.*

right column in Table 14.2). People have thus mistakenly taken the SOEs' share of output among total industrial enterprises (the left data series) and the SOEs' share of employment among independent accounting unit industrial enterprises at or above the county level (the right data series).

This rudimentary "mistake of comparison" made by so many economists inside and outside China for so many years results from the carelessness of editors at China's annual *China Statistical Yearbook*. They persistently and without explanation present as comparable certain figures based on different data universes (see, e.g., *China Statistical Yearbook* 1997, pp. 412–413).

TABLE 14. 2 Difference in China's Industry Statistics by Survey Level
Number of companies

Ownership	Total Industrial and Production (units)	Enterprises Units (%)	Independent Accounting Industrial Enterprises at or Above Village Level (units)	(%)
State-owned	118,000	1.6	118,000	23.1
Collective	1,465,628	20.0	363,840	71.3
Private	287,483	3.9	2,708	0.5
Individuals	5,403,643	73.6		
Joint	5,903	0.1	5,559	1.1
Stock	5,873	0.1	5,873	1.2
FIE	54,045	0.7	44,293	8.7
Others	942	0.0	583	0.1
Total	7,341,517	100.0	510,381	100.0

Year-end employees

Ownership	Total Industrial and Production (thou. persons)	Enterprises Units (%)	Independent Profit Industrial Enterprises at or Above Village Level (thou. persons)	(%)
State-owned	46,522	31.6	44,646	52.1
Collective	58,583	39.8	30,889	36.0
Private	4,906	3.3	165	0.2
Individuals	25,764	17.5		
Joint	874	0.6	854	1.0
Stock	2,548	1.7	2,530	3.0
FIE	8,078	5.5	6,605	7.7
Others	79	0.1	63	0.1
Total	147,355	100.0	85,756	100.0

Total value of production

Ownership	Total Industrial and Production (billion RMB)	Enterprises Units (%)	Independent Profit Industrial Enterprises at or Above Village Level (billion RMB)	(%)
State-owned	2,684	32.6	2,589	47.1
Collective	2,925	35.5	1,584	28.8
Private	234	2.8	15	0.3
Individuals	963	11.7		
Joint	67	0.8	65	1.2
Stock	275	3.3	273	5.0
FIE	1,072	13.0	964	17.5
Others	9	0.1	8	0.1
Total	8,230	100.0	5,495	100.0

Note: FIE indicates foreign companies and companies invested from Hong Kong, Macao, and Taiwan.
Source: The Data of the Third National Industrial Census of the People's Republic of China in 1995.

Operational Problems in
State-Owned Enterprises

The problem of losses by the SOEs became evident during the economic tightening following the Tiananmen Incident. This can be seen from Figure 14.4. From 1989 to 1990 total profits of all enterprises dropped by half. At the same time, the losses of lossmaking enterprises doubled. Thus the loss ratio curve (the ratio of profits of profitable enterprises to losses of lossmaking enterprises) rose dramatically. In the revitalized atmosphere following Deng Xiaoping's 1992 Southern Excursion Talks, SOE profits increased in 1993 and 1994, only to decline again sharply in 1995 and 1996. For this reason the line showing the loss ratio curve again turned sharply upward.

Many theories have been advanced to explain why SOEs have fallen so into the red. A commonsense view simply holds that state ownership engenders inefficiency. Due to limitations in the data, this is difficult to show statistically. Table 14.3 shows the lossmaking situation of Chinese industry as of year-end 1995, based on statistics gathered during the Third National Industrial Census. Of some 88,000 SOEs, some 30,000, or roughly one-third, were lossmakers. Taken by size, somewhat less than one-third of large firms, and somewhat more than one-third of small- and medium-sized enterprises, were making losses.

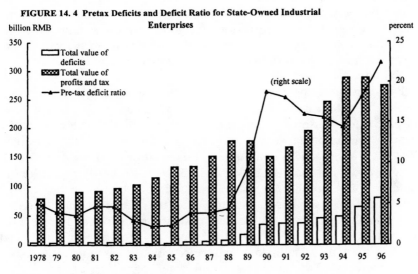

FIGURE 14. 4 Pretax Deficits and Deficit Ratio for State-Owned Industrial Enterprises

Source: *China Statistical Yearbook* 1997, p. 439.

TABLE 14. 3   Deficit Situation of China's Industrial Companies, 1995

Ownership	Total Number of Enterprises (a) (units)	Deficit (b) Enterprises (units)	(b) / (a) (%)	Total Loss of Deficits Ent. (c) (billion RMB)	Total Profits (d) (billion RMB)	Deficit Rate * (c) / (c+d) (%)
State-owned	87,905	29,668	33.8	64	67	49.0
of which:						
large scale	4,685	1,321	28.2	25	72	25.5
middle scale	10,983	3,830	34.9	19	-2	110.2
small scale	72,237	24,517	33.9	20	-4	124.6
Collective	363,840	76,845	21.1	27	38	41.6
Private	2,708	452	16.7	0.1	1	10.6
Joint	5,493	1,582	28.8	1.4	2	47.9
Stock	5,559	1,204	21.7	2.1	20	9.4
FIE	17,692	6,690	39.3	13	22	36.5
Hong Kong, Macao & Taiwan	26,601	11,064	41.6	13	14	47.4
Others	583	145	24.9	0.08	2	4.8
Total	510,381	127,920	25.1	120	163	42.3

Notes: [1]Figures are for independent accounting industrial enterprises at or above village level.
   [2]* deficit rate = c / (c+d) = value of losses of deficit enterprises / value of profits
   of profitable enterprises.
Source: *The Data of the Third National Industrial Census of the People's Republic of China in 1995.*

What about the actual amount of losses? For all SOEs we have total losses of RMB 63.9 billion, compared with total profits of RMB 66.5 billion. (Almost the same number!) If profits were used to subsidize losses, the result would appear to be a virtual offset. But the reality is different. Losses are kept at the enterprise level, whereas profits are remitted to the government treasury in the form of taxes and through the practice of "handing-up" (*shangjiao*), that is, giving profits to superior government authorities.

Based on value, the disparity according to enterprise scale is great. For large-scale enterprises, the value of losses of lossmakers against the value of profits for profitmakers is about 1:3. The loss ratio is 25 percent. By comparison, for both medium- and small-sized enterprises, the amount of losses is greater than the amount of profits, creating a net loss situation. In other words, the problem of losses in SOEs is primarily a problem in medium- and small-sized enterprises. What of losses for non-SOEs? Looking at the lossmaking enterprise ratio (the ratio of lossmaking enterprises to all enterprises) on the basis of total number of enterprises, FIEs and enterprises invested from Hong Kong and Macao actually exceed SOEs. The smallest lossmaking enterprise ratio is seen in privately operated enterprises. The pattern is the same for value of losses.

State-Owned Enterprises and Social Security

Under a combined attack from FIEs and township and village enterprises, SOEs have plenty to be worried about. But how do the SOEs themselves perceive their predicament?

Figure 14.5 illustrates the "social security" burdens of SOEs. The cost of providing housing, medical care, education, and the like accounts for 15–20 percent of the total investment of most enterprises. Ordinary schools, as opposed to technical schools, should of course be financed by society. Subsidized housing and medical care is an important benefit for employees. But the "cradle-to-grave" policy of providing housing to retired employees until death, and the policy of providing retirees the same level of medical care that current workers receive, is a heavy burden.

With respect to employees, apart from there being some 30 percent too many workers, the SOE is paying personnel costs for retired former cadres and retired workers, who constitute another 25 percent of the total workforce. In other words, the reality is that there are more hangers-on than real producers in SOEs. Converted to wage cost, the wages paid to workers actually engaged in production roughly equal the payments made to excess and retired personnel.

The excessively generous SOE pension system is effectively consuming all the resources, and this, more than anything else, is seen as a manifestation of the "superiority of socialism."

FIGURE 14. 5 The Weight of the "Social Security" Burden of State-Owned Enterprises

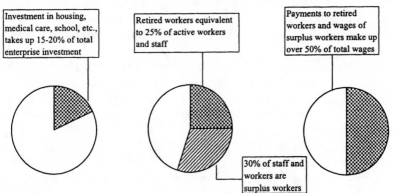

Source: "After All, How Should We View SOEs," *Economic Daily*, June 2, 1997.

Vagaries of State-Owned Enterprise Reform

China's groping for a way to reform SOEs was a concomitant of the Deng Xiaoping era and began at the same time. On July 13, 1979, the State Council handed down its "Decision Concerning the Expansion of Autonomy for State-Owned Enterprises." Phase One (1979–1984) began with this decision and extended to the introduction of the system of "converting profits to taxes" (*ligaishui*). The principal theme of this period was to "let go of authority and give up profits" (*fangquan rangli*), which meant devolving authority to enterprises and allowing enterprises to retain profits.

Phase Two (1984–1986) was the transition period of *ligaishui*, which meant converting from a system where all enterprise profits were remitted to the supervising state authority to one of taxing profits. Under this system, large- and medium-sized enterprises were obliged to pay an enterprises income tax of 55 percent. Any remaining profits were divided into an amount payable to the state and an amount that could be retained by the enterprises.

Phase Three (1987–1991) was the period of the "responsibility system" (*qingfuzhi*). The enterprise guaranteed a fixed amount of profit remittance to the state and was allowed to retain whatever remained. The principal theme of this phase was "separation of government and enterprises, separation of ownership and operation."

Phase Four dates from July 23, 1992, when the State Council promulgated its "Regulations on the Conversion of Operational System of Industrial Enterprises Owned by the Whole People." This was actually a concrete manifestation of the Party Central Document No. 4, drafted by then–vice premier Zhu Rongji on the basis of Deng Xiaoping's remarks during his southern excursion. The principal themes of this phase were "transforming the system of operation" and "establishing a modern enterprise system."

Phase Five followed the Fifteenth Party Congress in 1997, which adopted Jiang Zemin's government work report. Previous experiments were validated, and SOE reform was positioned to advance to a higher level. Most remarkable was the complete legitimization of the joint-stock company system.

Table 14.4 presents a rough summary of the issues raised in Jiang Zemin's report. Chinese enterprises had already been listed on such foreign stock exchanges as Hong Kong, New York, and London, and in China securities exchanges had been established in Shanghai and Shenzhen. In order to support the development and enlargement of China's better companies, which in most cases are small by international stan-

TABLE 14. 4 Direction and Strategy for State-Owned Enterprises Reform

---

Direction

- "Specify ownership rights, clarify authority and responsibility, separate government administration from enterprises, institute scientific management." Establish the modern enterprise system.
- *Corporatizing SOEs:* Reform large and medium-sized enterprises into corporations...establish legal person entities capable of competing in the market.
- *Separating government and SOEs:* The state will enjoy ownership rights in accordance with the amount of capital invested in enterprises; the state's liability for the debts of the enterprise will be limited. Enterprises will by law have autonomy in operations and will be solely responsible for their profits and losses.

Strategy

- *Form large enterprise groups:* Form large enterprise groups with large competitive strength and operations that transverse regions, sectors, ownership forms, and countries.
- *Freeing and vitalizing small SOEs:* Speed up liberalization and vitalization of small SOEs through reorganization, forming associations, mergers, leasing out facilities, contracting facilities to operators, converting to cooperative shareholding companies, or outright sales.

Related Reforms

- *Dealing with bankruptcy and unemployment:* Provide incentives for mergers; apply standards for bankruptcy. While raising enterprise performance by temporarily laying off or transferring personnel, implement reemployment programs.
- *Protecting state assets:* Preserve and increase the value of state-owned assets; prevent state assets flowing or being drained away.
- *Establish a society security system:* Institute an old-age and medical security insurance system, establish unemployment insurance and a social welfare system. Provide for the most basic societal needs.

Source: Jiang Zemin, "Political Work Report at the Fifteenth CCP Congress," *People's Daily*, September 22, 1997.

dards, a key policy was instituted to "nurture enterprises groups." Yet for small- and medium-sized SOEs, the new prescription included bankruptcy or merger or the adoption of a cooperative shareholding system (meaning share ownership by workers). The strategy is to nurture a "company mentality" among workers by making employees shareholders. This is a realistic strategy, since there is little chance that small- and medium-sized enterprises will be listed on stock exchanges.

The Framework of Public Ownership and Joint Stock Companies

Jiang Zemin's report offered the possibility that SOE reform could take many forms, but it was emphasized that any reform should support and not undermine "public ownership." Thus, if a socialist market economic system was to remain worthy of the name "socialism," nothing should be allowed to develop too far outside the framework of "public ownership." For sectors with a strong public interest, operations are placed in the hands of public enterprises, even in capitalist countries. This would become policy in China. In the countryside, however, the collective economy would combine collective ownership with private ownership. This is not much different than the "dual-level operation" (operations by the collective and by individual farm families) of the People's Communes period, where collective agriculture was the basic tenet.

In the "surnamed capitalism or surnamed socialism" (*xingsi, xingshe*) ideological debate, the corporate share system presents a particular problem. Is a limited-stock company privately owned or publicly owned? Chinese ideologues have managed to place share ownership in the publicly owned category by employing two artifices: First, they have endeavored to greatly broaden the category of public ownership; second, they have greatly narrowed the category of private ownership, which is theoretically two sides of the same coin.

In the first case, the focus has been placed on the owner or the controller of the shares. If the owner is not an individual, then it is not considered private ownership. On this theoretical basis, the shares of Japanese and U.S. companies owned by institutions—"corporate shares" in the Chinese context—would belong in the category of collective ownership. An example of the second case is the share cooperative system, in which the ownership of shares is with individuals, both investors and workers. In this case, private ownership of shares can be placed in the category of public ownership.

As the above illustrations make clear, the effort has been to avoid inconsistency by greatly expanding the category of public ownership, on the one hand, and narrowing, to the extent possible, the category of private ownership on the other (Figure 14.6). However, according to Deng Xiaoping, it should be possible to suspend fruitless and unproductive discussions as to whether something is "surnamed capitalist or surnamed socialist." The author (Yabuki) believes we are beginning to see that socialism with Chinese characteristics and concepts of the socialist market economy are nothing other than strategies meant to deceive China's conservative faction.

Formation of Large Group Companies

In 1991 the State Council put out its "Notice Concerning Selection and Implementation on an Experimental Basis of Some Large Scale Enterprise Groups" (State Council Notice No. 71). This launched a policy to form one hundred large-scale enterprise groups. At first, fifty-seven experi-

FIGURE 14. 6 Forms of Public Ownership

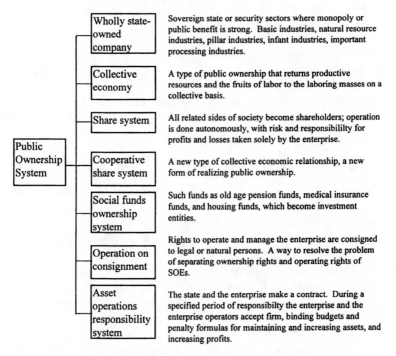

Source: Wang Maoling, "Actively Search for Various Forms of Realizing Public Ownership," *Economic Daily*, October 6, 1997.

mental group enterprises were approved. These were key enterprises, selected by the principal administrative departments in their respective sectors. Noteworthy was the inclusion of thirteen enterprises in the automotive, machinery, and like fields under the authority of the Ministry of Machinery Industry; six in electric power; and four each under the Ministries of Metallurgical Industry and Petrochemical Industry.

In April 1995 the State Council produced its "Temporary Regulations Concerning Formation and Management of Enterprise Groups," which elucidated the definition of enterprise groups. An *enterprise group* was now defined as "a united economic entity comprising many enterprises and businesses tied together through investment and production operations," or an enterprise group with a core enterprise as well as subsidiary enterprises. Subsidiary enterprises under the umbrella of the core enterprise would have corporate status; the enterprise group itself, however, would not be a corporate person. The basic principles of an enterprise group are as follows:

1. The group should be in conformity with the state's economic development strategy and industrial policy, having an important position in a sector's production or exports.
2. Enterprise groups should pursue fair competition across regional and administrative barriers.
3. Enterprise groups should implement the policy of "separating government and the enterprise."
4. In forming an enterprise group, the decisionmaking independence of invested enterprises should be upheld, subject to the leadership of the state.

The main features of enterprise groups are as follows:

1. The enterprise scale of the core enterprise should attain the standard for large-scale enterprises set by the state or have a registered capital of RMB 100 million or more.
2. The core enterprise should have at least five subsidiary enterprises.
3. The group should require that members of the group jointly observe and follow group standards and regulations, which include the group name, core enterprise name, address and operations location, form of association between member enterprises, specifics as to requirements for consultation and decisionmaking for group-related business activities, and registration of the core enterprise with the government administrative agencies.

Subsidiaries would be included in the following three cases:

1. Membership through shareholding occurs in cases where the core enterprise owns more than 50 percent of the subsidiary company's shares and where the accounts of both companies must be consolidated in financial statements.
2. Membership through share participation: The core company does not own more than 50 percent of the subsidiary company, but membership in the group has been approved in the group's articles and regulations.
3. Cooperative membership: designated member due to long and stable production, operation, or technical cooperation association with the core enterprise and approved in the group's articles and regulations.

In June 1997 the so-called State Experimental Enterprise Group work meeting was convened in Beijing. The development of large-scale enterprise groups was deemed a "task having strategic significance" for China's economic reform. Since the first designation (six years earlier), the power of enterprise groups had been greatly strengthened. The performance of many groups in economic development and structural adjustment was highly praised. Regarding future development, six issues were raised:

- Adopting the modern enterprise system;
- adapting to the market economy;
- promoting the development of enterprise groups in the context of structural adjustment; also, raising enterprise efficiency, avoiding duplicate investment within the group, and coordinating on new projects;
- strengthening the group's internal management system;
- strengthening management ranks; and
- continuing to promote reforms necessary to build the group.

At the same time, a second complement of sixty-three groups was approved. Noteworthy were fast-growing enterprises, which were benefiting from economic reforms in such sectors as agriculture, electronics, pharmaceuticals, and TVEs. Comparing the first complement to the second complement, we can perceive that China's economy is moving toward a market economy. Combining the first and second complements, then, these 120 groups now constitute the "backbone" of the national economy. Compared with assets, sales, and profits before tax of all independent accounting unit enterprises nationwide, these 120 constitute about one-fourth in each category and more than half of after-tax profits (Premier Li Peng, 1997).

—Yabuki

15

Unemployment

An Ambush of SOE Reform

Chinese-Style Unemployment: "Waiting for Work"

The conversion from a planned economy to a market economy is a Copernican transformation that is leaving many Chinese confused. Causing them greatest disquiet is the concept of unemployment. Unemployment is a feature of capitalism, but it is supposed to be nonexistent in the socialist system. Heretofore, in China there has been no such thing as the unemployed, but some people have been "waiting for employment" (*daiye*). There is a large, 1,672-page book called *A Comprehensive View of China's Social Security System* (Guo Jinping, ed., 1995). In this volume, the contradiction is resolved through a bold redefinition: "There is no difference between waiting for work and unemployment. Waiting for work is unemployment. Insurance for waiting for work is unemployment insurance. Since 1994 the concerned department of the state officially renamed waiting for work insurance unemployment insurance" (Guo Jinping, *A Comprehensive View*, p. 389).

The Difference Between "Waiting for Work" and Unemployment

Thus, the concept of unemployment has been officially accepted, but in the Chinese context "unemployment" does not adequately define many situations. For example, what is the difference between being unemployed and being laid off (*xiagang*). Let us again ascertain the official view of the State Council Ministry of Labor. According to an explanation by the Policy and Regulations Bureau of the Ministry of Labor, the difference between being laid off and unemployment is as follows: "Laid-off workers have been separated from their production posts because of the production and operations situation of the enterprise and they are not working at the workplace. [However,] they retain their employment relationship with that workplace." The meaning of the first sentence is that employed and laid-off workers are one and the same. But the second makes a distinction, that is, the unemployed are those who maintain no kind of employment relationship ("The Difference Between the Laid-Off and the Unemployed," *People's Daily*, October 24, 1997).

In recent years persons have explained (see the writings of Liu Changming among others) that "reasonable unemployment" is a characteristic of the market economy. In a market economy, the unemployed provide a labor pool. Thus, for a market economy to operate smoothly the unemployed are indispensable. If unemployment rises too high, labor will be wasted and social instability will ensue. This is the genesis of the concept in the West of "reasonable unemployment," which is defined as a 1–5 percent unemployment rate. At a 1 percent or lower rate of unemployment, enterprises find difficulty ensuring the availability of additional labor, whereas a 5 percent or higher rate invites social instability.

China's Reality: Vast Latent Unemployment

What, then, is the reality of unemployment in China? And what form does unemployment take? The distinctive form of unemployment in China is "disguised unemployment" (*yinxing shiye*) or "latent unemployment" (*qianzai shiye*). This is also called "unemployment in the workplace" (*zaizhi shiye*). It is said that more than 80 percent of Chinese enterprises carry 15–20 percent excess workers. In other words, "unemployment in the workplace" reaches 15 to 20 million people.

In the countryside, two-thirds of the labor force, or 130 to 150 million people, is excess labor. These people are waiting for other work opportunities.

Because of shortages in energy and raw materials, the situation of many enterprises is "three days operation, four days closed" or "four days operation, three days closed." The standard workday in SOEs is supposed to be eight hours, but in reality it is four or five hours.

With the labor force increasing along with an exploding population, the policy has been to allocate labor across a relatively smaller number of jobs. The result has been to lower wages to broaden the employment scope. The model has been, in other words, low wages and more jobs.

This has been rationalized as the realization of socialist egalitarianism. Its consequences have been a lack of interest in increasing labor productivity, loss of worker morale, and loss of enterprise competitiveness in the market. The special character of Chinese-style unemployment was adroitly explained in an article by Liu Changming, He Dingmeng, and Zhao Xiyu, 1997 (see references).

Measuring the Unemployed

The *China Statistical Yearbook* 1997 offers figures for jobseekers and the reemployment ratio as of 1996. On the national level, against 19.4 million jobseekers, there were 11 million job vacancies (i.e., job offers). The ratio of jobs sought to jobs given was 1.8:1. Reemployed people totaled 8.9 million, yielding a reemployment rate of 46 percent. Of the 19.4 million people registered as seeking work, rural laborers accounted for 6.09 million; city residents accounted for 13.3 million. Incidentally, until 1995 "registered urban unemployed" were counted as 5.2 million, and the "registered urban unemployment rate" was officially given as 2.9 percent (*China Statistical Yearbook* 1996, p. 114). This figure actually reflects only about one-half of the total unemployed. The real unemployment rate is generally estimated to be 6–7 percent. The *Yearbook* 1997 takes a new approach for calculating unemployment from concrete figures of jobseekers and job offers for each province. This is a big improvement. From Figure 15.1 we see a number of provinces where jobseekers exceeded 1 million, that is, where employment conditions are considered severe. The five worst were Henan at 2.1 million, Liaoning 1.2 million, Guangdong 1.2 million, Tianjin city 1.2 million, and Jiangsu 1.2 million. These were followed by Zhejiang, Heilongjiang, and Shandong.

Minister of Labor Li Boyong, in his first interview at the beginning of 1998, revealed that 8–10 million new layoffs were expected in 1998. More likely the number would exceed 20 million. However, as mentioned above, those who were laid off continued to hold employment contracts with their enterprise and received subsidy payments accordingly. This is not complete unemployment.

The difficulty attending the dismissal of workers is the most serious threat to SOE reform. A campaign to confront and address the problem was launched in 1997. The "reemployment project" (*zai jiuye gongcheng*) now seems to be the expression in vogue.

As we have pointed out, laid-off workers, during the period of their layoff, can receive either subsidies from the enterprise they work for or unemployment insurance payments. What is the status, then, of the unemployment insurance system?

The Unemployment Insurance System

In 1986 the "Provisional Regulations Governing Waiting for Work Insurance for Workers and Staff of State-Run Enterprises" were promulgated. This was the original form of unemployment insurance. In 1993 the "Regulations Governing Waiting for Work Insurance for Workers and Staff of State-Owned Enterprises" (State Council Order No. 110) were promul-

138

FIGURE 15. 1 Jobseekers / Reemployment Ratio at the Province Level

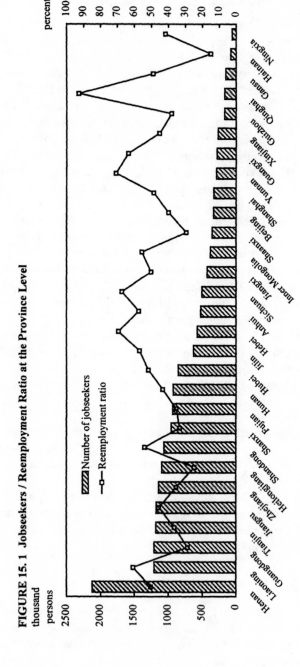

Source: China Statistical Yearbook 1997, p. 134.

gated (*People's Daily*, April 21, 1993). Deleting the word *provisional* from the title, this second set of rules was thus elevated to the status of "official" regulations. During this period as well, the state-*run* enterprise was changed to the state-*owned* enterprise. Hidden in this change in locution is the idea that in the state-*owned* enterprise ownership rights can rest with the state, and so-called operating rights can be exercised in many forms.

Let us compare the 1986 provisional regulations to the 1993 regulations. In the provisional regulations, persons qualified to receive unemployment insurance within the universe of state-run companies would be limited to the following categories: (1) staff and workers of enterprises that had declared bankruptcy; (2) workers and staff laid off during the legally sanctioned restructuring period by enterprises close to bankruptcy; (3) workers whose employment contract had been terminated by an enterprise; and (4) staff and workers who had retired from enterprises. In the 1993 regulations, three new categories were added to the four listed above: (5) staff and workers of enterprises disbanded in accordance with related regulations of the state; (6) staff and workers laid off or made redundant by enterprises in accordance with related regulations of the state; and (7) other staff and workers receiving unemployment insurance according to law or according to regulations of provincial governments. In this way, the categories of persons entitled to receive unemployment insurance were expanded, but basically payments remained limited to staff and workers of SOEs.

According to an article by Guo Qingsong and Yang Guang (1997), when the State Council's regulations concerning unemployment insurance were received, twenty-six provincial governments drafted their own unemployment insurance regulations. Among these, all but one expanded coverage to all urban enterprises (rural enterprises were excluded). As of the end of 1995, the number of staff and workers participating in unemployment insurance had reached 95 million. This, according to Guo, was 63.7 percent of 149 million total staff and workers.

Collecting and Using Unemployment Insurance Funds

The funding sources for China's system of unemployment insurance are insurance premiums collected by enterprises, interest on these funds, and subsidies from the state budget. In the provisional regulations the premium was set at 1 percent of the total standard base wages. Subsequently, the weight of the standard base wage in the total compensation declined, and so the 1993 regulations stipulated 0.6 percent of total wages paid. At the province level, premiums can be raised or lowered, but it is stipulated that premiums cannot exceed 1 percent of the total wage cost. Thus, in the eight years from 1987 to 1994, RMB 8.3 billion was accumulated in unemployment insurance funds. In 1995, RMB 3.53 billion was accumulated.

What about the payment period and payment rate? For staff and workers with more than five years' seniority, a maximum of twenty-four months of payments will be made. Those with more than one but less than five years' seniority may receive payments for twelve months. In the provisional regulations it was stipulated that in the first year a person can receive 60–75 percent of base wages; in the second year the figure was 50 percent. In the official regulations the payment is stipulated as "120–150 percent of the social welfare allotment" set by local civil and government departments. The social welfare allotment is a subsistence cash income level. Twenty to 50 percent above this level would still constitute less than 50 percent of the wage level. It would appear that the standard payment is being lowered in view of a shortage of funds.

In the six years from 1987 to 1992, insurance payments of RMB 144 million were paid to 650,000 unemployed persons nationwide. In 1993, RMB 288 million was paid for 1.03 million persons; in 1994, RMB 600 million was paid for 1.8 million persons. In 1995, however, RMB 1.5 *billion* was paid for 2.61 million persons.

Who is in charge of unemployment insurance? Under the provisional regulations, management was implemented through "labor service companies" subordinate to the main labor management departments at each level of government. Under the 1993 regulations the main labor management departments at each level of government (above the county level) take direct responsibility for managing unemployment insurance. Thus, management responsibility has been elevated from the "off-take destination" (service companies) to the government administration organs.

A System Still Being Built

What are the issues remaining? A participation rate of 63.7 percent means that 36.3 percent of staff and workers continue to fall outside the unemployment insurance scheme. The issue is whether to expand coverage to include these people.

In China, workers pay very little or no insurance premiums. As a result the cost is concentrated in the enterprise or the state. The basic character of unemployment insurance is mutual assistance, so a system of burden-sharing by three parties—workers, enterprises, and the state—should be established.

The unemployment payment level was changed from 60–75 percent—or 50 percent of the basic wage—to 20–50 percent higher than the social welfare allotment. However, only something like the minimum subsistence level in the locality or 30 percent of the wage level is actually being paid, and their are many cases of hardship. The 1995 payment of RMB 1.5 billion to 2.61 million persons means a per capita annual payment of RMB 578. In 1995 the national average annual wage was RMB 5,500. So the unemployment payment was only about 10 percent of the average wage. Moreover, if we consider that "reemployment promotion expenses" are included, the payment level is too low (Guo Qingsong and Yang Guang, 1997; incidentally, Guo is a researcher at the Population Research Institute of Beijing University).

If we look at China's unemployment policies, we can appreciate that the country is in the midst of establishing a system. At a stage like this, when it is said that SOE reforms will create 10 million layoffs, we must take into account the weight of the decisions being taken by Zhu Rongji and others.

—Yabuki

16

Township and Village Enterprises

*Engines of Transformation
for China's Villages*

The Great Leap Forward for Township and Village Enterprises

The concept of township and village enterprises first appeared in the March 1984 "Notice from the Chinese Communist Party Central Committee and the State Council" (*People's Daily*, March 18, 1984), confirming the "Report on Opening of a New Phase for Commune and Brigade Enterprises of the State Council Ministry of Agriculture, Animal Husbandry, and Fisheries." The notice announced, along with the dismantling of the people's communes, the policy of changing the name of the former commune and brigade enterprises to township and village enterprises. So-called peasants' joint capital enterprises and individual enterprises were recognized as "important component parts of multitype enterprise operation" and accorded the position of "important" sources of state revenue.

In 1992 during his Southern Excursion Talks, Deng Xiaoping praised the dynamism of TVEs, remarking they had "appeared out of nowhere like an ambushing army." It is certainly true that the TVEs have been a great engine for change in China's rural areas.

Figure 16.1 shows the dramatic growth in the number of TVEs, from 1.52 million in 1978 to 23 million in 1996, as well as the change in the business sector, from the predominance of manufacturing in 1993 to the predominance of service industries like commerce and food after 1994. A decline in the number of TVEs was observed in the postadjustment year of 1995 as many weak TVEs failed or were liquidated.

FIGURE 16. 1 Number of Township and Village Enterprises by Industry Sector

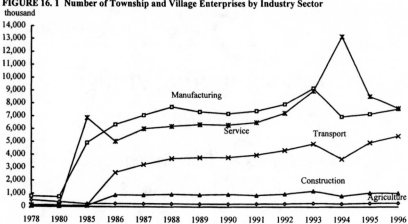

Source: *China Statistical Yearbook* 1997.

Figure 16.2 shows that employment in TVEs is approaching 130 million. This is nearly 30 percent of the 450 million laborers in the countryside. The illustrations show that the output of TVEs has risen to contribute some 70 percent of total output value from the rural economy. The largest part TVE production is found in such nonagricultural pursuits as manufacturing, services, transport, and construction, meaning that TVEs contribute close to three-fourths of total nonagricultural production in the countryside.

The greatest contributions of TVEs have been as a receptacle for absorbing excessive labor and as a driving force for reform in the countryside.

Ownership Modes of
Township and Village Enterprises

Industry is in the top position in terms of TVEs' total employees as well as their total output value. Looking at statistics for TVEs in 1995, industry (read: manufacturing) was the purpose of slightly more than 30 percent of enterprises. These enterprises employed slightly less than 60 percent of TVE employees and contributed slightly less than 70 percent of total TVE output value. Service occupations were the purpose of slightly less than 40 percent of TVEs, which is a high share, but output value was only 9 percent of total.

The 1996 *Chinese Industrial Development Report* provided an analysis of the ownership structure of TVEs for year-end 1994. Looking at the number of TVEs, those operated by individuals constituted 90 percent of the

FIGURE 16. 2 **Trends in the Number of Workers in Township and Village Enterprises and Ratio of Rural Laborers**

(trends in number of workers in township and village enterprises)

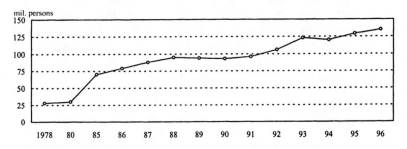

(Ratio of rural laborers in township and village enterprises)

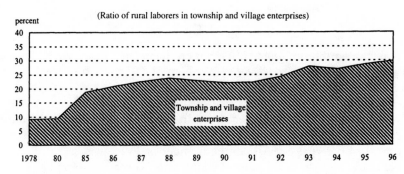

Source: *China Statistical Yearbook* 1996, p. 97.

total. However, on an output-value basis, township-operated enterprises constituted 35 percent and village-operated enterprises constituted 33 percent, for a combined share of more than two-thirds. In terms of form of ownership, TVEs operated jointly by several individuals were similar to individually operated enterprises in being closer to private ownership.

Using the standard for economic efficiency of pretax profit, we see that township- and village-operated enterprises contributed about one-third each, with individually operated enterprises contributing about one-third. In actuality, although many TVEs are typed as "township-operated" or "village-operated," they are in fact run by individuals or small groups of individuals.

Now let us try to clarify the distinction between TVEs and collectively owned enterprises. From the standpoint of ownership, China places enterprises in three large categories: state-owned, collectively owned, and privately owned. State-owned companies are not included among TVEs, even if they are established in the countryside. Put differently, to be designated a TVE an enterprise must meet three conditions: (1) it is located in

the countryside; (2) it is not state-owned; and (3) it is not a wholly for-
eign-owned enterprise.

Again from the standpoint of ownership, TVEs are separated into collectively owned enterprises (township-run or village-run enterprises) and
privately owned enterprises (individually owned and privately run enterprises). As noted above, the ratio of their respective shares is some 2:1.
The property rights of collectively owned enterprises in the countryside
are stipulated to belong to all of peasants in the concerned village under
the June 1990 "PRC Regulations on Township and Village Collectively
Owned Enterprises."

Position of Township and Village Industrial Enterprises

We have seen that industrial (read: manufacturing) enterprises make up
the bulk of TVEs. What, then, is the share of TVEs in China's overall industrial sector?

Figure 16.3 presents the position occupied by industrial TVEs in
China's overall industrial sector by three measures: number of enterprises, total employees, and total output value. Looking first at the total
number of enterprises, in 1995 the number of TVEs was 6.52 million, an
overwhelming, nearly 90 percent share. This is because of the large number of small and unsubstantial enterprises among TVEs. Total TVE employment was 7.3 million persons, about 50 percent of total sector employment. Total output value was RMB 3.6 trillion, a 44 percent share.

FIGURE 16. 3 Status of Township and Village Enterprises in China's Total Industrial Enterprises, 1995

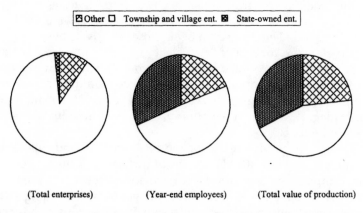

| ⊠ Other □   Township and village ent. ⊠   State-owned ent. |

(Total enterprises)   (Year-end employees)   (Total value of production)

Source : The Data of the Third National Industrial Census of the People's Republic of China in 1995.

These figures illustrate the significance of industrial TVEs within the Chinese economy. Above all, it is "effective absorption of labor." Employing excess labor is one the biggest issues in China. Because TVEs typically are pursuing labor-intensive activities, their contribution has been great. Moreover, they have been contributing significantly to overall output.

Another significance of TVEs is that they are located in the countryside. The widening income gap between the industrializing cities and the countryside is also a big problem needing resolution in China. However, the measures that can be taken to address this problem are limited. It can only be hoped that the countryside can self-reliantly carve out a position in the market economy. The TVEs are important in this sense as well.

—Yabuki

17

Regional Economics

Potential for a Yangtze River Economic Region

End of the Coastal Region Economic Development Strategy

It is often said that China is a land of "vast territory and abundant resources." Because of the expanse of territory north to south and east to west, different regions can have greatly different conditions. If we take the indicators of economic power (Table 17.1) and graph them, we create Figure 17.1.

Let us first divide China into its eastern coastal region and its central and western interior regions. Next, as a measure of the factors employable for economic activity, let us apply the yardsticks of each province's area and population. The eastern coastal region occupies less than 15 percent of China's total area, whereas the interior regions claim more than 85 percent. However, some 40 percent of the population lives in the coastal region, 60 percent in the interior. The 40 percent of the population available to participate in economic activity in the coastal region contributed 60 percent to total GDP, whereas the 60 percent of the people in the interior region contributed 40 percent of GDP. This is an interesting contrast.

Looking at the key component of GDP as well as the heretofore key driver of economic growth—the output value of industry—in 1995 the coastal region claimed a two-thirds share, whereas the interior region claimed only one-third.

The main underwriters and engines of industrialization during the Deng Xiaoping era were foreign-invested enterprises. Foreign enterprises chose to invest in the coastal region, economically more dynamic and with better infrastructure. In 1995, 85 percent of the foreign investment

FIGURE 17.1 Economic Power by Region, 1995

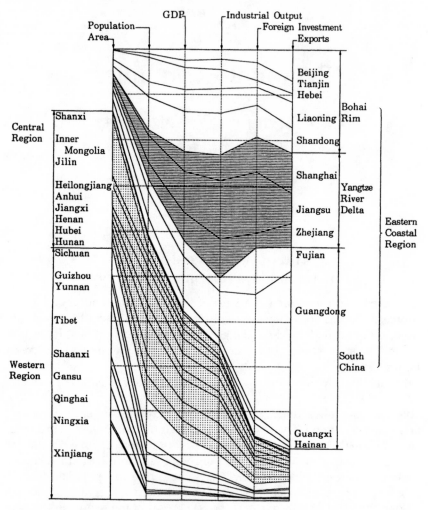

Note: The vertical axis aggregates to 100 percent of national total.
One section represents 10 percent.
Source: Table 17.1.

TABLE 17. 1 Financial Power of Regions in China

Region	Population 1995 year-end (mil. persons)	national proportion	GDP 1995 (bil. RMB)	national proportion	Total Value of Industrial Production 1995 (bil. RMB)	national proportion	Actual Use of Foreign Investment 1995 (mil.)	national proportion	Volume of Export 1995 (mil.)	national proportion
Beijing	12.5	1.0	139.5	2.4	190.9	2.1	1,106	2.8	10,250	6.9
Tianjin	9.4	0.8	92.0	1.6	209.4	2.3	1,587	4.0	4,064	2.7
Hebei	64.4	5.4	285.0	4.9	399.6	4.3	613	1.5	2,866	1.9
Liaoning	40.9	3.4	279.3	4.8	497.5	5.4	1,568	3.9	8,230	5.6
Shandong	87.1	7.2	500.2	8.7	845.6	9.2	2,765	7.0	8,160	5.5
Bohai Rim	214.3	17.8	1,296.0	22.5	2,143.0	23.3	7,640	19.2	33,570	22.7
Shanghai	14.2	1.2	246.3	4.3	512.9	5.6	3,005	7.6	12,964	8.7
Jiangsu	70.7	5.9	515.5	8.9	1,181.3	12.9	5,326	13.4	9,789	6.6
Zhejiang	43.2	3.5	352.5	6.1	808.8	8.8	1,290	3.2	7,693	5.2
Yangtze Delta	128.0	10.6	1,114.3	19.3	2,503.0	27.2	9,621	24.2	30,446	20.5
Fujian	32.4	2.7	216.1	3.7	280.1	3.0	4,149	10.4	7,908	5.3
Guangdong	68.7	5.7	538.2	9.3	953.5	10.4	10,670	26.9	56,573	38.2
Guangxi	45.4	3.8	160.6	2.8	166.6	1.8	708	1.8	1,702	1.1
Hainan	7.2	0.6	36.4	0.6	19.3	0.2	1,184	3.0	923	0.6
South China	153.7	12.8	951.3	16.5	1,419.5	15.4	16,711	42.1	67,107	45.3
Eastern Region	496.0	41.2	3,361.5	58.3	6,065.5	66.0	33,972	85.5	131,123	88.5
Shanxi	30.8	2.6	109.2	1.9	175.4	1.9	94	0.2	1,143	0.8
Inner Mongolia	22.8	1.9	83.3	1.4	78.2	0.9	89	0.2	500	0.3
Jilin	25.9	2.2	112.9	2.0	142.9	1.6	482	1.2	1,097	0.7
Heilongjiang	37.0	3.1	201.5	3.5	220.4	2.4	625	1.6	1,167	0.8
Anhui	60.1	5.0	200.4	3.5	315.6	3.4	516	1.3	1,693	0.9
Jiangxi	40.6	3.4	120.5	2.1	129.1	1.4	345	0.9	1,042	0.7
Henan	91.0	7.6	300.3	5.2	471.5	5.6	649	1.6	1,358	0.9
Hubei	57.7	4.8	239.1	4.1	410.3	4.5	887	2.2	1,400	0.9
Hunan	63.9	5.3	219.6	3.8	245.1	2.7	560	1.4	1,470	1.0
Central Region	429.9	35.7	1,586.8	27.5	2,188.4	23.8	4,247	10.7	10,568	7.1
Sichuan	113.3	9.4	353.4	6.1	442.6	4.8	619	1.6	2,270	1.5
Guizhou	35.1	2.9	63.0	1.1	55.7	0.6	90	0.2	443	0.3
Yunnan	39.9	3.3	120.7	2.1	120.7	1.3	120	0.3	1,258	0.8
Tibet	2.4	0.2	5.6	0.1	0.9	0.0	-	-	9	0.0
Shaanxi	35.1	2.9	100.0	1.7	118.3	1.3	392	1.0	1,270	0.9
Gansu	24.4	2.0	55.3	1.0	82.5	0.9	83	0.2	360	0.2
Qinghai	4.8	0.4	16.5	0.3	14.9	0.2	2	0.0	130	0.1
Ningxia	5.1	0.4	17.0	0.3	19.8	0.3	6	0.0	168	0.1
Xinjiang	16.6	1.4	83.5	1.4	80.2	0.9	189	0.5	592	0.4
Western Region	276.7	23.0	815.0	14.1	935.5	10.2	1,502	3.8	6,499	4.4
Inland	706.6	58.8	2,401.7	41.7	3,123.9	34.0	5,748	14.5	17,067	11.5
Total	1,202.6	100.0	5,763.3	100.0	9,189.4	100.0	39,721	100.0	148,190	100.0

Source: *China Statistical Yearbook* 1996.

went to the coastal region, only 15 percent to the interior. Share of value of exports was similar to that for foreign investment.

The economy of the coastal area, boosted by use of foreign capital, developed competitive industries and greatly increased the value of exports. This is a result of the coastal-region development strategy of the Deng Xiaoping era.

Five Economic Zones

Let us divide China into several economic regions or zones. In the coastal region, we have three zones: the Bohai Rim economic zone, the Yangtze Delta economic zone, and the South China economic zone. In the interior region we have two zones: the Central economic zone and the Western economic zone (Map 17.1).

Displaying the most dynamic activity is the South China economic zone, particularly Guangdong province. At the end of 1995 the population of Guangdong province was 68.7 million, only 5.7 percent of the national total. However, Guangdong's shares of national GDP and value of industrial output were 9.3 percent and 10.4 percent respectively. The reason for

MAP 17.1 Open Coastal Cities and Open Yangtze River Cities

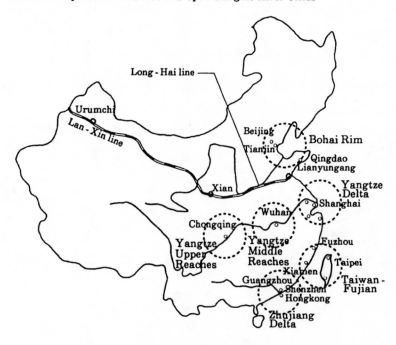

the outstanding industrial activity is clearly indicated by the province's receipt of a huge 26.9 percent share of total foreign investment in China. Foreign investment brings, together with management know-how, advanced technology and information, allowing for the production of competitive products. Guangdong province's share of total national exports value reached 38.2 percent. This shows that Guangdong has been the greatest beneficiary of the strategy of development of the coastal region economies and illustrates the vitality of this province, which is aiming to be the fifth Asian newly industrialized economy. The Shenzhen special economic zone played a leading role in the development of Guangdong's economy. We do not need to elaborate on the fact that most of the foreign investment in the Shenzhen special economic zone came from Hong Kong.

The northern Bohai Rim economic zone and the Yangtze Delta economic zone (alternatively the Shanghai economic zone) in central China are relatively equally matched in a competitive rivalry. Compared by GDP, the Bohai Rim claims 22.5 percent, whereas the Yangtze Delta takes 19.3 percent. In value of industrial output the Bohai Rim contributes 23.3 percent against the Yangtze Delta's 27.2 percent. For value of exports the Bohai Rim accounts for 22.7 percent against the Yangtze Delta's 20.5 percent. Although the two are roughly matched in economic power, the Bohai Rim has a population of 214 million against a population of 128 million for the Yangtze Delta. Thus, on a per capita basis the economic dominance of the Yangtze Delta economic zone is clear.

The disparity in economic power between the coastal region and the interior has been widely noticed. Beginning with the drafting of the Ninth Five Year Plan (1996–2000), voices ever more loudly have been stressing the necessity of developing the interior.

The Yangtze River Basin: The T-Shaped Development Strategy

The "T" is formed by drawing a horizontal line along the coastline of the coastal region and a vertical line from the intersection of the Yangtze River. The T-shaped opening strategy got its start after Deng Xiaoping's talks during his southern excursion. In 1992 the Communist Party Central Committee (in its Document No. 4) dictated a "multidirection, multistrata liberalization" in which the T-shaped strategy emerged as a core component.

The Yangtze River is often referred to as a dragon, Shanghai as the dragon's head. The Yangtze Delta economic zone, with Shanghai as its center and comprising fourteen cities including Nanjing, Zhenjiang, and Hangzhou in the provinces of Jiangsu and Zhejiang, possesses 10.6 percent of China's population and 19.3 percent of national GDP.

In the middle reaches of the Yangtze River are the four provinces of An-hui, Jiangxi, Hunan, and Hubei, with thirteen cities including Wuhan, Yichang, Changsha, and Jiujiang. The population is 18.5 percent of the national total; the share of GDP is 13.5 percent. If the Yangtze is the dragon, then this region is the dragon's torso. The Yangtze's upper reaches are the dragon's tail (in maps the Jinshajiang tributary is drawn as well, making the tail very long). In Sichuan province there are five cities including Chengdu, Panzhihua, and Luzhou. But the main previous city, Chongqing, was elevated to a directly administered municipality under the State Council in spring 1997. Share of total population is 9.4 percent, and that of GDP is 6.1 percent.

We have divided the dragon into three parts, from its head to its tail, each very different in terms of proportions of population and GDP. Notwithstanding the differences, if we combine the three regions they constitute 38.5 percent of national population and 38.9 percent of GDP. If the dragon recovers its vitality, it means the revival of 40 percent of the country. Thus, the strategic significance of this region is great (Table 17.2).

Birth of the Chongqing Directly Administered Municipality and the Three Gorges Dam Project

Chongqing is a port city located at the confluence of the Jialing River from the north and the Yangtze River from the west. Sitting within the confluence the city is an island shaped like a wedge. This is the center of the city of Chongqing. The main goods transport is via ship, with the routing upstream against the Yangtze current. In March 1997 the National People's Congress decided to upgrade Chongqing municipality (previously a city under the Sichuan provincial government) to a municipality directly under the Central government (a status enjoyed by only three other cities—Shanghai, Beijing, and Tianjin). The neighboring Quanxiang District (Quanxiang City, Wulong County, Qianjiang County, Xiyang County) and Wanxian District (Wanxian City, Wuxi County) were incorporated into the new Chongqing. From about 15 million, population roughly doubled to 30 million, creating a huge new municipality.

In the 1960s and 1970s as Sino-Soviet relations deteriorated and the Vietnam War escalated, China began to fear war with the United States. In this context, the Chinese government carried out a so-called Third Front construction initiative for national defense. At that time, the former Chongqing City incorporated surrounding farm districts, and a new Chongqing City was created as a Third Front construction base. Beginning with railway construction, heavy industries such as weapons manufacturing–related industries (for example, steelmaking and armaments

TABLE 17. 2   Three Economic Regions in the Yangtze River Basin

	Central City	Other Cities	Provinces and Cities	Share of National Population	Share of National GNP	Share of National Use of Foreign Capital
Yangtze delta	Shanghai	14 cities including Nanjing, Zhenjiang, Hangzhou	Shanghai, Jiangsu, Zhejiang	10.6%	19.3%	20.5%
Yangtze middle reaches	Wuhan	13 cities including Yichang, Changsha, Jiujiang	Anhui, Jiangxi, Hubei, Hunan	18.5%	13.5%	3.5%
Yangtze upper reaches	Chongqing	5 cities including Luzhou, Panzhihua, Chengdu	Chongqing, Sichuan	9.4%	6.1%	1.5%

Source: Table 17. 1.

industries) were developed. Based on the technological strength of these military industries, a transformation to civilian-related production began in the 1980s. A typical example was the formation of joint-venture companies with Japan's Honda and Yamaha to build motorcycles. The two companies that formed as a result of the introduction of Japanese technology have achieved a 60 percent national market share in motorcycles.

The full influence of reform and liberalization, including the ongoing construction of the Three Gorges dam, is being felt by Chongqing municipality. The first necessity is to resettle some 1 million persons who live in the flood area of the dam and will be forced out of their homes. When the dam is completed larger ships will be able to sail up the Yangtze River, and electric power and agricultural irrigation resources will be greatly expanded. Construction work on the dam is proceeding. While blocking of the river proceeds according to schedule, so does the opening of Chongqing to the outside world. An expressway partly built with World Bank funds linking Chengdu and Chongqing was opened in 1995. The Jiangbei Airport has been completed. With the completion of this transportation infrastructure, and by improving freight movement on the Yangtze River, Chongqing municipality should be able to overcome some of the handicap of being an interior-region city and to serve as a engine of growth for the regional economy.

—Yabuki

Part Three

State Finances, Financial Institutions and Markets, and Government Institution Reform

18

The State Budget, the Fiscal System, and Monetary Policy and Trends

State Budgetary Revenues and Expenditures

How much of the national product, we may ask, is collected as government budget revenues and redistributed either as budgetary expenditures or investments? Table 18.1 shows total budgetary revenues and expenditures and growth rates for the period 1978–1996. Three points are evident. First, the portion of government revenue (and, roughly, expenditure) to GDP has fallen steadily from about 31 percent in 1978, when the planning system and collectivized agriculture still prevailed, to 11 percent in 1996. Second, since 1990 the state budget has suffered from chronic and—until 1996—growing deficits. As a percentage of revenues, the deficit peaked at 11 percent in 1994, declined to 9.3 percent in 1995, and stood at 7.2 percent in 1996. And third, budget revenues and expenditures have been growing at divergent rates. From the mid-1980s until 1994 expenditures generally grew faster than total revenue, which is why deficits grew larger. This pernicious trend was reversed in 1995 on the heels of reforms initiated by Zhu Rongji in 1994 and saw further improvement in 1996.

Before making a judgment about budget trends we should examine where budgetary money comes from and, particularly, how it is used. Table 18.2 presents a summary of the state budget—combining local and Central budgets—in 1996. Chinese budgets at the local and Central levels are divided into current items and capital or construction items. Current items include expenditures for social development and welfare and expenditures for national defense, armed police, and administration. In 1996 total current expenditures consumed RMB 601.5 billion, or 76 percent of total state budgetary expenditures. Only RMB 192.2 billion, or 24 percent of expenditures, went to productive investments. On the revenue side, current revenues, primarily taxes, made up 96 percent of total rev-

TABLE 18. 1   Changes in the Ratio of State Fiscal Revenues and Expenditures to GDP

(unit: bil. RMB)

Year	Revenues (bil. RMB)	Growth Rate	Expenditures (bil. RMB)	Growth Rate	Balance (bil. RMB)	Revenues / GDP (%)
1978	113.2	29.5	112.2	33.0	1.0	31.2
1980	116.0	1.2	122.9	-4.1	-6.9	25.7
1985	200.5	22.0	200.4	17.8	0.06	22.3
1986	212.2	5.8	220.5	10.0	-8.3	20.8
1987	219.9	3.6	226.2	2.6	-6.3	18.4
1988	235.7	7.2	249.1	10.1	-13.4	15.8
1989	266.5	13.1	283.3	13.3	-15.9	15.8
1990	293.7	10.2	308.4	9.2	-14.6	15.8
1991	314.9	7.2	338.7	9.8	-23.7	14.5
1992	348.3	10.6	374.2	10.5	-25.9	13.1
1993	434.9	24.8	464.2	24.1	-29.3	12.6
1994	521.8	20.0	579.3	24.8	-57.5	11.2
1995	624.2	19.6	682.4	1?.8	-58.2	10.9
1996	740.8	18.7	793.8	16.3	-53.0	11.0

Notes: [1]Growth rate is YoY (%).
   [2]Figures for revenues exclude foreign and domestic borrowing.

Source: *China Statistical Yearbook* 1997, p. 236.

enues. There was a surplus of RMB 113.9 billion in current revenues over expenditures, and this was applied to the construction budget. Even so, the construction budget deficit was RMB 53 billion (compared with RMB 58 billion in 1995). The government issued domestic and foreign bonds, raising RMB 196.7 billion, RMB 60.9 billion of which was applied to cover the deficit in the Central construction budget; RMB 123.9 billion was applied to payments of interest and principal of previously issued debt.

Central and Local-Government Budgets

As mentioned, the state budget combines Central and provincial budgets. Table 18.3 and Figure 18.1 show budgetary figures for revenue and expenditure of Central and local governments. This shows that the Central government redistributes a significant part of Central revenues to local governments, the latter making most of the expenditures. In 1996 local governments carried out 73 percent of total expenditures and contributed some 51 percent of total revenues.

One of the most important trends in Chinese state finances has been the change in relative shares that Central and local governments have been contributing to or claiming from the state budget. Table 18.3 shows that from the early 1970s until 1996 the relative contributions and claims of the Central and local governments have dramatically changed. In the first half of the 1970s, local governments contributed 85 percent of revenues

TABLE 18. 2 Government Budget Accounts, 1996

Combined Central and Local Operating Budgets

Current Budget		(unit: billion RMB)	
Revenue		Expenditure	
Total taxes	657.1	Expenditure for nonproductive capital construction	28.9
Subsidies for lossmaking nonproductive enterprises	-12.9	Expenditure for social development and welfare	229.4
Revenue of the adjustment fund for the budget	1.1	Expenditure for national defense, armed police, and administration	184.9
Other current revenue	70.1	Price subsidies	45.4
		Other current expenditures	112.9
Total current revenue	715.4	Total current expenditures	601.5
		Current budget surplus	**113.9**

Constructive (Capital) Budget		(unit: billion RMB)	
Revenue		Expenditure	
Current budget surplus	113.9	Expenditure for productive capital construction	61.9
Special constructive revenue	46.2	Technological upgrading and new product trial production expenses	52.3
Subsidies for lossmaking productive enterprises	-20.8	Expenditures for supporting agricultural production	25.9
		Expenditure for city maintenance	33.6
		Other constructive expenditure	18.6
Total constructive revenue (+current surplus)	139.3	Total constructive expenditures	192.2
Total 1997 budgetary revenues	**740.8**	**Total 1997 budgetary expenditures**	**793.8**
1997 fiscal deficit	**-53.0**		

Central Government Financing Budget (1996)		(unit: billion RMB)	
Total financing revenue	196.7	Total financing expenditures	131.5
of which:		Principal and interest payments on domestic debt	122.3
(a) domestic debt issued to cover central deficit	60.9	Principal and interest payments on foreign debt	6.1
(b) borrowing to cover principal and interest payments on domestic debt	123.9	Interest payments on borrowing from PBOC	2.8
Direct foreign borrowing	11.6	Other	0.3
Other	0.3		
Net financing budget surplus: (carried over to next fiscal year)	65.2		

Source: Finance Yearbook of China 1997, pp. 391-392.

TABLE 18. 3 Central and Local Fiscal Revenue and Expenditure

(unit: bil. RMB, %)

Year	Revenue			Expenditure		
	Total	Central	Local	Total	Central	Local
1971-1975	392.0	57.6	334.3	391.9	212.5	179.4
(%)	100.0	14.7	85.3	100.0	54.2	45.8
1976-1980	509.0	90.4	418.5	528.2	262.5	265.7
(%)	100.0	17.8	82.2	100.0	49.7	50.3
1981-1985	740.3	258.3	482.0	748.3	372.6	375.8
(%)	100.0	34.9	65.1	100.0	49.8	50.2
1986-1990	1,228.1	410.4	817.6	1,286.6	442.0	844.5
(%)	100.0	33.4	66.6	100.0	34.4	65.6
1991-1995	2,244.2	903.8	1,340.4	2,438.7	732.3	1,706.4
(%)	100.0	40.3	59.7	100.0	30.0	70.0

Notes: [1]Revenue is for central and local governments.
[2]Revenue excludes domestic and foreign loans, and expenditure excludes foreign debt concerning expenses fees and repayment of principal and interests.

Source: *China Statistical Yearbook* 1997, p. 247.

FIGURE 18. 1 Revenue and Expenditure for Central and Local Fiscal

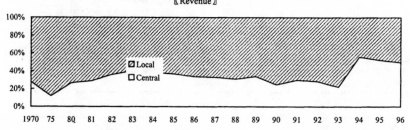

Source: *China Statistical Yearbook* 1997, p. 247.

and accounted for only 46 percent of expenditures. By the first half of the 1990s, they were contributing almost 60 percent of revenues but spending 70 percent. Looked at from the perspective of the Central government, it was taxing the localities to support national priorities during the 1970s. (Although by the 1990s it was transferring funds and spending authority to the provinces.) Needless to say, the allocation of budgetary revenues and expenditures is a critical political issue in China, as in other countries. It seems reasonable to conclude from the above that we have seen, and continue to see, two influences at work: (1) the gradual dismantling of central planning and direct budgetary allocations for state-run industries; and (2) the success of rich provinces, like Shanghai and Guangdong, in reducing or "capping" incremental payments of local-government revenues to Beijing.

Tax Collection and Reduction of Subsidies to State-Owned Enterprises

Officials in Beijing are often heard to complain that after attending to welfare and security requirements few tax revenues flow to the state to finance major capital construction projects. A major push has been under way since 1994 to improve the situation.

One element has been to improve tax collection. In 1994 a major reform was announced in the system of taxes and tax collection. Most dramatically, a value-added tax—at a high rate of 17 percent—was introduced for the first time. Perhaps equally important, it was decided that the Central and local governments should set up parallel tax collection systems throughout the country. Prior to the reform, local tax bureaus—under a "responsibility system"—had collected both taxes for both the Central government and for local governments. The system of clearly identifying taxes as Central, local, or "shared" remained. Immediately, in 1994, the VAT became the largest revenue earner. It is a "shared" tax, combining a 15 percent Central component and a 2 percent local component (hence the 17 percent rate). Evidencing the dissatisfaction with the results of the previous local responsibility system, collection of the VAT is now specifically entrusted to Central tax collection units. Other key Central taxes are enterprises income tax for Central-level, state-owned companies (total 33 percent, actually shared 30 percent for Central, 3 percent for localities) and consumption taxes. Local taxes include individual income taxes, income taxes for local and collective enterprises, land appreciation taxes, and excise taxes. Table 18.4 shows tax revenues by type.

As is often the case, Central's policy objectives have to some extent been frustrated by local resistance. In the three years since the new sys-

TABLE 18. 4   Categories of Tax Revenues

(unit: bil. RMB, %)

Year	Total Tax Revenue (%)	Industrial and Commercial Tax (%)	Tariffs (%)	Agricultural and Animal Husbandry Taxes (%)	State-Owned Enterprises Income Tax (%)	Collectively Owned Enterprises Income Tax (%)
1980	57.2 (100)	51.1 (89.3)	3.4 (5.9)	2.8 (4.8)		
1985	204.1 (100)	109.7 (53.8)	20.5 (10.1)	4.2 (2.1)	59.6 (29.2)	10.0 (4.9)
1990	282.2 (100)	185.9 (65.9)	15.9 (5.6)	8.8 (3.1)	60.4 (21.4)	11.2 (4.0)
1995	603.8 (100)	459.0 (76.0)	29.2 (4.8)	27.8 (4.6)	75.9 (12.6)	11.9 (2.0)
1996	691.0 (100)	527.0 (76.3)	30.2 (4.4)	36.9 (5.4)	82.2 (11.9)	14.6 (2.1)

Source: China Statistical Yearbook 1997, p. 240.

tem was announced, separate Central and local tax bureaus have been set up in Beijing and Guangzhou. Taxpayers fill out separate returns for each bureau and pay taxes separately. However, as at late 1997 the Shanghai tax bureau had refused to allow the separate Central tax collector to operate, so taxes are paid against only one return that is filed with the local bureau. The Shanghai tax bureau continues to argue that separate returns and tax collectors will inconvenience taxpayers, but the real reason for its resistance is the bargaining power it gains from possessing the money; determining how to share revenues, or even defining what are Central and local revenues, remain unclear.

In 1994 and 1995, as the reforms began, Central revenues grew more rapidly than local revenues, but in 1996 the opposite was true. We can safely assume that local creativity of the kind seen in Shanghai was the cause of the reversal. Preliminary figures for tax collections in 1997 indicate that Central again turned the tide by increasing tax revenues 19.3 percent, to RMB 426.1 billion, while local collections increased 14.6 percent, to RMB 328.7 billion. Central tax collections thereby accounted for 56.4 percent of total tax collections, 0.9 percentage points higher than the share in 1996 (Shanghai Securities News, January 1, 1998).

Another key reform has been to reduce subsidies to lossmaking SOEs. In 1994, 1995, and 1996 subsidies to lossmaking SOEs amounted to RMB 36.6 billion, 32.8 billion, and 33.7 billion respectively. This was equivalent to 7.0 percent, 5.3 percent, and 4.6 percent of government revenues in 1994, 1995, and 1996, representing 63.7 percent, 56.4 percent, and 63.7 percent of the respective fiscal deficits (Table 18.5).

Principal Sources of Capital Investment Funds: Bank Loans and "Off-Budget" Funds

These budget figures clearly point out that Central and local-government budgets are not the most important conduit for investment capital in

TABLE 18. 5 Scale of Deficit Subsidies to State-Owned Enterprises

(unit: bil. RMB)

Year	Fiscal Revenue (a)	Fiscal Deficits (b)	Deficit Subsidies to State-Owned Enterprises (c)	(c) / (a) (%)	(c) / (b) (%)
1985	200.5	--	50.7	25.3	--
1990	293.7	14.6	57.9	19.7	395.2
1991	314.9	23.7	51.0	16.2	215.2
1992	348.3	25.9	44.5	12.8	171.9
1993	434.9	29.3	41.1	9.5	140.2
1994	521.8	57.5	36.6	7.0	63.7
1995	624.2	58.2	32.8	5.3	56.4
1996	740.8	53.0	33.7	4.6	63.7

Source: China Statistical Yearbook 1997, p. 249.

China. When the government is a major source of funds, the mechanism tends to be funding from state policy banks, particularly the State Development Bank. More often, during the days of the planned economy, as well as today, investment funds have come from China's state-owned banks in the form of loans to SOEs and infrastructure projects. These loans have actually been quasi–equity infusions, since repayment in most cases required the success of the funded investments. Because of this, economists have begun to look at the loans on the books of state-owned banks as disguised government deficit spending. The writer is in sympathy with this interpretation, which, if accepted, requires a recalculation of China's domestic government debt.

Another major source of investment funds is the "off-budget" funds collected and allocated by virtually every ministry and subsidiary unit (e.g., provincial and local bureaus). The source of these funds is levies placed on services—for example, electric power, roads, telephone communications—provided by or through government agencies.

Table 18.6 shows off-budget funds accumulated on a national basis during the ten-year period 1987–1996. We observe two points clearly: (1) the amount of off-budget funds is enormous (RMB 389.3 billion in 1996, or close to 50 percent of the on-budget revenues); and (2) almost all of the collections—93 percent in 1995—are made by the enterprises or quasi-enterprises run by the government. Off-budget funds have been and continue to be a major source of nondebt financing for projects at all levels in China. Table 18.7 provides data for on- and off-budget revenues and expenditures at the province level for 1996.

Government Debt Financing

In 1994, as part of several measures to combat inflation, an important decision was taken by the State Council: The Ministry of Finance (MOF)

State Budget, Fiscal System, and Monetary Trends

TABLE 18. 6 Off-Budget Funds by Revenue Category

(unit: billion RMB)

Year	Total	Local Fiscal Admin. Off-Budget Funds	Administrative Units and Institutions Off-Budget Funds	State-Owned Ent. and Main Dept. Off-Budget Funds	Ratio of Off-Budget Revenue to On-Budget Funds (%)
1987	202.9	4.46	35.84	162.58	92.2
1988	236.1	4.89	43.89	187.29	100.1
1989	265.9	5.44	50.07	210.38	99.7
1990	270.9	6.06	57.70	207.11	92.2
1991	324.3	6.88	69.70	247.75	103.0
1992	385.5	9.09	88.55	287.86	110.7
1993	143.3	11.47	131.78		32.9
1994	186.3	14.00	172.25		35.7
1995	240.7	17.17	223.49		38.6
1996	389.3				52.6

Notes: The scope for off-budget funds in 1993-1995 and 1996 was changed, so they are not comparable to prior years.
Source: Finance Yearbook of China 1997, p. 466.

could no longer borrow funds from the People's Bank of China to finance its deficits. The ministry was therefore left with only one deficit-financing method: the issuance of treasury securities to the Chinese public. The treasury had been issuing debt securities since 1981, but since the 1994 decision the volume and variety of debt issues has exploded. In 1997 issuance volume was RMB 241.8 billion, compared with RMB 212.6 billion in 1996. A trend is the issuance of more voucher-form T-bonds with maturities of three and five years, aimed at the individual investor market.

The government debt market is still underdeveloped, and the state's resort to public debt issuance falls far short of what would be expected and appropriate considering the investment needs of the government. To date, the reliance on "directed" lending from banks has allowed governments at all levels to achieve indirect financing of investment needs. This system is out of date and incompatible with the idea of reforming banks into real commercial lenders. In the future we should expect to see the government access the domestic debt market much more actively. One step in this direction was taken by the Ministry of Finance in March 1998, when it issued RMB 270 billion in bonds to begin to recapitalize the state banks.

A salutary side-effect of the growth and variety of government debt issues has been the development of a vital secondary treasury securities market. This market, in time, will be instrumental in enabling the Central Bank to begin to exercise indirect control over the money supply and interest rates through open market operations.

Monetary Policy and Money Supply Trends

From the 1950s through the 1970s many in China thought it desirable to hold the money supply to one-eighth of the gross value of retail transactions (Yang Peixin, 1990). Officials postulated that the money supply

TABLE 18. 7 On- and Off-budget Revenues and Expenditures by Province in 1996

(unit: million RMB)

Region	Revenue			Expenditure		
	Total Revenue	On-Budget	Off-Budget	Total Expenditure	On-Budget	Off-Budget
Total	124,192	80,204	43,989	121,495	79,561	41,934
Beijing	1,000	816	184	1,228	1,014	214
Tianjin	1,032	729	302	803	512	292
Hebei	5,453	3,366	2,087	4,467	2,525	1,941
Shanxi	2,043	1,620	423	1,962	1,541	421
Inner Mongolia	1,801	1,550	251	1,847	1,612	235
Liaoning	3,908	2,692	1,217	4,494	3,215	1,278
in which: Dalian	840	598	242	772	531	242
Jilin	1,294	771	522	1,824	1,303	521
Heilongjiang	1,784	1,434	350	1,925	1,585	340
Shanghai	3,637	2,526	1,111	3,794	2,799	995
Jiangsu	12,570	6,456	6,114	11,491	6,029	5,463
Zhejiang	10,496	5,588	4,908	8,897	3,748	5,149
in which: Ningbo	1,797	895	902	1,574	620	954
Anhui	7,507	4,392	3,115	6,781	3,935	2,846
Fujian	6,267	3,821	2,446	5,202	2,692	2,510
in which: Xiamen	238	142	96	232	153	79
Jiangxi	3,346	2,615	731	3,011	2,350	661
Shandong	11,724	5,745	5,979	12,284	6,636	5,648
in which: Qingdao	860	522	338	843	516	327
Henan	6,515	4,390	2,124	6,681	4,703	1,978
Hubei	4,181	3,240	941	3,872	3,103	769
Hunan	6,613	3,687	2,926	5,318	2,577	2,741
Guangdong	10,414	6,691	2,724	12,342	8,604	3,738
in which: Shenzhen	1,109	359	750	1,342	600	742
Guangxi	2,724	2,612	112	2,788	2,690	98
Hainan	529	512	17	773	758	16
Sichuan	9,210	6,067	3,143	8,174	5,197	2,977
in which: Chongqing	1,222	818	404	1,306	914	392
Guizhou	2,171	1,851	319	1,910	1,635	275
Yunnan	4,253	4,107	146	4,758	4,636	121
Shaanxi	2,142	1,653	489	2,110	1,684	426
Gansu	865	725	140	1,255	1,141	114
Qinghai	107	93	13	168	155	13
Ningxia	177	120	56	239	186	53
Xinjiang	433	334	98	1,095	995	99

Source: *Finance Yearbook of China* 1997, pp. 476-477.

would turn over eight times on average and that the money stock would be 12.5 percent of the value of retail transactions, but if it rose to 16.5 percent of this value there would a risk of inflation. Amid the 1980s economic reforms, adherence to these standards was abandoned.

China's monetary definitions are the same as in other countries: M0 is currency in circulation; M1 (or "money") is currency in circulation plus demand deposits; and M2 is M1 plus "quasimoney" (time deposits plus savings deposits plus other deposits). In China, because of the prevalence

TABLE 18. 8 M0, M1, M2, Year-on-Year Increase, and Growth Rate

(unit: billion RMB)

Year	M0	M0 YoY Increase	M0 Growth Rate (%)	M1	M1 YoY Increase	M1 Growth Rate (%)	M2	M2 YoY Increase	M2 Growth Rate (%)
1986	122	23	23.3	386	85	28	672	152	29.3
1987	146	24	19.4	448	63	16.2	844	172	25.6
1988	213	68	46.7	549	101	22.5	1010	166	19.7
1989	234	21	9.8	584	35	6.3	1,195	185	18.3
1990	264	30	12.8	695	112	19.1	1,529	334	28.0
1991	318	53	20.2	863	168	24.2	1,935	406	26.5
1992	434	116	36.4	1,173	310	35.9	2,540	605	31.3
1993	587	153	35.3	1,628	455	38.8	3,488	948	37.3
1994	729	142	24.3	2,054	426	26.2	4,692	1,204	34.5
1995	789	60	8.2	2,399	345	16.8	6,075	1,383	29.5
1996	880	92	11.6	2,852	453	18.9	7,610	1,534	25.3
1997	1,018	138	15.6	3,483	631	22.1	9,100	1,490	19.6

Sources: The People's Daily, March 8, 1998;
        PBOC, *The People's Bank of China Quarterly Statistical Bulletin*, vol. 8, 1998.

FIGURE 18. 2 Growth Rate of M0, M1, M2

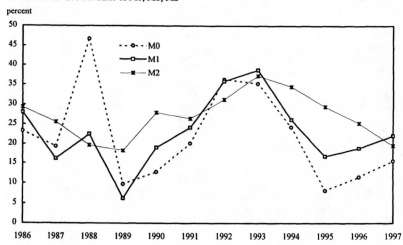

Source: Table 18. 8.

of cash settlements both for individual and company purchases, M0 is the measure most closely tied to price movements. M1 and M2 movements tend to move in opposite directions to goods prices.

Table 18.8 and Figure 18.2 show that China's figures for growth in its money supply have fluctuated drastically since 1986. The growth rate of M0 shot above 45 percent in 1988 amid a "goods panic," then crashed to 10 percent the next year in the chill of the Tiananmen Incident. Growth rates leaped again in 1993 and 1994 to more than 35 percent. Double-digit inflation accompanied this monetary growth. A second correction followed after Zhu Rongji seized control of the financial system in mid-1993, and M0 growth touched bottom in 1995 at less than 10 percent. In 1997 the growth rates were 15.6 percent for M0, 22.1 percent for M1, and 19.6 percent for M2. PBOC's targets for growth in 1998 are M0 15 percent, M1 17 percent, and M2 16 percent. Based on past evidence this would be in line with the government's target for inflation of less than 5 percent.

—*Harner*

19

China's Banking System

From the Planned Economy to
True Financial Intermediation

The Unibank Period of
the People's Bank of China

The devastation China suffered as a consequence of adopting Soviet-style central planning was hardest felt in the banking system. By the 1940s Chinese as well as foreign banking institutions had reached a high level of sophistication in the country's commercial centers, and modernization was making headway in the hinterlands. However, Soviet-style central planning offered no role for independent financial intermediaries like commercial banks, which borrowed funds from savers and lended to investors while also performing the critical function of risk evaluation. During the 1950s China's many commercial banks were closed. In their place appeared a sole entity, the People's Bank of China, a so-called unibank whose function within the planning system was primarily to disburse investment and operating funds to state-run enterprises according to annual plans. By the late 1970s, when the decision was taken to adopt a market system, China's leadership was confronted with a truly terrible reality: As in Europe when it emerged from the Dark Ages, it became necessary not only to rebuild the institutions of a modern financial system but also to relearn everything about modern banking and finance. The Chinese people, among the world's most capable bankers abroad, had totally lost their art in their homeland.

Rebuilding the Banking Institutions

Reestablishing the institutional framework of the banking system began with Deng Xiaoping's reforms in 1979, one of the first steps being to renew an independent identity and role for the Agricultural Bank of China (which had been established in 1955, only to be merged with PBOC in 1957). The Bank of China, previously the PBOC department specializing in foreign exchange business, was segregated from PBOC that same year (1979). In September 1983 the State Council formally adopted a plan to transform PBOC into the Central Bank and to transfer its commercial banking functions to "specialized banks." ABC was already in this category. In 1983 the People's Construction Bank of China (now the China Construction Bank), which had operated as the conduit for budgetary allocations for infrastructure and capital construction projects under the Ministry of Finance, was established as a separate entity, and its credit plan was brought under PBOC's overall credit system. Another major step was the establishment, in early 1984, of the Industrial and Commercial Bank of China to take over the industrial and commercial business portfolio of PBOC. In 1987 the Bank of Communications was reestablished as the country's first shareholding bank. During the late 1980s and early 1990s a number of new Chinese banks were established as "commercial banks" by local governments and major groups (Figure 19.1).

Yet rebuilding the institutional structure of the banking system was only the first step. By the early 1990s it was announced that the goal would be to remake China's banking system into one suitable for the "socialist market economy," that is, banks would actually perform the financial intermediation function of allocating the system's liquidity toward its most productive and efficient uses based on an objective analysis of risk and return.

Impediments to Effective Financial Intermediation

Anyone close to the reality in China during the early 1990s saw two huge obstacles to rapid realization of this new vision. One was the growing weakness, indeed, the effective bankruptcy of the SOE sector, which constituted by far the largest customer base of the four former specialized banks, which still provided close to 80 percent of the total credit in the economy (Table 19.1). The other was the Chinese banks' lack of independence from local governments and the influence of local and even national officials over lending decisions. A concomitant feature was the lack of professional expertise and standards in management and staff at Chinese banks, especially in the critical area of credit risk assessment.

The reality of China during the 1980s and into the mid-1990s was that Chinese banks continued in most cases to act as they had in the past—advancing funds to SOEs without expectation of repayment and supporting projects sponsored by local political interests without regard to the economic value or debt service capability of these projects.

FIGURE 19.1 Financial Institutions Under the People's
Bank of China

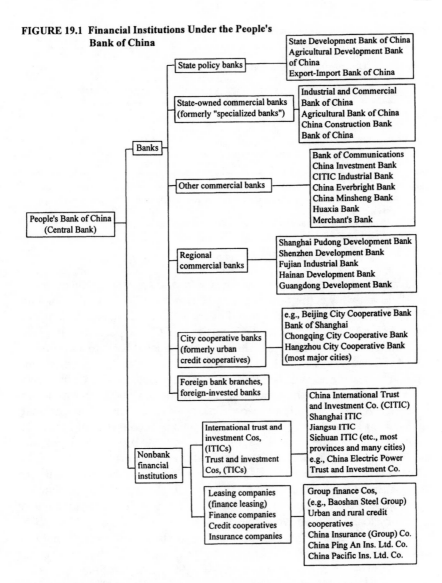

Note: Securities companies, formerly supervised by PBOC, are deemed to be supervised primarily
by the China Securities Regulatory Commission (CSRC).
Sources: *The People's Bank of China Quarterly Statistical Bulletin*, vol. 3, 1997; *Almanac of China's Finance
and Banking* 1997.

TABLE 19.1   Share of Commercial Financing by Financial Institutions

(unit: bil. RMB, %)

Year/Month	Total Volume of Commercial Financing (bil. RMB)	State-Owned Commercial Banks (bil. RMB)	(%)	Other Commercial Banks (bil. RMB)	Rural Credit Cooperatives (bil. RMB)	Urban Credit Cooperatives (bil. RMB)	Finance Companies (bil. RMB)
Dec. 1993	3,089	2,558	83	124	314	78	16
Dec. 1994	3,864	3,100	80	179	417	144	25
Dec. 1995	4,809	3,756	78	281	523	207	41
Dec. 1996	5,823	4,448	76	409	636	263	67
Dec. 1997	7,145	5,437	76	430	766	352	83

Note: State-owned commercial banks indicate Industrial and Commercial Bank of China,
         Agricultural Bank of China, China Construction Bank, and Bank of China (previously
         "specialized banks").
Source: PBOC, *The People's Bank of China Quarterly Statistical Bulletin*, vol. 8, 1998.

Basic Banking Legislation

A major step in reforming the banking system and addressing the problems described above was the promulgation of two basic laws in 1995: the Law of the People's Bank of China, passed by the National People's Congress on March 18, and the Commercial Banking Laws of China, passed by the NPC Standing Committee on May 5. These laws gave legal basis to a number of critical reform elements such as the PBOC's role as the Central Bank and chief supervisor and regulator of the banking system. The Commercial Banking Law's ninety-one articles lay out the details and authority for reforms in five key areas: (1) converting the specialized banks into commercial banks; (2) converting credit cooperatives into commercial banks; (3) granting greater autonomy to commercial banks; (4) protecting depositors; and (5) introducing prudential standards and regulations.

Three new, state-level policy banks—the State Development Bank, the Agricultural Development Bank, and the China Export-Import Bank—were established to take over policy lending (and, perhaps, accept some of the policy loan portfolio weighing down the other banks). By 1994 PBOC had already established basic guidelines and standards for asset liability and risk management for banks (Table 19.2). In reality, these standards were out of reach for the major banks in 1994, and compliance was expected to take until at least 2000. In any event, the two 1995 banking laws and additional institutional, legal, and policy changes are helping Chinese banks to progress toward the goal of becoming real commercial banks.

The Gargantuan Scale of China's State-Owned Banks

Chinese banks are massive, not only in terms of assets but also in terms of physical presence and people. The banks' complicated, multitier organi-

TABLE 19. 2 PBOC Guidelines for Asset-Liability Management for Commercial Banks (promulgated February 1994)

Capital Adequacy

    a. Total capital not less than 8 percent of risk-weighted assets.

        Formula: The month-end average balance of total capital divided by the month-end average balance of risk weighted assets should be equal or greater than 8 percent.

    b. Primary capital not less than 4 percent of risk-weighted assets.

        Formula: The month-end average balance of primary capital divided by the month-end average balance of risk assets should be equal or greater than 4 percent.

Loan-Deposit Ratio

    All categories of loans should not exceed 75 percent of all categories of deposits.

    a. Total balance basis (applied to commercial banks: including Bank of Communications, Citic Industrial Bank, Everbright Bank, Huaxia Bank)

        Formula: Period-end average balance of all types of loans divided by period-end average balance of all types of deposits should equal or be less than 75 percent.

    b. Increased volume basis (applied to specialized banks: ICBC, ABC, BOC, CCB)

        Formula: Period-end average increase in all categories of loans divided by period-end average increase in all categories of deposits should equal or be less than 75 percent.

Medium- and Long-Term Loan Ratios

    Medium- and long-term loans exceeding one year (including one-year) may not exceed 120 percent of deposits over one year.

        Formula: Average month-end balances of medium- and long-term loans over one year (including one-year) divided by average month-end balances of deposits over one year (including one-year) should equal or be less than 120 percent.

Asset Liquidity Ratio

    The ratio of liquid assets must not be below 25 percent of all categories, liquid liabilities.

    a. Current assets defined as assets convertible to cash within one month, including cash in hand, deposits with PBOC, interbank placements, one month or less interbank money market (net) loans, treasury bills, loans maturing within one month, and banker's acceptance drafts maturing within one month.

    b. Liquid liabilities defined as deposits and net interbank borrowing maturing within one month.

        Formula: Period-end balance of liquid assets divided by the period-end balance of liquid liabilities should equal or exceed 25 percent.

Cash Reserve Ratio

    Reserve deposits with the PBOC and cash in hand should not be less than 5-7 percent (actual ratio to be determined by PBOC from time to time).

Single Borrower Lending Limit

    a. Loans to a single borrower cannot exceed 15 percent of total capital.

    b. Loans to the ten largest borrowers cannot exceed 50 percent of all categories of capital.

Interbank Money Market Funding Ratios

    a. Interbank money market borrowing cannot exceed 4 percent of the balance of all categories of deposits.

    b. Interbank money market lending cannot exceed 8 percent of all categories of deposits.

Loans to Shareholders

    Loans to shareholders may not exceed 100 percent of the value of the capital paid in by the shareholder. Terms and conditions of loans to shareholders should be no more favorable than those for other customers for the same type of loan.

Loan Quality

    The balance of overdue loans (*yuqi daikuan*) should not exceed 8 percent of the total loans balance; non-performing loans (*daizhi daikuan*) should not exceed 5 percent of total loans; and bad debts (*daizhang daikuan*) should not exceed 2 percent of total loans.

        Formulas:

        Overdue loans: Month-end average balance of overdue loans divided by month-end average balance of all categories of loans equal or less than 8 percent.

        Non-performing loans: Month-end average balance of nonperforming loans divided by month-end balance of all categories of loans equal or less than 5 percent.

        Bad debts: Month-end average balance of bad debts divided by month-end average balance of all loans equal or less than 2 percent.

Source: Appendix in Hu Zhanghong, *The Competitive Strategy of Chinese Commercial Banks* 1996, pp. 323-327.

TABLE 19. 3 Personnel and Various-Level Organizational Units for State-Owned Banks, 1996

	Total	PBOC	ICBC	ABC	BOC	CCB
Year-end employees	1,915,947	189,195	565,955	538,780	198,555	383,593
in which: headquarters		2,512	742	740	2,362	1,030
Year-end No. of organizations	157,365	2,448	38,219	65,870	13,863	35,117
in which: headquarters	9	2	1	1	1	1
branches at province level		30	29	30	30	30
branches in cities at prefectural level		16	14	14	15	14
local branches		319	362	324	253	325
branches at county level		1,982	1,981	2,391	1,522	2,002
city offices		8	1,642	896	1,690	3,550
operation units			370	701		506
local offices			5,972	33,260	3,546	4,738
savings depositories			23,670	26,470	6,788	20,256
others		91	4,149	1,687	-	2,860

Source: Almanac of China's Finance and Banking 1997, p. 592.

zational system extends from Beijing to the lowest districts and townships and villages throughout China. In 1996 the Industrial and Commercial Bank of China employed a total of 565,955 persons, including 121,140 at the township and village level, in 38,219 branches, subbranches, and offices nationwide. The Agricultural Bank of China employed 538,780 in 65,870 branches, subbranches, and offices nationwide. The total employment of China's state-owned commercial banks, policy banks, and the People's Bank of China at year-end 1996 was 1,915,947 persons in 157,365 branches, subbranches, and offices nationwide (Table 19.3).

The enormous scale and scope of China's state banking operations make efficiency, accountability, and risk control impossible.

Interest, Loan, and Reserve Rates of Chinese Banks

PBOC set deposit and lending rates for RMB for all financial institutions in China. From 1991 to July 1993, a period of quickening inflation, the trend for rates was up. Since July 1993 the trend has been down, so that the standard one-year deposit rate in May 1998 was 5.22 percent and the one-year loan rate was 7.92 percent (Table 19.4). This built-in spread of 2.7 percent appears rich but actually is not, considering the huge costs borne by Chinese banks from operations, the "drag" of bad debts, and high taxes.

The banks have also traditionally been forced to place large reserves with PBOC. Prior to March 25, 1998, the combined requirement for two categories of reserves was 18–20 percent of deposits (Table 19.5). As part of reform measures being instituted to improve bank economics and bolster banks' capital, PBOC lowered the reserve requirement to 8 percent effective March 25, 1998.

TABLE 19. 4   Bank Deposit and Loan Interest Rates in China

Deposits

	5/15/1993	7/11/1993	5/1/1996	8/23/1996	10/23/1997	3/25/1998
Demand	2.16	3.15	2.97	1.98	1.71	1.71
3-month deposit	4.86	6.66	4.86	3.33	2.88	2.88
6-month deposit	7.20	9.00	7.20	5.40	4.14	4.14
1-year deposit	9.18	10.98	9.18	7.47	5.67	5.22
3-year deposit	10.80	12.24	10.80	8.28	6.21	6.21

Loans

	7/11/1993	1/1/1995	7/1/1995	5/1/1996	8/23/1996	10/23/1997	3/25/1998
People's Bank standard interest rate							
6 months	9.00	9.00	10.08	9.72	9.18	7.65	7.02
1 year	10.98	10.98	12.06	10.98	10.08	8.64	7.92
3 years	12.24	12.96	13.50	13.14	10.98	9.36	9.00
Maximum interest rate							
6 months	10.80	10.80	12.10	10.69	10.10	8.42	7.72
1 year	13.18	13.18	14.47	12.08	11.09	9.50	8.71
3 years	14.69	15.55	16.20	14.45	12.08	10.30	9.90

Notes: [1]Banks were permitted by PBOC to add a 20% surcharge on loan interest rate in 1993-1995.
[2]The permitted surcharge was reduced to 10% on May 1, 1996.

Source: PBOC, *The People's Bank of China Quarterly Statistical Bulletin*, vol. 10, 1998.

TABLE 19. 5   Reserve Requirements for Chinese Banks

Percentage of deposits	Prior to March 25, 1998	After March 25, 1998
Legal reserves	13%	8%
Special withdrawal preparation reserves	5-7%	abolished

Source: PBOC.

Clearly PBOC has sought to maintain a fairly stable or widening net spread between lending and deposit (borrowing) rates for banks. PBOC policy is also based, of course, on its intentions toward the customers of the banks: borrowers, especially state-owned companies, and savers, particularly consumers.

The Massive Scale of the Banking System's Bad Debts

In the alarmed and self-searching atmosphere of early 1998, there was some unusual candor about the extent of bad debts on the books of China's banks. *Xinhua Financial News* (January 12, 1998), citing "estimates of the People's Bank of China," put the level at 20 percent of loans, or more than RMB 1 trillion. This is almost certainly an underestimate. The main borrowers of the system are SOEs and state projects. Perhaps half of these borrowers are losing money and not properly servicing debt. PRC accounting standards and bank management practice make it easy for both borrower and bank to not recognize bad debts. In reality, probably 30–40 percent or more of the banking system's assets are nonperforming and uncollectible and should be written off. The value would be some RMB 1,630–2,175 billion at the end of 1997, about 25 percent of GDP. This means that the Chinese banking system is actually insolvent (although as long as government backing is unquestioned, as it will remain, failure is highly unlikely). It also illustrates the huge cost and burden of restructuring the system.

Outlook for Chinese Bank Reform

The Asian financial crisis—and the fear that it would spread to China—raised financial policy and reform to an unprecedentedly high level of priority for the Chinese government in late 1997 and early 1998. Previously, financial policy was treated by the political cadres and engineers who populated China's leadership as an esoteric field to be handled by specialists and technocrats. In late 1997 and early 1998, however, Beijing held a series of high-level meetings including participants in the financial system. The need for reform was elucidated, and, more important, party and government leadership lined up in support of urgent action.

What kinds of reform are needed? We would identify three major categories: (1) cleaning out bad debts and recapitalizing the banks; (2) reorganizing and downsizing bank organizations; and (3) modernizing and improving management and accountability.

Cleaning Up the Banks and Raising New Bank Capital

The first urgent task is to clean up the banks and recapitalize their balance sheets. The urgency was evidenced by the State Council's surprise decision under Zhu Rongji in March 1998 to issue RMB 270 billion in Ministry of Finance bonds for the specific purpose of increasing the capital of state-owned commercial banks. Given our estimate of bad debts (RMB 1,630–2,175 billion at the end of 1997), we can see that this is some one-tenth the volume of new capital needed to put banks on secure footing.

Three approaches are possible for going forward: (1) issuing government bonds to the public and injecting proceeds into the banks; (2) allowing the banks to raise capital directly by issuing convertible debentures and stock to the public and enterprises; and (3) converting loans to equity in enterprises. All three approaches are likely to be followed to some degree during the next decade. The second will require "corporatizing" and converting the banks to shareholding companies.

Reorganizing and Downsizing Bank Organizations

This process started in 1997 and will gain momentum in 1998–2000. The many overlapping layers and coverage areas of offices and branches of Chinese banks will be pared down. In particular, ICBC, BOC, and the China Construction Bank (CCB) will retrench their operations in the countryside, concentrating activities in the cities. The hugely overstaffed and inefficient workforce must be scaled down.

Modernizing and Improving Management and Accountability

This is the greatest challenge. China has employed consultants and instituted training programs to devise and implement management information systems and to institute new management disciplines. The vast scale of the banking system adds a degree of difficulty and ensures slow progress. And there remain all the impediments and obstacles and temptations that have frustrated progress in the past. No doubt within three years much progress will be made, but the task will only have begun.

—Harner

20

China's Stock Markets

*Effecting Fundamental Changes in
China's Economic and Social Life*

The Shanghai and Shenzhen
Securities Exchanges

Next to decollectivization of agriculture and introduction of foreign investment, probably the most important and profound innovation during the Deng Xiaoping era was the opening of stock exchanges in Shenzhen and Shanghai in 1990. Similar to the way in which effective ownership of land restored the entrepreneurial spirit of farmers and produced surpluses that supported rapid development during the 1980s and 1990s, the advent of Chinese stock markets has: (1) turned the Chinese public into vicarious entrepreneurs; (2) created a financial knowledge industry that is disseminating modern concepts and standards concerning corporate strategy, enterprise management, risk management, cost of capital, and shareholder value; (3) heightened transparency of Chinese corporations and accountability of management; and, of course, (4) provided a source of capital that will be essential for the restructuring and reform of productive enterprises in China.

Securities listed in Shenzhen or Shanghai can only be traded on their respective exchanges, and there is no system of dual listing on the two exchanges. Chinese investors buy and sell listed securities through brokerage firms that are members of the securities exchanges. At the end of 1997 some 470 brokerage firms from every province of China except Taiwan, as well as some seventy foreign firms, were members of the Shanghai exchange, and a similar number are members of the Shenzhen exchange. Brokers are linked to the exchanges through a computerized, satellite-linked trading and communications system as modern as any in the world. At the end of 1997 there were more than 32 million investment account holders in the two securities exchanges, up from 21 million in 1996. The total turnover on the two Chinese exchanges exceeded RMB 3 trillion in 1997, and the market value of shares was RMB 1,753 billion, nearly 25 percent of GDP (Table 20.1).

The Volatile History of the Stock Indexes

Chinese stock markets began with great fanfare but few listed securities. During 1991, the first full year of operation, only thirty securities were listed on the Shanghai exchange. These included, as today, treasury bonds, corporate bonds, financial bonds, investment funds, and "A" and "B" shares. At the beginning only eight stocks were listed. Listed Chinese companies have increased from 9 in 1990 to 882 at year-end 1997. In the first few years of the markets, most stock listings were of "local" companies in Shanghai and Guangdong province. In recent years virtually every province has been able to list some companies (Table 20.2).

From mid-1992 through mid-1993 the markets soared under the influence of speculative fever, the shortage of stocks available for purchase, and, most important, massive infusions of "hot money" diverted by enterprises and financial institutions from core businesses to the stock market. Bust followed boom—punctuated by occasional speculative bubbles—in 1994 and most of 1995, as Zhu Rongji implemented a financial tightening and cracked down on bank involvement in securities speculation. During 1996, 1997, and into 1998 the stock markets continued to experience volatility, and there was evidence of a continuing lack of sophistication by Chinese investors, but the situation is much improved compared to the stock markets' early years. Chinese regulatory authorities are evidently serious about policing improper or illegal behavior and punishing wrongdoing. Several prominent heads of financial institutions, including Shen Ruolei, president of the Shanghai branch of the Industrial and Commercial Bank of China, were fired during 1997 as punishment for involvement in prohibited stock market activities.

China Securities Regulatory Commission: Supreme Regulator

As part of Zhu Rongji's plans for improving regulatory effectiveness in the financial sector, the China Securities Regulatory Commission (CSRC), which is directly under the State Council, has been given supreme authority to regulate and police China's securities markets and institutions.

TABLE 20. 1   Comparison of Shanghai and Shenzhen Securities Exchanges

	Listings		Market Capitalization (mil. RMB)	No. of Transactions (mil. shares)		Value of Transactions (mil. RMB)	
	1996	1997	1997 / 12	1996	1997	1996	1997
			Shanghai Securities Exchange				
A shares	287	372	903,245	106,924	116,601	901,916	1,355,024
B shares	42	50	18,561	2,770	4,967	9,457	21,293
Funds	15	16		12,735	5,556	49,738	21,953
Discount T-bills							
spot	9	9		434	315	496,237	346,840
repo	8	8		1,238	1,191	1,243,916	1,191,216
Corp./Financial bonds	7	5		0	0	0	0
			Shenzhen Securities Exchange				
A shares	227	348	812,174	138,187	148,500	1,203,205	1,674,497
B shares	43	51	18,943	3,974	3,863	18,530	21,369
Funds	10	10		34,535	16,433	106,912	58,838
Discount T-bills							
spot	9	9		6	11	6,687	11,435
repo	9	9		56	96	56,948	96,391
Corp. bonds	1	1		0	0	30	258

Source: *Shanghai Securities News,* January 1, 1998.

TABLE 20. 2   Listed Companies by Province, City, and Autonomous Region

(unit: case)

Region	Total	1990	1991	1992	1993	1994	1995	1996	1997
Shanghai	111	7		20	43	24	2	10	5
Guangdong	105	1	4	13	23	25	9	15	15
Sichuan	41				10	6	5	8	12
Liaoning	38			1	4	3	2	13	15
Jiangsu	36				4	5	2	11	14
Shandong	35				4	2	1	16	12
Fujian	32				10	2	1	11	8
Zhejiang	28	1			5	6		7	9
Hubei	28			1	4	1	1	13	8
Beijing	23				2	4		5	12
Jilin	21				5	2		10	4
Hainan	19			4	1	5		4	5
Hunan	18				2			9	7
Heilongjiang	17				1	4		7	5
Chongqing	16				3	2	1	6	4
Shaanxi	16				1	4		5	6
Total	718	9	4	39	130	109	32	207	188

Notes: [1]Cases in 1997 are from January to September.
   [2]Cases for other regions: Hebei 14, Anhui 13, Tianjin 11, Inner Mongolia 11, Henan 11,
   Xinjiang Autonomous Region 10, Shanxi, Jiangxi, Yunnan 9, Guangxi Autonomous Region,
   Gansu 8, Guizhou, Qinghai 6, Tibet 5, Ningxia Autonomous Region 4.
Source: *Shanghai Securities News,* October 5, 1997.

Prior to March 1998 the China Securities Policy Commission had set policy, which was then implemented through the CSRC. The former office was abolished during the governmental reforms of March 1998.

In mid-1997 the new head of the CSRC, Zhou Zhengqing, under expanded Central authority, took effective control of the Shanghai and Shenzhen exchanges by firing the incumbent presidents and appointing new ones from Beijing. Thus, the exchanges, which had been administered by the governments in Shanghai and Shenzhen, were brought under the direct authority of CSRC. This consolidation of power over the exchanges by the Central government shows that Beijing plans to prevent competition between Shanghai and Shenzhen and try to instill more discipline at the exchanges. One problem in securities regulation is that as of September 1998 China had not yet adopted a comprehensive securities law. Many drafts of such a law have reportedly been reviewed by the State Council, but conflicting interests have thus far prevented passage.

Effecting Fundamental Changes in Corporate Management

China's stock markets will play a critical role in the reform and restructuring of China's industrial and commercial enterprises. Indeed, the stock markets have already begun to play such a role. Even when the state continues to hold a majority of shares in an enterprise after its listing, which is usually the case, new disclosure requirements and public accountability have a profound and positive effect on the enterprises' managers. A listed company is under constant scrutiny by the Chinese financial press as well as institutional and individual investors. Every March and April companies now publish their detailed financial reports. These are carefully analyzed and provide the basis for detailed comparisons and critiques of company performances. Since the development of China's stock markets, it is increasingly difficult for managers to get by with excuses and cultivating *guanxi* (relationships) with administrative superiors, as in the old days. Now real performance, as measured by profits and shareholder value, is what counts.

—*Harner*

21

China in the International Financial Markets

Becoming a Major Factor

The Early 1980s Emergence from Financial Autarchy

Since 1982, China has emerged as a major player in the international capital markets, and the pace and magnitude of its involvement virtually exploded during the heady days of Asian finance in the five years leading up to mid-1997. The Asian financial crisis that began in summer 1997 substantially cooled international investor capital interest in new "emerging market" investments, including those in Chinese equity and debt. In reality, however, most of the capital streaming into Chinese equity and debt issues in the years leading up to mid-1997 was from "local" Hong Kong or Asian investors—individuals and institutions. These investors in particular were hard hit by the crisis. The result was that the flurry of activity in international fund-raising by Chinese issuers seen in the first half of 1997 slowed markedly in the third quarter 1997 and virtually stalled in the fourth quarter of 1997 and the first half of 1998. As of October 1998 suppliers of new debt or equity capital in international markets—and particularly in China's major market, Hong Kong—are hard to find. Notwithstanding the current slowdown and gloom, the market will eventually recover, and when investor sentiment warms we can expect China and Chinese enterprises to be in the front of the queue to receive new capital.

We distinguish between capital markets transactions—where the provider of finance is a private investor or lender—and finance provided by foreign, state, or international financial institutions, like the World Bank, which may be considered foreign government–source finance. Since at least the mid-1980s, private-sector capital, channeled through international capital markets, has been the most important component of investment and debt capital flows from the developed to the developing world, overwhelming government or multilateral sources. Developing and developed countries around the world compete to gain access to the enormous capital resources in the international capital markets. China has emerged as one of the most aggressive and successful competitors and is benefiting tremendously as a result.

CITIC Issues China's First Foreign Bonds in 1982

During the 1980s, China's approach to international capital markets was principally as a borrower. The government signaled its intention to aggressively seek international capital to invest in projects when it set up the China International Trust and Investment Company (CITIC) under the State Council during the early 1980s. CITIC conducted China's first international bond issue in 1982 in Japan. Subsequently other leading state banks, including the Bank of China, proceeded to float bonds in the markets available to them at the time, primarily the Eurobond market. Additional large sums of capital were borrowed under finance leases through such agencies as the Civil Aviation Administration of China to finance major equipment purchases. Certain large projects, such as Baogang Steel in Shanghai, also sought and received international funds, but often this was quasi–state financing in the form of soft loans loosely tied to importation of equipment from the extending country.

The Shift from Foreign Debt to Equity

During the 1990s, reflecting the liberalization of China's domestic financial markets and new openings for foreign investment, Chinese municipalities, government ministries, agencies, and enterprises have—with the assistance in international investment banks—found an increasing number of ways to tap international capital markets, particularly through the "window" on Hong Kong. Some of methods have been as follows:

"B," "H," "N," and "L" Shares

These are shares of Chinese enterprises issued to foreign investors and traded on stock exchanges. "B" shares are listed and traded on China's own stock exchanges. "H" shares are listed and traded on the Hong Kong securities exchange. "N" and "L" shares refer to the very few Chinese issues listed in New York and London. As of December 1997 there were some 101 "B" shares. New listings during 1997 and through March 1998 are presented in Table 21.1.

TABLE 21. 1 New Listings of "B"-Shares and "S"-Shares, January 1997–March 1998

Listed Date	Company Name	Total Funds Raised (US$ million)
	Shanghai "B" Share	
08-Jan-97	Shanghai Kai Kai Industrial	20.5
17-Jun-97	Jinan Qingqi Motorcycle Group	110.9
26-Jun-97	Hainan Airlines	33.4
05-Aug-97	Shanghai Zhenhua Port Machinery	43.0
08-Aug-97	Inner Mongolia Yitai Coal	67.6
23-Sep-97	Zhejiang Southeast Electric	207.6
16-Oct-97	Jiangsu Wuling Diesel Engine	52.0
21-Oct-97	Dalian Chemical Industry	31.1
	Shenzhen "B" Share	
25-Mar-97	Wafangdian Bearing	44.6
15-Mar-97	Hubei Sanonda	51.7
22-Mar-97	Nanjing Telecommunications	31.4
26-Mar-97	Shandong Chenming	65.8
10-Jun-97	Beijing Orient Electronics	45.7
08-Jul-97	Bengang Steel Plates	122.9
19-Aug-97	Luthai Textile Joint Stock	19.9
23-Sep-97	Yantai Changyu Pioneer Wine	36.9
20-Mar-98	Dailian Refrigeration	46.8
	Singapore	
27-Jun-97	Tianjin Zhong Xin Pharmaceutical	68.0

Source: *DMG China Digest*, April 1998.

Because of the limitations of the Shanghai and Shenzhen stock exchanges, "B" share listings have been less important and raised less capital for issuers than "H" shares, which are placed and traded in the deep Hong Kong market. As of the end of January 1998 there had been 41 Chinese "H" share issues, which had raised over $US7 billion for their issuers (Table 21.2). For both "B" and "H" shares, new listings virtually stopped in the depressed international capital market environment during early and mid-1998. The same market situation—and pause in new issues—confronted "Red Chips" in Hong Kong.

Equity Fund-Raising by PRC-Controlled Companies: "Red Chips"

In 1995, 1996, and 1997 Hong Kong's capital market was tapped for both equity and debt capital by Hong Kong–registered companies that are controlled by Chinese cities, government departments, or state agencies (see Relation Chart, Figure 21.1). These "Red chips" grew in number and im-

TABLE 21. 2 Chinese "H"-Share IPOs

Listed Date	Company Name	Total Funds Raised (US$ million)
01-Jul-93	Tsingtao Brewery	114.7
16-Jul-93	Shanghai Petrochemical	342.4
22-Jul-93	Guangzhou Shipyard International	38.9
23-Jul-93	Beiren Printing Machinery Holdings	29.7
15-Oct-93	Maanshan Iron & Steel	509.2
07-Dec-93	Kunming Machine Tool Plant	17.8
14-Mar-94	Yizheng Chemical Fibre	308.1
03-May-94	Tianjin Bohai Chemical Fibre	52.8
18-May-94	Dongfang Electrical Machinery	62.0
16-Jun-94	Luoyang Glass	118.1
16-Jul-94	Qingling Motors	132.7
26-Oct-94	Shanghai Haixing Shipping	204.1
10-Nov-94	Zhenhai Refining and Chemical	184.7
23-Nov-94	Chengdu Telecommunications Cable	58.0
05-Dec-94	Harbin Power Equipment	145.1
19-May-95	Jilin Chemical Industrial	200.2
22-Jun-95	Northeast Electrical Trans & Transfer	60.0
18-Jan-96	Jingwei Textile Machinery	30.0
24-Apr-96	Nanjing Panda Electronics	66.9
10-May-96	Guangshen Railway	543.9
18-Jul-96	Guangdong Kelon Electrical Bldgs.	96.6
28-Oct-96	Anhui Expressway	112.9
12-Dec-96	Shandong Xinhua Pharmaceutical	33.0
05-Feb-97	China Eastern Airline	279.1
12-Mar-97	Shenzhen Expressway	212.3
21-Mar-97	Beijing Datang Power	465.4
14-May-97	Beijing North Star	219.0
15-May-97	Zhejiang Expressway	440.5
12-Jun-97	Jiangxi Copper Industry Co.	380.7
23-Jun-97	First Tractor Engineering	194.6
25-Jun-97	Beijing Yanhua	229.9
27-Jun-97	Jiaangsu Expressway	490.6
25-Jul-97	Angang New Steel	187.3
31-Jul-97	China Southern Airline	712.4
29-Sep-97	CATIC Shenzhen Holdings	49.1
07-Oct-97	Sichuan Expressway	179.1
17-Oct-97	Chongqing Iron & Steel	91.4
21-Oct-97	Anhui Conch Cement	106.3
30-Oct-97	Guangzhou Pharmaceutical	46.8
21-Jan-98	Huaneng Power International *	NA

Note: * means listing by way of introduction; IPO price was the first transaction price.

Sources: *DMG China Digest*, April 1998; *International Financing Review*, September 1997.

FIGURE 21. 1   Relation Chart of Chinese Companies Listed Abroad

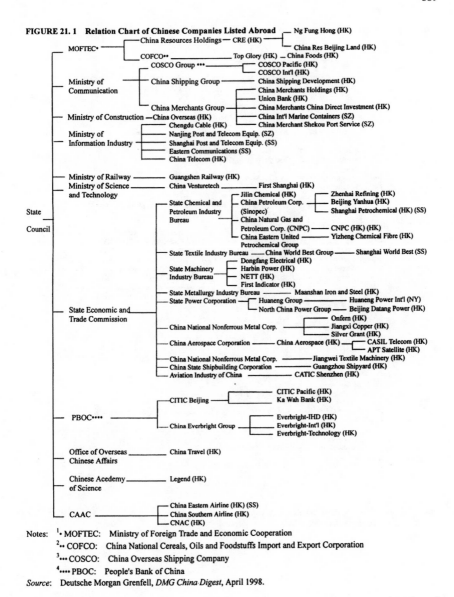

Notes: [1]• MOFTEC: Ministry of Foreign Trade and Economic Cooperation

[2]•• COFCO: China National Cereals, Oils and Foodstuffs Import and Export Corporation

[3]••• COSCO: China Overseas Shipping Company

[4]•••• PBOC: People's Bank of China

Source: Deutsche Morgan Grenfell, *DMG China Digest*, April 1998.

(continues)

190

FIGURE 21. 1   Relation Chart of Chinese Companies Listed Abroad (cont'd)

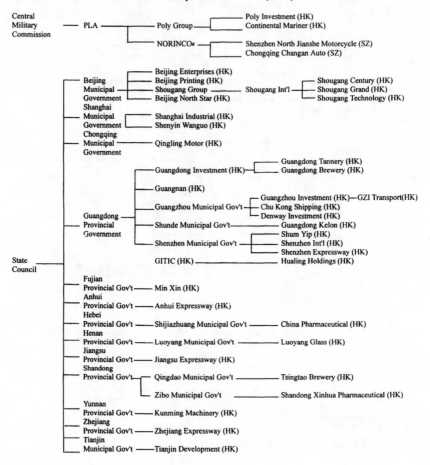

Note: #NORINCO: China North Industries Group
Source: Deutsche Morgan Grenfell, *DMG China Digest*, April 1998.

portance during 1996 and 1997, when the Hong Kong–based "window" companies of Chinese municipalities and provinces made initial public offerings (IPOs) in the Hong Kong market. Such companies as Shanghai Industrial, Beijing Enterprises, Guangdong Investment, Tianjin Development, and China Telecom (Hong Kong), which alone raised almost US$4 billion from its October 23, 1997, IPO, came to market, and found extraordinary interest among investors. Hong Kong and foreign investors observed that these companies were being permitted to buy, at cheap prices, high-quality assets in China under the control of their "parents." Shanghai Industrial, for example, came to market with a portfolio of Shanghai investments including tobacco, pharmaceuticals, and cosmetics. After the IPO the Shanghai government transferred to the company, at a good price, Shanghai's toll-road assets.

With the huge success of Shanghai Industrial and Beijing Enterprises (which raised US$242 million in May 1997), other Hong Kong window companies of Chinese provinces, municipalities, ministries, and agencies that have not made IPOs are hoping to do so.

Thus, Shanghai Industrial, Beijing Enterprises, Tianjin Development, and other Red chips and provincial and ministry window companies have become specialized investment banks. They are raising capital from the international market and investing it in projects in China (or even outside China) for the benefit of shareholders. Investors need not doubt the fact that when the Shanghai government offers "foreign" equity in an attractive project in Shanghai the first party to receive the offer will be Shanghai Industrial.

Hong Kong as China's Strategic International Capital Market

Hong Kong is without a doubt, and will remain, China's indispensable market for raising international capital, especially international equity capital. It is also a market where more and more innovations in structured finance for Chinese companies, Red chips, and windows are being seen. Unlike anywhere on the mainland, Hong Kong possesses all the elements necessary for financial innovation: a sophisticated investor market, experienced and reputable commercial and investment bankers, a body of financial law, sophisticated legal and accounting services, and a stable, strong, and convertible currency.

Practitioners, like the author, observe clearly that there is a "Beijing–Hong Kong axis" for major structured and corporate financing. Chinese ministries or large national companies formed from ministries in Beijing hatch plans for major restructuring and investments, inside and outside of China, which are then executed through sophisticated fund-raising in Hong Kong.

FIGURE 21. 2   Corporate Structure of the CHINA TELECOM (HK) Group upon Completion of the Acquisition of Jiangsu Mobile, April 28, 1998

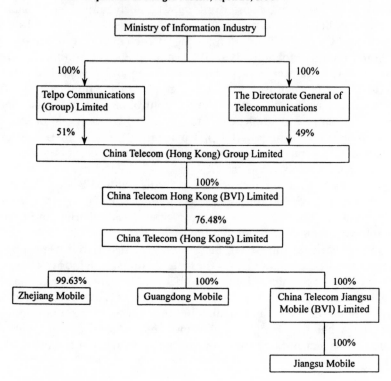

Source: South China Morning Post, April 29, 1998.

An excellent example is China Telecom (Hong Kong). This Red chip subsidiary of the former Ministry of Post and Telecommunications (now the Ministry of Information Industry) in Beijing was IPO'ed in October 1997, having been infused with the excellent assets of the mobile telecommunications system of Guangdong and Zhejiang provinces. As mentioned, it raised US$3.9 billion. In May 1998 the company announced it was acquiring the mobile telecommunication system of Jiangsu province, investing the HK dollar equivalent of US$2.9 billion (see Figure 21.2 for corporate structure after the acquisition). This is a pattern we will see repeated.

International Bond Issues

In May 1997 Standard and Poor's (S&P) raised China's sovereign credit rating to BBB+. A combined Moody's/S&P rating of A3/BBB+ meant that

TABLE 21. 3 China's Foreign Investment in Oil Resources

Kazakhstan--June 1997: China National Petroleum Corp. (CNPC) buys 60 percent of Aktyubinskmunai Production Association for US$4.3 billion. Estimated reserves: 140 million tons. August 1997: CNPC buys 60 percent of Uzen field for $1.3 billion. Estimated reserves: 200 million tons.
Bashkir, Autonomous Republic, Russia--1997: CNPC negotiates joint venture with Bashneft state oil company.
Italy--1997: CNPC signs joint venture with Italy's AGIP to develop oil fields in Central Asia and Africa.
Venezuela--June 1997: CNPC buys Caracoles block for $240 million and Intercampo Norte block for $118 million. Total estimated reserves: 100 million tons.
Peru--1993: CNPC buys Talara block. Reserves unknown.
Sudan--May 1997: CNPC buys 40 percent of Heglig field for $1 billion. Reserves unknown.
Iraq- -June 1997: CNPC buys 50 percent of Al Ahdab field for $1.2 billion. Estimated reserves: 140 million.
Turkmenistan--1998: CNPC negotiating with government for oil concessions.

Source: *Far Eastern Economic Review*, February 26, 1998, p. 47.

Chinese sovereign credit was considered highly safe by the credit-rating agencies. Although China had ample foreign currency reserves of some US$140 billion at the end of 1997, Chinese entities still issued international notes and bonds in order to raise liquidity, to raise project funds, or simply to keep China's name in front of international investors. As can be expected, Chinese entities with sovereign or quasisovereign status have been paying very low interest rates in the face of very strong investor interest. In June 1996 the PRC issued a global five-year U.S. dollar bond in the amount of US$700 million at a price of 0.80 percent per annum over U.S. Treasury yields. In May 1997 the Ministry of Finance issued 500 million deutsche marks in five-year bonds at a rate of 0.55 percent over the level of five-year German government bonds.

Chinese entities conducted thirty-three international bond issues during 1994, 1995, and 1996 (for details see *Almanac of China's Finance and Banking*, 1997, p. 477). It is interesting to note that whereas Europe was the principal market for raising funds during the 1980s, China during the 1990s has become more obviously a bankable risk, and as U.S. funds managers have become more aggressive international investors, U.S. markets, together with Japan, are proving most receptive to Chinese debt.

A New Trend: Chinese Investment Abroad

In summary, the advance of Chinese entities into the international financial marketplace during the past few years has been phenomenal. As Figure 21.1 (produced by the investment bank Deutsche Morgan Grenfell) shows, through subsidiaries or agencies the State Council, virtually every PRC ministry, many agencies, and many cities and provinces have gained direct access to the international capital markets through overseas listings.

With this access to foreign capital, and with the abundance of savings at home, we are beginning to see a new phenomenon: aggressive Chinese investments abroad. To date, the most impressive activity has been seen from China National Petroleum Corporation (see Table 21.3), which purchased blocks in two oil fields in Venezuela for some US$350 million, bought 50 percent of Al Ahdab field in Iraq for US$1.2 billion, and reportedly bought controlling shares in oil fields in Kazakhstan for more than US$5 billion. This is a pattern seen in Japan during the 1980s: Where there will be a long-term importing need, there is a tendency to try to own the resource. This is even more likely when speaking of a strategic resource like energy.

—Harner

22

Foreign Financial Institutions in China

Yearning to Play a Larger Role

Chinese Ambivalence Toward Foreign Banks

The first representative office of a foreign bank was allowed to open in China (Beijing) in 1979. At the time, China's financial system was still largely locked in a rudimentary stage within a Stalinist system of planning. During the 1980s, as China went about constituting—more or less along Western lines—banking, insurance, and, later, securities institutions that could finance development and China's transition to a market economy, the attitude toward the role of foreign financial institutions in the Chinese system was ambivalent. On the one hand, there was the desire to learn from foreign financial institutions and to "cooperate" with them to the extent that this could help China access foreign capital to finance its development. On the other hand, there was the great—and well-founded—fear that if foreign financial institutions were allowed to compete directly with Chinese financial institutions, the latter would be hopelessly out-classed and even weakened.

From Protectionism to "National Treatment"

Around the world, policies of financial supervisory authorities toward foreign financial institutions generally fall into three categories: protectionism, reciprocity, and "national treatment." From the first granting of licenses to foreign banks to open branches in the special economic zones in the mid-1980s, to the major step of opening Shanghai to foreign branch banking in 1991, until this writing in mid-1998, the dominant principle of the PBOC with respect to foreign banks has been protectionism. This is admitted openly and unapologetically. The most fundamental protectionist policy is the prohibition against handling local currency—RMB—and engaging in local currency business (with the exceptional circumstance of some banks in Shanghai; see below).

With a few exceptions, foreign banks can offer and conduct banking business—loans, deposits, trade transactions, foreign exchange trade— only in foreign currency. Because Chinese companies are in general not permitted to hold foreign currency accounts or to borrow foreign currency without special approval, foreign banks are effectively cut off from the broad market of Chinese companies (where they would compete directly with Chinese banks) and are forced to concentrate on providing services to foreign-invested companies and to certain projects or sectors (e.g., aircraft financing) where special access has been accorded by the Chinese authorities.

At a financial meeting at Beijing University in September 1997, PBOC Vice Governor Chen Yuan affirmed that the policy of the Chinese Central Bank is to move gradually from protectionism to national treatment for foreign financial institutions. Additional and more equal access would first be given in the banking sector, then in insurance and securities.

The RMB Experiment in Pudong

A first step in this respect was the December 1996 granting, to nine foreign banks in Shanghai, of the right to handle RMB on an "experimental" basis. On August 11, 1998, PBOC announced that an additional ten foreign banks in Shanghai would be licensed to join the "experiment" in Pudong before the end of 1998. It was also announced that the experiment would be extended geographically to the Shenzhen special economic zone. Thus, foreign economic banks within the Shenzhen zone could now apply for licenses to conduct business in RMB.

In practice, the operating restrictions placed on foreign banks are such that the expansion in scope is still not meaningful: (1) The foreign banks may offer RMB services only to foreign-invested companies; (2) services can only be offered within the geographic limits of Shanghai for the Shanghai-licensed banks and Shenzhen for the Shenzhen-licensed banks; (3) foreign banks may not fund themselves from other Chinese banks or from the Chinese interbank money market; and (4) the "swap" facility offered by PBOC is for only US$4 million, which provides about RMB 30 million for the banks to lend. (On August 11, 1998, this swap facility was increased to RMB 100 million for "qualifying" banks, but the amount is still ridiculously small.) Of all the restrictions, that on funding is curtailing business most severely. The banks can accept deposits only from FIEs, which with few exceptions are borrowers, not depositors. Under the circumstances, the banks involved have made heroic progress. According to

PBOC statistics, at the end of June 1998 the banks were reporting total RMB assets of RMB 1,160 million (equivalent to US$140 million), total RMB loans of RMB 603 million (US$73.5 million), and total RMB deposits of RMB 763 million (US$93.1 million).

In spite of the restrictions, the banks involved and others hope to see the restrictions gradually relaxed. And in another move toward national treatment, during 1996 the PBOC brought foreign banks into the system for foreign currency transactions existing for local banks, thus establishing equality. Taxation of income of foreign banks (currently at 15 percent on foreign currency business) is to be unified with that of domestic banks (33 percent); this has already been done in the case of the RMB business being conducted by the select banks.

Operational Results of Foreign Banks in Shanghai

With all the restrictions, have foreign banks been able to do much business in China? Actually, they have accomplished a lot in the last six to seven years (Table 22.1). According to PBOC figures, at year-end 1997 total assets of foreign banks were US$37.9 billion, up 27 percent over the previous year. Their outstanding loans and deposits rose by 42 percent and 15 percent to US$27.5 billion and US$4.5 billion respectively. By the end of 1997, even on a national level, foreign banks had become a significant factor in China's financial system, accounting for 4.4 percent (up from 3.13 percent in 1996) of China's total financial assets, about 20 percent of total foreign exchange assets of all banks in China.

As would be expected from its putative position as China's financial center, Shanghai has emerged as the location for the largest number of foreign financial institutions, and most actual banking business is being conducted there. Every March the PBOC's Shanghai branch releases a ranking of the foreign banks operating in Shanghai in terms of business performance. This annual "league table" ranking is anxiously awaited by the foreign banking community in Shanghai. Table 22.2 is the top-ten ranking (out of forty-five total) for 1997 (released in March 1998). It shows clear dominance by Japanese banks, particularly Bank of Tokyo–Mitsubishi and Hong Kong and Shanghai Bank (HSBC in the table). Citibank is in the top ten in several categories (it is twelfth in after-tax profit). The two German banks with branches in Shanghai, Commerzbank and Dresdner Bank, also rank highly. In general the ranking reflects the aggressiveness of the banks and the existence in and around Shanghai of subsidiaries of customers, that is, in the case of Japanese banks, FIEs invested by Japanese companies who are global customers of the banks. Incidentally, apart from Citibank, the other American banks with branches in Shanghai in early 1998 were Bank of America and Chase Manhattan

TABLE 22. 1 Number and Business Volumes of Foreign Financial Institutions in China
Number of Foreign Financial Institutions (year-end 1997)

	Total China (of which: Japan)	Shanghai (of which: Japan)	Ratio of Shanghai (%)
Representative Offices			
Banks	288	65 (21)	20.8
Insurance companies	152	49 (10)	27.0
Securities companies	53	35 (6)	60.4
Business Operations	173	51	28.8
Foreign bank branches	142 (30)	39 (11)	28.2
Chinese bank established			
with foreign investment	5	0 (0)	18.2
Foreign finance companies	6	4 (0)	60.0
Foreign insurance companies	11	4 (1)	37.5
Sino-foreign JV banks	7	2 (-)	-

Business Volumes of Foreign Banks (year-end 1997)   (unit: US$ billion)

Index	Total China		Shanghai		(b) / (a)
	Value (a)	Growth Rate YoY (%)	Value (b)	Growth Rate YoY (%)	(%)
Total assets	37.9	27	17.7	29	45
Loans	27.5	42	13.4	48	49
Deposits	4.5	15	1.9	39	43
Profits after tax	0.0	31	0.0	28	26

Source: PBOC, *The People's Bank of China Quarterly Statistical Bulletin, vol. 10, 1998.*

Bank. Bank of America, in business since 1991, ranked twentieth in terms of loans and twenty-fifth in profits. Chase, newly licensed in 1997, ranked fortieth in loans and posted a loss for the year.

Restrictions on Foreign Insurance and Securities Firms

As explained by Chen Yuan, then the deputy governor of PBOC, liberalization of foreign access to China's market will proceed first with banks, second with insurance companies, and last with foreign securities companies. We should not be surprised to learn, then, that as restricted as foreign banks are they still have more access than do foreign insurance companies. As of mid-1998 China had licensed only a handful of foreign insurance companies and had imposed severe geographic and business-scope restrictions. Foreign securities can effectively do nothing in China. What business they do conduct—and in any event, under various restrictions—is limited to underwriting and trading the securities of Chinese issuers outside China.

TABLE 22. 2 Top-Ten Ranking of Foreign Financial Institutions in Shanghai, 1997

Rank	Total Assets	Foreign Currency Loans	Foreign Currency Deposits	After-Tax Profit	Export Settlements
1	Tokyo-Mitsubishi	Tokyo-Mitsubishi	Tokyo-Mitsubishi	Tokyo-Mitsubishi	HSBC
2	HSBC	Sanwa	HSBC	HSBC	Sanwa
3	Sumitomo	Sumitomo	Citibank	East Asia	Tokyo-Mitsubishi
4	Sanwa	HSBC	Sumitomo	Sumitomo	Citibank
5	IBJ	IBJ	Sanwa	Sanwa	Dai Ichi Kangyo
6	Dai Ichi Kangyo	Dai Ichi Kangyo	IBJ	Dai Ichi Kangyo	Sakura
7	Citibank	Fuji	Korea Dev. Bank	Royal Bank Canada	A.B.N. Amro
8	A.B.N. Amro	Sakura	Dai Ichi Kangyo	IBJ	Bangkok
9	Commerzbank	Commerzbank	Standard Chartered	Commerzbank	Standard Chartered
10	Fuji	Citibank	Chia Tai Finance	Dresdner	Fuji

Notes: [1]Total assets, loans and deposits are balances at end of December 1997.

[2]Exports bills are listed in terms of total export bills of 1997 of each institution.

Source: Hand-out announcement from PBOC Shanghai Branch, March 10, 1998.

Notwithstanding some progress, foreign banks and other financial institutions will undoubtedly continue to operate under severe restrictions in the years ahead. Although PBOC appears willing to further liberalize, strong resistance continues from Chinese banks, insurance firms, and securities companies, which are afraid of being defeated or weakened by foreign competitors. The banks, in particular, find support in the State Council for their argument that with the legacy of planning and policy lending to state-run enterprises, they have inevitably come to bear the burden of bad loans. They need to rebuild their capital bases by doing more profitable business with the best Chinese companies while reducing exposure to the weak companies. If foreign banks are allowed into the Chinese corporate market, they will surely pursue the best and most credit-worthy companies. And if the foreign banks were to capture a significant part of this market, it would leave Chinese banks with an even higher proportion of bad risk.

—Harner

23

Corporate and Project
Finance in China

The Fundamental Flaw in
China's Investment System

One of the key realities and strengths of the Chinese economy is its massive annual capital accumulation and investment. National savings (equal to investment plus net exports) reached 42 percent of GDP in 1993 and have been in the 35–40 percent range since 1980 (Table 23.1). Had China put this massive savings into productive investment during the last forty years, it would today be a world power. Unfortunately, the inefficiencies of central planning caused much of the invested capital surpluses to be wasted. Sadly too, it is probably true that the system of market socialism introduced during the 1980s has been even more wasteful than planning.

The fundamental flaw in the Chinese system, from the standpoint efficient use of investment resources, has been the combination of two things: (1) control over investment funds and their allocations in the hands of government officials and bureaucrat-managers at the Central, provincial, and local levels; and (2) the prevailing system of state ownership with the predominant social and political, as well as economic, roles of state-owned firms. The result of this flaw has been an excessive allocation of investment resources to the state-owned sector (61.1 percent of all fixed-assets investment from 1981 to 1995; see Figure 23.1) but with increasingly diminishing returns.

The realization that market socialism has squandered vast amounts of precious investment capital was part of the reason the Fifteenth Party Congress decided to effectively privatize much of the industrial and commercial economies. The same realization provided impetus to the decision to drastically reform the government administrative structure (see Chapter 25). However, until privatization is accomplished or the government is effectively withdrawn from corporate decisionmaking, bureaucratic allocation of investment capital—and the resulting inefficiencies—

TABLE 23. 1 Ratio of Total Investment in China's Gross Domestic Expenditure
(unit: RMB, %)

Year	Gross Domestic Expenditure billion	Gross Consumption billion	%	Total Investment billion	%	Net Exports billion	%
1980	455.1	297.6	65.4	159.0	34.9	-1.5	-0.3
1985	879.2	577.3	65.7	338.6	38.5	-36.7	-4.2
1986	1,013.3	654.2	64.6	384.6	38.0	-25.5	-2.6
1987	1,178.4	745.1	63.2	432.2	36.7	1.1	0.1
1988	1,470.4	936.0	63.7	549.5	37.4	-15.1	-1.1
1989	1,646.6	1,055.7	64.1	609.5	37.0	-18.6	-1.1
1990	1,832.0	1,136.5	62.0	644.4	35.2	51.0	2.8
1991	2,128.0	1,314.6	61.8	751.7	35.3	61.8	2.9
1992	2,586.4	1,595.2	61.7	963.6	37.3	27.6	1.0
1993	3,450.1	2,018.2	58.5	1,499.8	43.5	-68.0	-2.0
1994	4,711.1	2,721.6	57.8	1,926.1	40.9	63.4	1.3
1995	5,940.5	3,452.9	58.1	2,387.7	40.2	99.9	1.7
1996	6,849.8	4,017.2	58.6	2,686.7	39.2	145.9	2.2

Original note: Disparities in figures for total output and total production due to
calculation errors.

Source: China Statistical Yearbook 1997.

FIGURE 23. 1 Ratio of the State-Owned Sector in Total Value of Fixed-Assets Investment

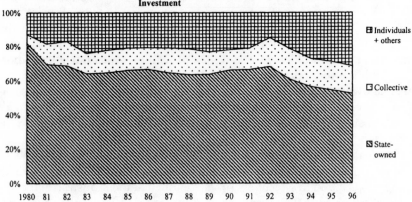

Notes: [1]Fixed-assets investment is equal to sum of public investment and nonpublic equipment investment.

[2]"Others" includes jointly operated, stock ownership system, and foreign-invested enterprises.

Source: China Statistical Yearbook 1997, p. 152.

will remain the reality. The good news, perhaps, is that in China, unlike in other systems, a relatively small proportion of investment funds is allocated directly through the national budget.

China's Domestic Capital Allocation System

Nineteen ninety-eight is likely to see the beginnings of substantial changes in how China allocates capital, with the "market" and "commercialized" banks having a more decisive role. But as of September 1998, how this will happen is unclear, and in any event changes are likely to be gradual.

Although changes seem to be possible under the Zhu Rongji economic regime, during the mid- and late 1990s (and until this writing in mid-1998) it is accurate to say that China's domestic capital allocation system has distinguished between (a) investment capital—used by corporations to fund fixed assets like land, equipment, and factory buildings and by governments to fund infrastructure projects—and (b) working capital—used primarily by enterprises to fund inventories of raw materials and finished goods and sales receivables. Working capital funding to enterprises is made through short-term bank loans, which constitute "recycling" of short-term deposits and are not considered to contribute to the money stock. Therefore, short-term working capital financing has been increasingly freed from administrative control and left to the banks based on their ability to raise short-term deposits so that their short-term loan-to-deposit ratio is 0.75:1 or less.

The regime for allocating investment capital has been much more rigid and structured (Figure 23.2). Each year, a national budget for investment capital allocation has been drawn up by the former State Planning Commission in consultation with various Central ministries and agencies under the State Council, including the PBOC, because most of the investment capital resources will flow through the banking system and all credit extension, particularly investment capital credit, needs to be kept within the overall national credit plan. China's "policy banks" are also involved. The former SPC was the most powerful arbitrator in the division and distribution of the national investment capital budget "pie," keeping most for itself (for allocation to major state projects) and for provincial planning commissions (for allocation to key provincial projects). Some budget is given to each ministry and some to banks, particularly the state policy banks. During the year, planning commissions at the Central and provincial levels will review all significant infrastructure and enterprise fixed-asset investments and allocate (or, often, refuse to allocate) "quota" authority for the project to receive investment capital financing, either in

204

FIGURE 23. 2 China's Planned Allocation System for Investment Capital and Foreign Debt, situation obtaining in early 1998

Decision and Allocation System for RMB "Fixed Asset Investment" Funds *

The total "scale" (*guimo*) of fixed asset investment funds is determined by the SPC in consultation with the PBOC. Lending authority and "scale" volumes are approved for Chinese financial institutions by the PBOC. Before applying to the planning commissions for project approval, sponsors of projects that wish to borrow funds find a bank that has sufficient unused fixed assets lending "scale" to support the project's fixed asset investment needs. If the bank has sufficient "scale" it will check whether the project is on the list of projects that the local planning commission has already approved in principle. Only projects that have arranged financing from banks in this way will be approved by the planning commission.

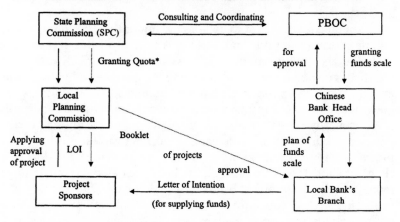

Foreign Currency Funds-Raising Quota *

The State Planning Commission allocates the national foreign currency debt-raising quota to (1) "Windows," including some Chinese bank head offices and central and provincial international trust and investment companies (ITICs); (2) Provincial and municipal planning commissions; and (3) ministries. The State Administration of Foreign Exchange (SAFE), under PBOC, is responsible for administration of the quota allocation. Banks may use their quota to borrow foreign funds for general banking purposes. ITICs generally use the quota to support local projects by borrowing and directly on-lending of foreign currency to projects or by guaranteeing the project's foreign currency borrowing. Planning commissions allocate quotas to projects at the time of project approval.

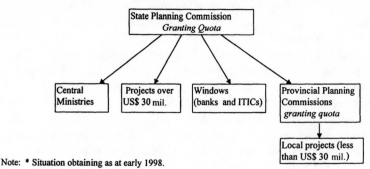

Note: * Situation obtaining as at early 1998.
Source: S. Harner.

TABLE 23. 2   Sources of Financing for Investment in Fixed Assets by State-Owned Enterprises
(unit: bil. RMB, (%))

Year	Investment in Fixed Assets (%)		State Budgetary Appropriation (%)		Domestic Loans (%)		Foreign Loans (%)		"Own Funds" (%)		Other (%)	
1985	168	100	40	24	39	23.0	9	5.3	68	40.4	12	7.3
1990	299	100	39	13	71	23.6	27	9.1	129	43.2	36	11.9
1995	1,090	100	54	5	258	23.7	86	7.9	531	48.7	173	15.9

Source: China Statistical Yearbook 1997.

the form of equity from sponsors or in the form of fixed-asset investment loans from the banking system

One of the greatest financing obstacles facing most Chinese enterprises and projects has been getting an investment capital quota allocation from the planning commission, either for their own equity investment or, particularly, for borrowing RMB long-term (more than three years) for fixed-asset investment. Normally, infrastructure projects and large state-owned companies could hope to receive so-called quota allocations from the planning commission. Foreign-invested companies almost never qualified. The rationale of the planners was that foreign investors were expected to bring in their own investment capital, not take any of China's scarce capital. Table 23.2 presents official statistics on sources of capital for investments in fixed assets by SOEs.

Working Capital Financing

Getting short-term working capital financing has been relatively easy for credit-worthy Chinese companies and FIEs if the amount was small and within the funding capability of the local branch of the Chinese bank. Problems have arisen when the amount is large (RMB 10 million by Chinese bank standards) or when the local bank has exhausted its resources on loans, particularly overdue loans, to weak state-owned companies. For a number of years PBOC has introduced some discretion for banks to add a surcharge to its base lending rates; banks could then differentiate, however modestly, quality of credit risks.

Debt Financing in Foreign Currency

Foreign currency borrowing by Chinese and FIEs is not allocated in the same way as RMB funds. A separate control regime exists with a fundamentally different purpose: to control China's foreign debt. In this regime PBOC and the State Administration of Foreign Exchange (SAFE) are the key regulators. Prior to 1998 the former SPC and the Ministry of Finance were also key policymakers. It is unclear whether this will change.

Every year a foreign debt–raising plan is agreed upon. The debt may be in the form of direct borrowing by projects or enterprises or foreign borrowing by government ministries and departments (including MOF and the Chinese state itself) by, for example, issuance of foreign bonds or acceptance of foreign loans. Also, PBOC can authorize Chinese banks to issue foreign debt securities or take loans abroad. Funds raised through these means are available for on-lending to enterprises and projects in China that need foreign currency to purchase goods and services from abroad.

Prior to 1998 the former SPC allocated the annual incremental foreign debt budget to Chinese projects and enterprises either directly or through allocations to ministries and provincial planning commissions. Under the Zhu Rongji regime, there appears to be a desire to let the "market" play a greater role in allocating this resource, but the mechanism is not yet clear.

SAFE regulations allow FIEs to incur foreign debt by, for example, borrowing from foreign banks in China without a quota allocation. They need only register foreign debt with SAFE so that it can be monitored for statistical purposes. (This looks like a huge "hole" in China's foreign debt management system but it is not. The reason is that PBOC has required main offices of foreign banks to commit that they will, if necessary, assume all liabilities of branches in China.)

Equity Financing for Chinese Corporations and Projects

China's postliberation adoption of socialism and the lack of a system of property laws and regulations for most of the last forty years has meant that little attention was paid to the question of ownership of Chinese enterprises, especially those owned by "the whole people." A new enterprise or factory would be established on land owned by a local district, funds would be contributed for buildings by one or more bureaus under the city or provincial governments, and equipment might be provided for "gratis equity" by another factory. Through it all, there would be little effort by any unit to clearly define ownership shares, rights, or obligations. The situation may have been slightly better for collectively owned enterprises, where the parties often had direct entrepreneurial interest—and therefore calculated ownership shares more carefully.

In China today equity contributions in new enterprises are normally clearly specified in approval documents presented to the approving authority, especially local planning commissions. Ownership equity in Chinese companies now comes from other Chinese companies, investment funds, trust and investment companies under provincial or local governments, and special investment holding companies formed during the past two or three years under previous government bureaus for the specific purpose of managing and investing state assets. Major government projects, especially infrastructure projects like dams, power plants, roads, bridges, and ports, still receive direct equity investment from local, provincial, and Central ministries and bureaus.

Of course, another source of equity financing is selling shares to the Chinese public through listing on the Shanghai or Shenzhen stock exchanges.

Equity in Foreign-Funded Enterprises and Projects

Equity in FIEs has normally come directly from foreign strategic investors setting up manufacturing facilities, on the one hand, and from Chinese partners on the other. In most cases, the foreign investor has provided cash and the Chinese partner has provided in-kind equity in the form of land use rights, factory buildings, and equipment. In wholly owned FIEs, all equity capital has come from abroad.

Although foreign investment in certain sectors has been restricted and foreigners have been required to take partners and share 50 percent of equity in certain projects (e.g., automobile assembly plants), China has placed few restrictions on the amount of capital that can be brought in. Unlike foreign borrowing, foreign equity investment does not have to be repaid.

—Harner

24

Shanghai

China's Commercial and Trading Center

The 1930s: Shanghai's Golden Age

It is no longer politically incorrect for Chinese, particularly Shanghainese, to speak of Shanghai's glorious past before "liberation." In the 1930s Shanghai was the largest and richest city in Asia, and it held a unique position (now shared in Asia by Tokyo, Hong Kong, and Singapore) as the region's financial center. In 1935 there were 164 banks in China; fifty-eight had their head offices in Shanghai. Of the forty-three largest Chinese banks, thirty-five were headquartered in Shanghai. Twenty-eight international banks—the leading banks of the period—had branches in Shanghai. Shanghai provided a long-term capital market through a stock exchange and a short-term money market through bills as well as short-term interbank money markets. In addition, insurance companies, shipping companies, and commodities markets provided all the support necessary for China's international and domestic trade.

Falling Far Behind in the 1980s

During the 1980s, Shanghai's economy and society were falling behind. Figure 24.1 shows that during most of the 1980s, Shanghai's growth rate was below that of China as a whole. From 1980 to 1990, Shanghai's growth rate lagged behind the national average (not just behind the advanced regions) by a total of 17.2 points. Obviously, then, Shanghai was growing much more slowly than the fastest-growing provinces. The reason for Shanghai's poor performance was twofold: (1) the fastest-growing provinces—Guangdong and Jiangsu—were succeeding by virtue of foreign investment and TVE development, whereas Shanghai's economic assets were still overwhelmingly state-owned (Figure 24.2), and industrial SOEs were increasingly unable to compete in China's liberalizing econ-

210

FIGURE 24. 1 Disparity in GDP Growth Rate for Shanghai and China

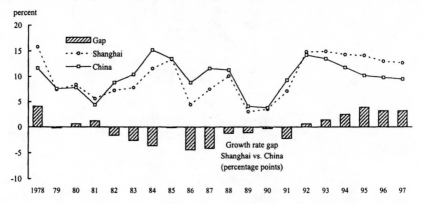

Sources: *China Statistical Yearbook* (each year); *Shanghai Statistical Yearbook* (each year); *Shanghai Economic Monthly*, vol. 1 1998.

FIGURE 24. 2 Composition of Shanghai's Total Value of Industrial Production

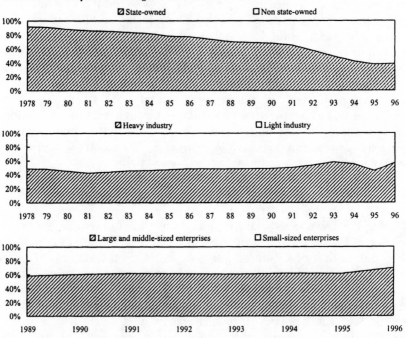

Sources: *China's Regional Economy Through Seventeen Years of Reform and Opening-Up; Shanghai Statistical Yearbook* 1997.

omy; and (2) Shanghai was still transferring a large part of its fiscal revenues to the Central government, which meant it had fewer funds to invest and a reduced level of local consumption.

Net Outflows of Revenues to Central

According to the calculations of Professor Sun Haiming (1997; see Figure 24.3), during the 1980s Shanghai "lost" through net out-transfers 24 percent of its GDP. During the Sixth Five Year Plan period (1981–1985) the figure was 42 percent. The result: Throughout the 1980s Shanghai was a truly pathetic and depressing city, trapped in the political and economic stagnation of the planned economy, with no alternative private economy to stimulate growth. Table 24.1 presents figures for Shanghai's total financial revenues (including revenues from Central units, like the Shanghai ports, and Central-owned enterprises), local financial revenues, and local financial expenditures. The numbers show that in terms of local fiscal revenues and spending, Shanghai was a huge net contributor to the rest of the country until 1994. Looking at total revenue and local spending, it can be seen that Shanghai continued during the first half of the 1990s to transfer huge funds, totaling some RMB 170 billion, or about 22 percent of GDP, to the Central government, a level not much different from that in the 1980s.

Targeting Development into China's Commercial and Financial Center

It can be said that Shanghai began to reclaim its role as China's economic, trading, and financial center in 1990. In this year the Shanghai securities exchange was established, and Shanghai was declared an "open city" for the establishment of branches of foreign banks and for foreign investment. In addition, in 1990 Shanghai finally received the approval—and financial support—of Beijing to develop Pudong as a special economic zone and a manufacturing, trading, and financial center. According to plans developed in the late 1980s, from 1990 to 1997 Shanghai has constructed the Lujiazui special zone to cater to financial and trading firms, the Jinqiao export processing zone to cater to foreign manufacturing and export processing firms, and the Waigaoqiao free trade zone to cater to trading firms (Map 24.1). At the end of 1997 and the beginning of 1998, Pudong, notwithstanding a glut in real estate investment, was an overwhelming success for the Shanghai government and for China in general. The Lujiazui area will certainly become the center for the Shanghai (and national) securities industry with the relocation of the Shanghai securities exchange to its new building in December 1997. Also, all Shanghai

FIGURE 24.3 Financial Outflow and Direct Investment for Shanghai

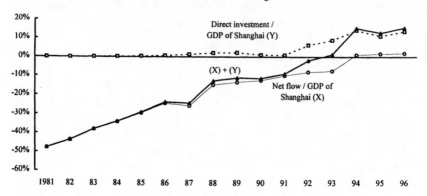

Source: Table 24.1.

TABLE 24.1 Fiscal Resources Outflow and Foreign Direct Investment for Shanghai

(unit: million RMB)

Year	Local (a) Fiscal Revenue	Local (b) Fiscal Expenditure	Net Flow (c) (b) - (a)	(c) / GDP of Shanghai	Direct (d) Investment	(d) / GDP of Shanghai
1981	17,435	1,906	-15,529	-47.8%	5	0.0%
1982	16,799	2,068	-14,731	-43.7%	6	0.0%
1983	15,639	2,239	-13,400	-38.1%	21	0.1%
1984	16,396	3,032	-13,364	-34.2%	66	0.2%
1985	18,423	4,607	-13,816	-29.6%	183	0.4%
1981-1985	102,165	15,770	-86,395	-39.6%	281	0.2%
1986	17,946	5,908	-12,038	-24.5%	337	0.7%
1987	16,897	5,385	-11,512	-25.8%	789	1.4%
1988	16,162	6,588	-9,574	-14.8%	1,355	2.1%
1989	16,688	7,331	-9,357	-13.4%	1,589	2.3%
1990	17,003	7,556	-9,447	-12.5%	848	1.1%
1986-1990	84,696	32,768	-51,928	-17.1%	4,918	2.3%
1991	17,553	8,605	-8,948	-10.0%	933	1.0%
1992	18,556	9,499	-9,057	-8.1%	6,943	6.2%
1993	24,234	12,926	-11,308	-7.5%	13,354	8.8%
1994	17,533	19,692	2,159	1.1%	27,847	14.1%
1995	22,730	26,789	4,059	1.7%	27,142	11.0%
1991-1995	100,606	77,511	75,023	9.4%	76,219	9.6%
1996	28,849	34,266	5,417	1.9%	39,208	13.5%

Note: U.S. dollars denominated foreign direct investment converted to RMB at each year's average
exchange rate.

Sources: *Shanghai Statistical Yearbook* 1997; Sun Haimin, *Financial and Economic Research*, vol.10, 1997.

MAP 24.1 Financial and Trade Areas of Shanghai's Pudong New Area

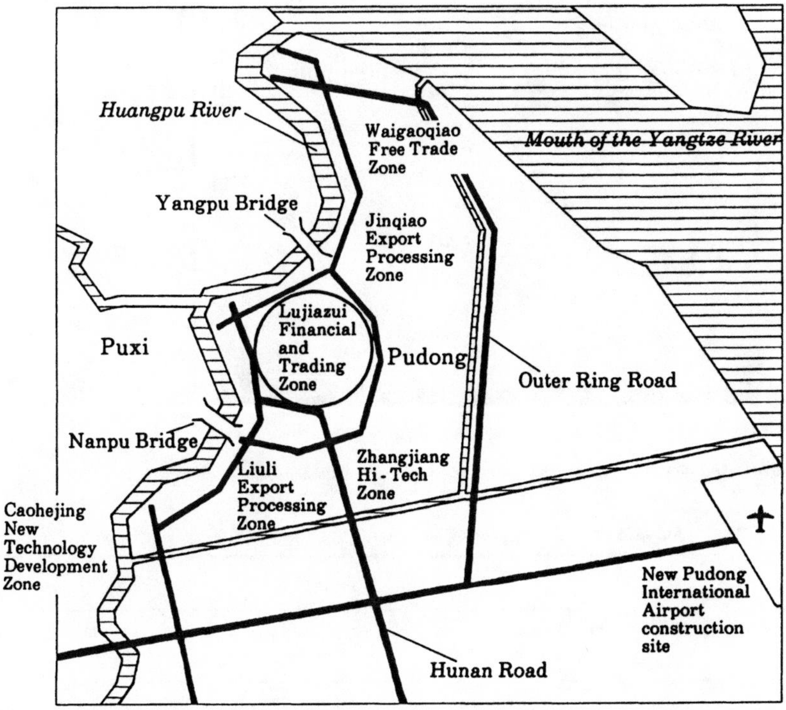

branches of Chinese banks, and most foreign banks, will move to Lujiazui by 1999. By 2000 Shanghai will develop in Pudong a major container port, Waigaoqiao (adding to Shanghai's three existing container ports), and China's largest and most advanced international airport, the New Pudong International Airport.

Changes in Shanghai's Economic Structure Since 1990

The changing structure of Shanghai's economy during the 1980s and through 1996 is illustrated in Figure 24.4. Three elements and trends have been fundamental and decisive in Shanghai's economy: (1) the predominant share of large state-owned enterprises and manufacturing; (2) the increasing contribution to GDP of the tertiary sector, particularly the securities, banking, and transportation industries during the 1990s; and (3) the very substantial role of FIEs in manufacturing and international trade by 1996.

FIGURE 24. 4 Trends in Composition of Shanghai's GDP

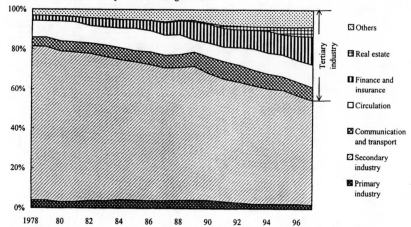

Sources : *Shanghai Statistical Yearbook* 1997, pp. 44-45; *Shanghai Economic Monthly,* vol. 1, 3, 1998.

TABLE 24. 2   Actual 1997 Performance of Shanghai's Economy

	1997		
	Production *(bil. RMB)*	*Growth Rate* *(%)*	*Ratio* *(%)*
GDP	336	12.7	100.0
Primary industry	7.6	4.2	2.3
Secondary industry	175.4	10.6	52.2
Tertiary industry	153	17.7	45.5
of which: banking			
and insurance	47.2	26.2	21.1
Total value of industrial			
Production	560.6	14.6	100.0
of which: light industry	257.9	13.4	46.0
heavy industry	302.7	15.6	54.0

Source: *Shanghai Economic Monthly* (Shanghai Statistics Bureau), vols. 1 and 2, 1998.

Table 24.2 presents actual economic performance for Shanghai in 1997. These data illustrate that Shanghai's economy has become, in line with the earlier plans of China's Central leaders, "special." The increasing importance of tertiary industry, particularly securities and banking, has allowed Shanghai to defy the economic cycles—related to the planning system—that have characterized the Chinese economy. (Shanghai is unlikely to avoid the cyclical correction resulting from overbuilding of real estate. By mid-1998, the seriousness of the overbuilding and excess capacity problem in Shanghai had become undeniable. A severe correction in real estate will likely be a drag on overall economic performance until 2000 at the earliest.)

The Role of Foreign Capital in Shanghai's "Takeoff"

In Shanghai, perhaps more so than in any other city in China, a driving force for modernization and change has been foreign investment. Indeed, from 1993 to 1998 the skyline and industrial landscape of Shanghai were transformed by foreign funds and foreign-invested enterprises of all kinds. In the formerly developed "Puxi" region of Shanghai west of the Huangpu River, most of the sparkling new skyscrapers along such famous streets as Huaihai Road and Nanjing Road, and in new areas like Hongqiao and Xujiahui, large foreign developers, especially from Hong Kong, Taiwan, and Southeast Asia, are investing. China's largest and most profitable joint venture (US$7 billion sales in 1996) is the 50-50 joint venture between Volkswagen and Shanghai Automotive Industrial Corporation (SAIC) located in Anting. Pudong, the new area east of the Huangpu River, has become the location of large factories of foreign companies such as General Motors (also joint-venturing with SAIC to produce Buick sedans with total investment of US$1.7 billion), Sharp, Intel, Hitachi, and Siemens. Many companies like C. Itoh, Manubeni, Mitsubishi, Mitsui, Daewoo, and General Motors have taken advantage of the policies of the Waigaoqiao free trade zone. Table 24.3 presents statistics showing that by 1996 FIEs were employing 16 percent of the workforce in Shanghai, contributing 34.8 percent of the total value of industrial production. More than half the value of all FIE production was being exported. These data are illustrated in Figure 24.5.

Professor Sun Haiming illustrates the impact and importance of foreign investment on Shanghai in Figure 24.3. The large net inflow of foreign capital to Shanghai during the early 1990s offset and exceeded the net outflow of GDP, which had been sapping Shanghai's aggregate demand and investment.

Toward Becoming One of Asia's Financial Centers

How long will it take Shanghai to fully regain its position as China's leading commercial, trading, and financial center? When it comes to commerce and trading, including international trade, Shanghai had in 1996 already captured one-tenth of China's total volume of freight traffic and one-fifth of total import and export cargoes. By these measures, by the late 1990s Shanghai, certainly qualified as China's leading commercial

TABLE 24. 3 Position of Foreign-Invested Enterprises in Shanghai Industry, 1996

Ownership	Number of Enterprises (No.)	Number of Employees (thousand persons)	Total Value of Industrial Production (billion RMB)	Sales (billion RMB)	Of Which, Exports (billion RMB)
State-owned ent.	3,612	1,382	168	167	22
(percentage)	23.2%	45.5%	38.8%	39.3%	29.8%
Collective ent.	7,607	718	53	52	5
Jointly operated ent.	1,195	231	24	23	3
Stock ent.	49	198	35	35	4
FIEs	3,008	486	151	146	39
(percentage)	19.3%	16.0%	34.8%	34.4%	53.1%
Others	124	20	3	2	0.1
Total	15,595	3,035	433	426	74

Note: Figures for industrial enterprises at or above the village level.
Source: Shanghai Statistical Yearbook 1997.

FIGURE 24. 5 Status of Shanghai Industry in Foreign-Invested Companies

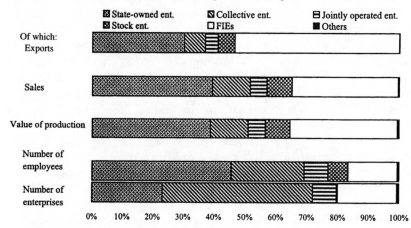

Source: Table 24. 3.

and trading center, was already playing its role as "dragon's head" for the interior provinces along the Yangtze River.

As for Shanghai's role as a financial center, as of mid-1998 Shanghai's stock exchange was the country's largest and most active. Shanghai is home to the national interbank funds market, the interbank foreign exchange trading system, and boasted a variety of national commodities exchanges. By mid-1998 there were some fifty foreign financial institutions with business operations in Shanghai, the largest concentration in China. All of China's national banks, securities companies, insurance companies, and other major financial institutions have significant operations in Shanghai. However, Shanghai is the headquarters of only one major bank, the Bank of Communications. The four big "specialized" banks all have headquarters in Beijing, as is the case with China's new policy banks, other large financial institutions such as the People's Insurance Co. of China, and, of course, the central bank, PBOC. The China Securities Regulatory Commission, which runs the securities exchanges, is also in Beijing. In sum, by mid-1998 Shanghai had become a center for many key financial markets like money markets, capital markets, and commodity markets. By virtue of the presence of so many foreign banks, it was and should continue to be the center of onshore international banking (including, perhaps, offshore banking).

However, as of mid-1998, and more clearly after the assumption to the premiership of Zhu Rongji, it is clear that, for the foreseeable future, financial policymaking and most of China's key financial institutions will remain concentrated in China's political center, Beijing. How long will it take Shanghai to recapture its role as an Asian or world financial center? One condition would be the free convertibility of RMB on capital account. Another is the development of skilled financial specialists, few of whom are in China today. Another is a qualitative improvement in the management and financial strength of China's banks. A final requirement would be relaxation of travel and information restrictions on Chinese citizens. The Shanghai government itself speaks of a target of the year 2010. Given the challenges ahead, that seems like an ambitious target.

—Harner

25

Government Administrative Structure Reform

Breaking Down "Little Empires"

Government Bureaucracy as an Obstacle to Reform

From the early 1990s, when the need to fundamentally restructure China's state-run economy became clear, Chinese leaders have realized that China's government administrative structure is an obstacle to reform. The administrative structures of Central-level ministries responsible for specific industries, subordinate provincial-level bureaus, and enterprises under the direct control of administrative ministries and bureaus were established as an organic part of Central planning. However, that very structure contributed to many of the problems that burden China's economy today: political interference, which leads to misallocation of resources; the prevalence of dozens or hundreds of enterprises in each province producing similar products in low volume and with low quality; and wasteful overinvestment and duplicative investment by enterprises.

The Imperative of Multilevel Reform

The historical legacy of planning in China has been a massive nationwide bureaucracy organized along vertical lines from *ministries* in the center, Beijing, to *bureaus* under the provincial governments, to *offices, commissions, and committees* in cities, wards, and districts. That structure may look like systems in the West, but the difference is that Western bureaucracies have been involved only in policymaking and regulation. Under China's socialist system, in contrast, bureaucracies have been running factories, corporations, theaters, markets, schools, and hospitals.

Why has China's system proven to be such a barrier to reform? The reasons are many, but certainly two are key. First, bureaucrats have enjoyed enormous and largely unchecked power by virtue of direct operational control of society's "factors of production" as well as other nonproductive assets. The system was constituted so that bureaucracies at each level could enjoy such powers. This was the benefit of Central-level, provincial-level, and local-level factories, companies, schools, and so on. The system thus produced strong vested interests in the status quo. Second, the system of vertical regimentation and organization has meant that reform at any level has been difficult or, for practical purposes, ineffective, without reform at all levels up and down the bureaucratic chain. In this sense, fundamental reform and change were possible only if initiated and pushed from the top of the superstructure, that is, at the ministry level in Beijing.

The Connection to
State-Owned Enterprise Reform

By the mid-1990s it was clear that without breaking down the network of institutional interests in the status quo, successful reform of the SOE system would be impossible. What was needed was a sectoral adjustment: closing down hundreds of money-losing factories, expanding strong enterprises through merger and acquisition across industry and administrative lines, nurturing national markets for products and materials, promoting market-based competition for resources; all required the removal of administrative controls and interests. This was obvious to all observers. Also obvious was the huge cost in terms of inefficiency, duplicate investment, and actual enterprise losses of the system.

Zhu Rongji Drives Massive
Government Administration Reform

At the National People's Congress meeting in March 1998, a massive reform of the Central government's bureaucracy was announced and approved. The architect and driver of this reform was the new premier, Zhu Rongji. According to a report by Luo Gan, the secretary of the State Council, the number of departments directly under the State Council was to be reduced from forty to twenty-nine. The departments' functions would fall into one of four categories: (1) macro-control; (2) specialized economic management; (3) education, science, and technology, culture, social security, and natural resource management; and (4) state affairs (Table 25.1). A key feature of the reform was the reform and restructuring of industrial ministries. For instance, the former Ministry of Coal Industry was formed into new "bureaus" responsible (like government bureaus in the West) only for regulation and policymaking under the powerful new State Economic and Trade Commission. Another change was made in the min-

TABLE 25.1 State Council Institutions Reform, March 1998

Macro Control Departments		
New Name	Old Name	Explanation
1. State Development Planning Commission (name change)	1. State Planning Commission	
2. State Economic and Trade Commission	2. State Economic and Trade Commission	2. Expanded authority.
3. Ministry of Finance	3. Ministry of Finance	3. No change.
4. People's Bank of China State Economic System Reform Commission	4. People's Bank of China State Economic System Reform Committee	4. Elevated to high level institution under the State Council. Premier to serve concurrently as chairman, membership comprises ministers of related ministries.

Specialized Economic Management Departments		
5. Ministry of Railways	5. Ministry of Railways	5. No change
6. Ministry of Communications	6. Ministry of Communications	6. No change
7. Ministry of Construction	7. Ministry of Construction	7. No change
8. Ministry of Agriculture	8. Ministry of Agriculture	8. No change
9. Ministry of Water Resources	9. Ministry of Water Resources	9. No change
10. Ministry of Foreign Trade and Economic Cooperation	10. Ministry of Foreign Trade and Economic Cooperation	10. No change
11. Ministry of Information Industry (MII)	11. (Ministry of Post & Telecommunications (MPT) + Ministry of Electronics Industry (MEI)	11. On the foundation of the MPT and MEI, absorbing the information management functions of the Ministry of Radio, Film, and Television, China Aeronautical and Space General Corp., and Aviation Industry General Corp. Further, newly establish a State Postal Bureau and place it under management of MII.
12. Commission of Science, Technology, and Industry for National Defense (newly organized)	12. Commission of Science, Technology, and Industry for National Defense	Absorbs the functions of defense industries under control of the Commission for Science, technology, and Industry for National Defense, of the national defense division of the State Planning Commission, and the government functions of all the military industry general corporations. All military industry general corporations to be restructured into enterprise general corporations. The State Aeronautical and Space Bureau and the State Atomic Energy institutions will be main institutions under the Commission of Science, Technology, and Industry for National Defense.

(continues)

TABLE 25.1 *(continued)*

State Coal Industry Bureau	Ministry of Coal Industry	Under management of the State Economic and Trade Commission
State Machinery Industry Bureau	Ministry of Machinery Industry	Under management of the State Economic and Trade Commission
State Metallurgical Industry Bureau	Ministry of Metallurgical Industry	Under management of the State Economic and Trade Commission
State Internal Trade Bureau	Ministry of Internal Trade	Under management of the State Economic and Trade Commission
State Light Industry Bureau	Light Industry Association	Under management of the State Economic and Trade Commission
State Textile Industry Bureau	Textile Council	Under management of the State Economic and Trade Commission
State Electric Power Corporation	Ministry of Electric Power	Government functions within the electric power industry will be transferred to the State Economic and Trade Commission
State Grain Reserve Bureau	State Grain Reserve Bureau	Elevated to state bureau under management of the State Economic and Trade Commission
State Petrochemical Industry Bureau	Ministry of Petrochemical Industry, China National Petroleum and Natural Gas Corporation, China National Petrochemical Corporation	Combining the government functions of one ministry and two national corporations, to be placed under management of the State Economic and Trade Commission. The resources under the one ministry and two companies, including gas fields, refineries, petrochemical industries, chemical fertilizer and chemical fiber industries, oil companies, and gasoline stations will be organized on the principle of vertical integration into two large petrochemical groups, some large chemical fertilizer, and chemical products companies.
State Forestry Bureau	Ministry of Forest Industry	Becomes organ directly under State Council.

Education, Science and Technology, Social Security, Natural Resources Management Departments

13. Ministry of Science and Technology (name changed)	State Science and Technology Commission	
14. Ministry of Education (name changed)	State Education Commission	
15. Ministry of Personnel	Ministry of Personnel	15. Adjustment of functions. Will comprehensively manage technologists and state public servants. Will appoint and dismiss leaders of large enterprises under State Council supervision.
16. Ministry of Labor and Social Security (new)	Ministry of Labor	16. Will build a unified social security administration agency on the basis of the Ministry of Labor. Will centralize and manage social security programs of the labor, personnel, civil affairs, and present industrial ministries.
17. Ministry of Land and Natural Resources (new)	Ministry of Geology and Mineral Resources, State Land Administration, State Oceanography Bureau, State Bureau of Surveying and Mapping	17. State Oceanography Bureau and State Bureau of Surveying and Mapping will be retained as state-level bureaus under the Ministry of Land and Natural Resources. Becomes organ directly under State Council.
State Bureau of Radio, Film, and Television	Ministry of Radio, Film, and Television	

(continues)

TABLE 25.1 *(continued)*

State Affairs Departments

18.	Ministry of Foreign Affairs	Ministry of Foreign Affairs	No change
19.	Ministry of National Defense	Ministry of National Defense	No change
20.	Ministry of Culture	Ministry of Culture	No change
21.	Ministry of Health	Ministry of Health	No change
22.	State Family Planning Commission	State Family Planning Commission	No change
23.	State Ethnic Affairs Commission	State Ethnic Affairs Commission	No change
24.	Ministry of Justice	Ministry of Justice	No change
25.	Ministry of Public Security	Ministry of Public Security	No change
26.	Ministry of State Security	Ministry of State Security	No change
27.	Ministry of Civil Affairs	Ministry of Civil Affairs	No change
28.	Ministry of Supervision	Ministry of Supervision	No change
29.	State Auditing Administration	State Auditing Administration	No change

Note: Numbers before new name indicate State Council ministry-level institution.
Source: Explanation by Luo Gan, *People's Daily*, March 7, 1998.

istries' authority for ownership and operation of factories, mines, and other enterprises, which would now be transferred to newly created national "corporations." This is the model for the State Power Corporation, created in 1997 under the former Ministry of Power Industry to act as the owner, operator, and manager of all the assets previously owned by the ministry. These include five major-group companies owning and operating the five major interprovincial and interregional power grids. Previously the State Council created some companies, like Sinopec and CNPC, which now have completely replaced ministries and come directly under the State Council. This is the pattern we expect to see repeated.

An elemental part of Zhu Rongji's strategy is to reduce the number of bureaucrats, variously counted at 10–12 million. This would primarily be a matter of reassigning people from government departments to the new corporations.

Zhu Rongji announced that the intended reform should be completed within three years and pledged to "exert my utmost efforts even unto death" to overcome the huge obstacles involved. Those obstacles are not to be underestimated. What Zhu's determination shows is the indispensability of administrative reform to the overall success of China's economic reform plans.

Administrative Reform Stalled
Under Li Peng and Yao Yilin

Mao Zedong attacked the bureaucracy during the Cultural Revolution and greatly simplified as well as "politicized" government departments. The result was a breakdown in administration. The bureaucracy was rebuilt under Hua Guofeng so that in 1981 the number of organs directly under the State Council rose to fifty-two (Table 25.2).

Under the Zhao Ziyang premiership in 1983 the number was reduced by seven to forty-five. In 1988, under Li Peng (with Yao Yilin actually in charge), a further reduction of four organs was accomplished. Looking at the Li Peng/Yao Yilin reform we see some streamlining, but we also can perceive a substantive bureaucratic counterattack (Table 25.3). An organ that has played a key role in progress toward a market economy—the State Economic Commission—was disbanded. The power balance became one of a small State Council and a big State Planning Commission. In the second term of Li Peng's premiership beginning in 1993, the Yao Yilin system was continued in basic form.

Zhu Rongji's "MITI":
The State Economic and Trade Commission

Table 25.3 sketches the roles played by two key policy commissions since 1952: the State Planning Commission and the State Economic Commission under the State Council. In Zhu Rongji's March 1998 reform, both commissions were substantially reformed. The State Planning Commission was reorganized and renamed the State Development Planning Commission (SDPC). In fact, the SDPC, formerly the most powerful economic bureaucracy in China, was targeted for downsizing and diminution of its roles and powers. In the past virtually all large projects and investments in China had to be approved by the SPC, a process that often took years. The iron grip of the SPC had multiple pernicious effects and few perceptible benefits. The approval process had demonstrably failed to stop duplicate investment or promote industrial rationalization. On the contrary, the process of getting approval was so long and painful that projects were regularly padded with extras so that subsequent applications could be avoided. Once the painstaking approval process was complete, projects would be pushed ahead even if market conditions had changed and the investment was no longer justified, because no one wanted to repeat the application process.

Under Zhu Rongji's State Council, the State Economic and Trade Commission (SETC) will act like the Japanese Ministry of International Trade and Industry (MITI) in setting government policy toward and coordinat-

TABLE 25. 2 Changes in Organs Under the State Council Since 1981

Hua Guofeng Structure 1981	Zhao Ziyang Structure 1983	Li Peng (Yao Yilin) Structure 1988	Li Peng Structure 1993	Zhu Rongji Structure 1998
1 Ministry of Foreign Affairs	1 Ministry of Foreign Affairs	1 Ministry of Foreign Affairs	1 Ministry of Foreign Affairs	1 Min. of Foreign Affairs
2 Ministry of National Defense	2 Ministry of National Defense	2 Min. of National Defense	2 Min. of National Defense	2 Ministry of Nat'l Defense
3 State Planning Commission	3 State Planning Commission	3 State Planning Com.	3 State Planning Commission	3 State Development Planning Com.
4 State Economy Commission	4 State Economy Commission	4 State Com. for Economic Restructuring	4 State Economic and Trade Com.	4 State Economic and Trade Com.
5 State Agriculture Com.	5 State Com. for Economic Restructuring	5 State Education Com.	5 State Com. for Economic Restructuring	5 Ministry of Education
6 State Basic Construction Com.	6 Min. of Science and Technology Com.	6 Min. of Science and Technology Com.	6 State Education Com.	6 Min. of Science and Tech.
7 State Machinery Industry Com.	7 Com. of Science, Technology of Industry for Nat'l Defense	7 Com. of Science, Tech., and Industry for Nat'l Defense	7 Ministry of Science and Technology Commission	7 Com. of Science, Tech., and Industry for Nat'l Defense
8 State Energy Commission	8 State Ethnic Affairs Com.	8 State Ethnic Affairs Com.	8 Com. of Science, Tech., and Industry for Nat'l Defense	8 State Ethnic Affairs Com.
9 Min. of Bldg. Material Industry	9 Ministry of Public Security	9 Min. of Public Security	9 State Ethnic Affairs Com.	9 Min. of Public Security
10 Ministry of Science and Technology Commission	10 Ministry of State Security	10 Ministry of State Security	10 Ministry of Public Security	10 Ministry of State Security
11 State Ethnic Affairs Com.	11 Ministry of Civil Affairs	11 Ministry of Supervision	11 Ministry of State Security	11 Ministry of Supervision
12 Ministry of Public Security	12 Ministry of Justice	12 Ministry of Civil Affairs	12 Ministry of Supervision	12 Ministry of Civil Affairs
13 Ministry of Civil Affairs	13 Ministry of Finance	13 Ministry of Justice	13 Ministry of Civil Affairs	13 Ministry of Justice
14 Ministry of Justice	14 State Auditing Admin.	14 Ministry of Finance	14 Ministry of Justice	14 Ministry of Finance
15 Ministry of Finance	15 People's Bank of China	15 Ministry of Personnel	15 Ministry of Finance	15 Ministry of Personnel
16 People's Bank of China	16 Ministry of Commerce	16 Ministry of Labor	16 Ministry of Personnel	16 Min. of Labor and Social Security
17 Ministry of Commerce	17 Ministry of Foreign Economic Relations and Trade	17 Min. of Geology and Mineral Resources	17 Ministry of Labor	17 Min. of Land and Natural Resources
18 All China Supply and Marketing Cooperatives	18 Min. of General Farming and Fishery	18 Min. of Construction	18 Min. of Geology and Mineral Resources	18 Ministry of Construction
19 Ministry of Grain	19 Ministry of Forestry	19 Ministry of Energy	19 Ministry of Construction	19 Ministry of Railways
20 Ministry of Foreign Trade	20 Min. of Water Resources and Electric Power	20 Ministry of Railways	20 Min. of Electric Power Industry	20 Min. of Communications
21 Ministry of Foreign Economic Relations	21 Min. of Urban and Rural Environment Protection	21 Min. of Communications	21 Min. of Coal Industry	21 Min. of Info. Industry
22 Foreign Investment Management Com.	22 Min. of Geology and Mineral Resources	22 Min. of Machinery and Electronics Industry	22 Min. of Machine Building	22 Min. of Water Resources
23 Imports and Exports Management Com.	23 Min. of Metallurgical Industry	23 Min. of Aeronautical and Space Industry	23 Min. of Electronics Industry	23 Ministry of Agriculture
24 Ministry of Agriculture	24 Ministry of Machine Building	24 Min. of Metallurgical Industry	24 Min. of Metallurgical Industry	24 Min. of Foreign Trade and Economic Cooperation
25 Min. of Land Reclamation	25 Ministry of Nuclear Industry	25 Min. of Chemical Industry	25 Min. of Chemical Industry	25 Ministry of Culture
26 Ministry of Forestry	26 Min. of Aviation Industry	26 Ministry of Light Industry	26 Ministry of Railways	26 Ministry of Health
27 Ministry of Water Resources	27 Min. of Electric Power Industry	27 Ministry of Textile	27 Min. of Communications	27 State Family Planning Com.
28 Min. of Electric Power Industry	28 Ministry of Weapon Industry	28 Min. of Posts and Telcom.	28 Min. of Posts and Telcom.	28 People's Bank of China
29 Min. of Metallurgical Industry	29 Ministry of Space Industry	29 Min. of Water Resources	29 Min. of Water Resources	29 State Auditing Admin.
30 Min. of Metallurgical Industry	30 Ministry of Coal Industry	30 Ministry of Agriculture	30 Ministry of Agriculture	
31 Min. of First Machinery Industry	31 Min. of Petroleum Industry	31 Ministry of Forestry	31 Ministry of Forestry	
32 Min. of Agric. Machinery	32 Min. of Chemical Industry	32 Ministry of Commerce	32 Min. of Internal Trade	
33 Min. of Second Machinery Industry (Nuclear)	33 Ministry of Textile	33 Min. of Foreign Economic Relations and Trade	33 Min. of Foreign Trade and Economic Cooperation	
34 Min. of Third Machinery Industry (Aviation)	34 Ministry of Light Industry	34 Ministry of Materials	34 Ministry of Culture	
35 Min. of Fourth Machinery Industry (Electronics)	35 Ministry of Railways	35 Ministry of Culture	35 Min. of Radio, Film and TV	
36 Min. of Fifth Machinery Industry (Weapon)	36 Min. of Communications	36 Min. of Radio, Film, and TV	36 Ministry of Health	
37 Min. of Sixth Machinery Industry (Ships)	37 Min. of Posts and Telcom.	37 Ministry of Health	37 State Physical Culture and Sports Commission	
38 Min. of Seventh Machinery Industry (Space)	38 Min. of Labor and Personnel	38 State Physical Culture and Sports Commission	38 State Family Planning Com.	
39 Ministry of Coal Industry	39 Ministry of Culture	39 State Family Planning Com.	39 People's Bank of China	
40 Min. of Petroleum Industry	40 Xinhua News Agency	40 People's Bank of China	40 State Auditing Admin.	
41 Min. of Chemical Industry	41 Min. of Radio, Film, and Television	41 State Auditing Admin.		
42 Ministry of Textile	42 Ministry of Education			
43 Ministry of Light Industry	43 Ministry of Health			
44 Ministry of Railways	44 State Physical Culture and Sports Commission			
45 Ministry of Communications	45 State Family Planning Com.			
46 Min. of Posts and Telecom.				
47 Ministry of Culture				
48 Foreign Culture Liasion Com.				
49 Ministry of Education				
50 State Family Planning Com.				
51 State Physical Culture and Sports Commission				
52 State Family Planning Com.				

Source: Mitsubishi Research Institute, Inc., *Chugoku Joho* (*China Information*), vol. 14, 1998.

TABLE 25. 3 **The State Planning Commission and State Economic (and Trade) Commission**

	Direction Toward Centrally Planned Economy	*Direction Toward Market Economy*
Establishment period	Nov. 1952: State Planning Commission established	May 1956: State Economic Commission established
Period of the "big" State Planning Commission	1970: "big" State Planning Commission	During the Cultural Revolution, the State Economic Commission was disbanded after its chairman, Bo Yipo, was criticized. Its functions were absorbed by the SPC.
Establishment period		March 1978: State Economic Commission revived. Kang Shien became chairman.
Period of the "big" State Planning Commission	April 1988: "big" State Planning Commission (Yao Yilin, chairman)	State Economic Commission is absorbed into the SPC.
Toward a "big" Economic Commission		June 1991: Zhu Rongji starts the State Council Office of Production and becomes its chairman. June 1992: Zhu Rongji starts the State Council Office of Economy and Trade. (Wang Zhongyu chairman.) June 1993: Zhu Rongji starts the State Economic and Trade Commission. (Wang Zhongyu chairman.)
Period of the "big" Economic Commission	March 1998: State Planning Commission reorganized as the State Development Planning Commission	March 1998: Broad functions of the former State Planning Commission are absorbed into the State Economic and Trade Commission

ing the development of China's industrial economy through its industrial bureaus. Having been in charge of the predecessor of SETC, and having a view of how it should operate to effect changes needed in a market economy, this new "Chinese MITI" will clearly be Zhu Rongji's key bureaucratic tool in carrying out his reform program.

Administrative Reform in Shanghai

What form will the reformed administrative structure take at the local level? To answer this question we look at steps already taken in Shanghai, one of the cities leading the reform process since 1995.

One reform has been to transform several industrial bureaus into industrial holding companies and group companies. The purpose is twofold: (1) to separate government from enterprise management so that enterprises can operate more like businesses; and (2) to put control of state assets—ownership control over state companies, land rights, and

TABLE 25. 4 Government Administration Reform in Shanghai, 1998

Industry-Related Bureaus under the Municipal Government	
Electric Power Industry Bureau	Post and Telecommunications Bureau
Railway Bureau	Water Resources Bureau
Harbor Bureau	Materials Bureau
Agriculture Bureau	

Bureaus That Have Been Reorganized into Group Companies

Instrument Industry Bureau + Electric Instrument Bureau ⟶	Shanghai Instrument and Telecommunications Industry Holding (Group) Company
Machinery Industry Bureau + Electric Machinery Industry Bureau ⟶	Shanghai Machine Building and Electrical Industry Holding (Group) Company
Textile Industry Bureau ⟶	Shanghai Textile Industry Holding (Group) Company
Construction Engineering Bureau ⟶	Shanghai Construction Engineering Holding (Group) Company
Building Materials Bureau ⟶	Shanghai Building Materials Industry (Group) Company
Metallurgical Industry Bureau ⟶	Shanghai Metallurgical Industry Holding (Group) Company
Light Industry Bureau ⟶	Shanghai Light Industry Holding (Group) Company
Transportation and Communications Bureau ⟶	Transport and Communications (Group) Company
Pharmaceutical Administration Bureau + Chemical Industry Bureau ⟶	Huayi Group Company

fixed assets—into the hands of "managers" who will be responsible for asset management (*zichan guanli*). Some holding companies are in charge of entire sectors—for example, the textile industry—and should be able to allocate investment resources productively to the better enterprises and to organize restructurings and mergers within the entire sector.

By 1995 Shanghai had already restructured and combined many industrial bureaus into the enterprise group holding companies. This process was continued in 1996 and 1997, so that by 1998 few government bureaus remained (Table 25.4).

Notwithstanding what appears to be impressive reform, officials in Shanghai concede that much remains to be done in government administration downsizing, and they will be called upon, in line with Beijing, to make significant cuts during the next three years. There remain hundreds of offices, agencies, commissions, institutes, and departments under the Shanghai government that are unproductive or counterproductive and grossly overstaffed. It will take a major political effort, and the example of substantive progress at the Central level, to achieve significant results.

—Harner and Yabuki

Part Four

Foreign Trade, Foreign Capital, and External Economic Relations

26

Foreign Trade

Movement Toward an
Open Economic System

The Expanded Role of Foreign Trade

The most symbolic feature of China's opening under the reform and liberalization policy has been the rapid advance of foreign trade. From US$20.6 billion in 1978 (the start of the Deng Xiaoping era) to US$325.1 billion in 1997, during the nineteen years of the Deng Xiaoping era foreign trade grew fifteenfold, with an average annual rate of growth of more than 16 percent (Figure 26.1). This performance is on a par with top trading nations such as South Korea and Taiwan.

Let us look at the trade balance. During the Mao Zedong era, because the volume of imports was decided based on the outlook for foreign exchange receipts, the pattern reflected a small annual remaining surplus. When a deficit occurred in one year, it was quickly corrected by a surplus the following year, so a strict multiyear balance was maintained. This policy was followed in the early Deng Xiaoping era, and no significant imbalances were seen through 1984.

However, in 1985 and 1986 deficits of more than US$10 billion continued for two consecutive years. This was a result of the "reform leap." In October 1984 the decision to reform the economic system was taken, and actual reform activities were begun in the local governmental and industrial fields. Broad new authority to use foreign currency was granted to provinces and large enterprises, with the result that control over imports was lost and deficits occurred. After this, though the size of the deficit was reduced, it continued through 1989. With the tightening of economic policy after the Tiananmen Incident and pursuant to an export drive, surpluses were restored in 1990 through 1992. In 1993 domestic demand strengthened in the context of a building boom. Exports declined and imports increased. Thereafter, macroeconomic control measures were imple-

FIGURE 26. 1 **Trends in China's Exports and Imports**

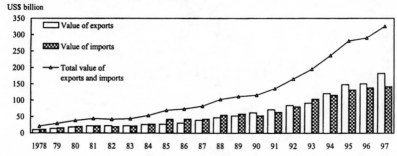

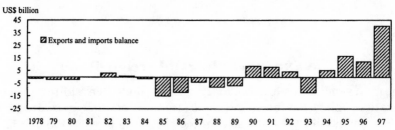

Sources: *China Statistical Yearbook* 1997, p. 588; 1997 figures from "Bulletin on National Economic and Social
Development for 1997," *Economic Daily*, March 5, 1998.

mented and, in the context of a soft-landing policy, exports and the trade
surplus grew steadily. The surplus in 1997 was US$40.1 billion.

Looking at China's export dependency ratio (value of exports divided
by GNP), we see that the ratio was 4.6 percent in 1978, rose to 8–9 percent
during the first half of the 1980s, and reached 12–13 percent during the
second half of the 1980s. By the mid-1990s, as the export drive reached
fruition, the ratio was trending around the 20 percent level (Figure 26.2).

Changes in Commodity Composition
of Imports and Exports

Table 26.1 presents the top-ten products in China's trade in five-year intervals to 1995. Looking first at exports, from 1980 through 1985 crude petroleum and petroleum products took first and second place; garments and
cotton fabric were third and fourth. In 1995 garments had assumed the
undisputed top position, followed by toys, cotton fabric, knitted cotton
goods, shoes, and other knitted goods. Petroleum had fallen to seventh
place. Thus, we can see that the leading role previously played by petroleum products has been taken over by textiles and miscellaneous goods.

As for imports, there has also been a big change. During the ten years
1985–1995 the top import was steel products, but the proportion has been

FIGURE 26. 2 China's Degree of Export Dependency

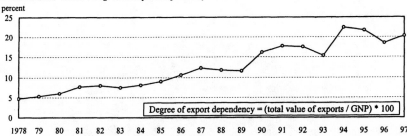

Sources: *China Statistical Yearbook* 1997, p. 588; 1997 figures from "Bulletin on National Economic and Social Development for 1997," *Economic Daily*, March 5, 1998.

TABLE 26. 1 Changes in the Top-Ten Commodities in China's Trade

Exports

Rank	1980 Item	%	1985 Item	%	1990 Item	%	1995 Item	%
1	crude oil	14.9	crude oil	19.2	garments	6.4	garments	9.1
2	processed oil	6.6	processed oil	5.3	crude oil	5.5	toys	2.3
3	garments	6.2	garments	4.4	cotton cloth	2.6	cotton cloth	2.3
4	cotton cloth	4.0	cotton cloth	3.6	aquatic prod.	2.1	cotton knits	2.0
5	rice	2.1	cotton	1.6	cotton knits	1.6	leather goods	1.8
6	coal	1.4	canned goods	1.4	processed oil	1.4	other knits	1.8
7	tea leaves	1.3	mixed yarn	1.3	silk goods	1.2	crude oil	1.5
8	slaughter hogs	1.3	coal	1.2	steel prod.	1.1	steel products	1.5
9	silks goods	1.1	silk goods	1.1	canned goods	1.1	aquatic prod.	1.4
10	rattan goods	1.1	tea leaves	1.1	coal	1.1	pharmaceuticals	1.1

Imports

Rank	1980 Item	%	1985 Item	%	1990 Item	%	1995 Item	%
1	wheat	10.9	steel products	14.9	steel products	9.7	steel products	4.9
2	steel products	7.4	televisions	2.4	wheat	8.4	paper, paperbd.	1.8
3	raw cotton	7.3	trucks	2.3	urea	4.5	machine tools	1.7
4	urea	3.4	wheat	2.1	automobiles	2.9	wheat	1.5
5	ethylene	3.1	logs	1.9	cotton	2.8	autos, chassis	1.2
6	trucks	2.4	urea	1.7	paper, paperbd.	2.6	edible oil	1.1
7	synthetic fiber	1.9	synthetic fiber	1.7	synthetic fiber	2.1	polyethylene	1.1
8	natural gas	1.7	aluminum	1.4	edible oil	2.0	raw cotton	1.1
9	sugar	1.7	ships	1.3	machine tools	1.9	urea	1.0
10	corn	1.4	copper alloys	1.2	ships	1.8	synthetic fiber	1.0

Sources: Figures for 1980 and 1985, *China's Commercial and Foreign Economic Statistical Materials, 1952-1988*, pp. 464-475. Figures for 1990 and 1995, *China Statistical Yearbook*, 1995 and 1996 editions.

234

FIGURE 26.3 Trends in Shares of China's Trade by Country and Region

【Exports】

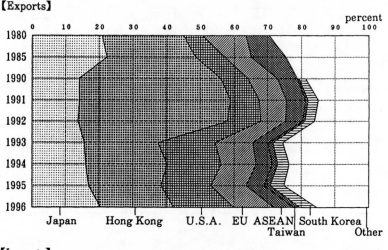

【Imports】

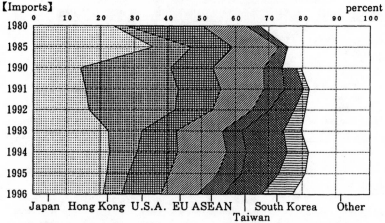

Notes: ¹ EU includes Germany, Italy, U.K., Netherlands, Belgium, Spain.
² ASEAN includes Indonesia, Malaysia, Singapore, Philippines, Thailand.
³ Statistics for Taiwan and South Korea reported from 1990.
⁴ Method of compiling and calculating Hong Kong's reexports changed substantially in 1993. Figures prior to and after 1993 are not comparable.

Sources: *China's Foreign Economic Statistics*, *China Statistical Yearbook*.

steadily declining and in 1995 was one-third of peak volume. The goods occupying second and third place have changed frequently. In 1985 they were color TVs and trucks, in 1990 wheat and urea, and in 1995 paper and cardboard and machine tools.

Changes in Foreign Trade Counterparties

The top panel of Figure 26.3 presents a view of counterparty shares of China's exports by country and region. (Please note we are using Chinese statistics; U.S. statistics show a sharply different pattern, presented in Chapter 30.) At the beginning of the 1990s, Hong Kong's share was overwhelming. Afterward it appears to decline by half, but this is because after 1993 reexports from Hong Kong were included in statistics for the final destination countries. Due to this change, the shares of the United States, Japan, the Association of Southeast Asian Nations, and Taiwan seemed to take a big jump. In 1996 three destinations—Hong Kong (24 percent), Japan (19 percent), and the United States (17 percent)—occupied about 20 percent each, with a combined share of 60 percent. Next are the European Union (EU) and ASEAN. In recent years the shares of Taiwan and South Korea have become prominent.

The bottom panel of Figure 26.3 presents a view of counterparty shares of China's imports by country and region. In 1996 Japan occupied the top position, with a 22 percent share. Following Japan were the United States (12 percent) and the EU (12 percent). Mainly, China is importing from these advanced countries industrial products that China is not yet able to produce itself. The shares of such partners as Taiwan (12 percent), South Korea (9 percent), and ASEAN (7 percent) are increasing rapidly. It remains to be seen whether the late-1990s Asian financial crisis will result in substantially changed trade flows between China and the crisis countries.

Looking at the structure of export destinations and import sources, we see a tendency toward concentration export destinations, on the one hand, and diversification of import sources on the other.

Changes in the Structure of Foreign Trade and the Role of Foreign Capital

Table 26.2 presents a view of the large proportion of China's trade carried out under processing trade arrangements. *Processing trade* describes transactions whereby foreign capital brings raw materials, patterns and designs, and parts into China (imports), which are processed in Chinese factories; the foreign investor then takes the goods back (exports), paying only a processing fee. After 1995, exports under processing trade exceeded exports under general trade. As for imports, processing trade–

TABLE 26. 2 Share of Processing Trade in China's Total Trade

(unit: US$ billions, percent)

Form of Trade	1992	1993	1994	1995	1996
Export value	84.9	91.7	121.0	148.8	151.1
of which:					
share of normal trade	51.4%	50.7%	50.9%	48.0%	41.6%
share of processing trade	46.6%	48.2%	47.1%	49.5%	55.8%
Import value	80.6	104.0	115.6	132.1	133.8
of which:					
share of normal trade	41.7%	41.2%	33.2%	32.8%	29.4%
share of processing trade	39.1%	35.0%	41.1%	44.2%	46.5%
share of goods and equipment					
imported for FIE investments	9.9%	16.0%	17.5%	14.2%	18.6%
Total trade value	165.5	195.7	236.6	280.9	289.9
of which:					
share of normal trade	46.7%	45.6%	42.2%	40.9%	35.3%
share of processing trade	43.0%	41.2%	44.2%	47.0%	50.6%
share of goods and equipment					
imported for FIE investments	4.8%	8.5%	8.6%	6.7%	8.6%

Source: Customs Statistics Yearbook of China, each year.

related imports switched positions with general trade imports during the period 1993–1994. From an examination of Chinese customs statistics we can find that SOEs are dominant in general trade, whereas FIEs play the leading role in processing trade.

Figure 26.4 illustrates the proportionate position of FIEs in the volume and value of China's imports and exports. In 1996 this share in the value of exports was US$61.5 billion and in the value of imports US$75.6 billion, resulting in net imports of US$14.1 billion. This level of net imports is equivalent to the value of equipment and goods (19 percent of imports; see Table 26.2) imported by FIEs as they began to set up operations. FIEs claim more than 40 percent of value of exports and more than 50 percent of the value of imports. From this graph we can appreciate the fact that the impetus for the rapid growth of China's imports and exports during the 1990s has come thanks to foreign-invested enterprises.

The Question of WTO Accession

In 1995 China's exports totaled US$148.8 billion and constituted 3 percent of world exports, eleventh worldwide. China's 1995 imports totaled US$132.1 billion, accounting for 2.6 percent of world imports, twelfth worldwide. Against this trade performance, and in view of the significant position now reached in global trade flows, it is unreasonable, according to the Chinese government, to exclude China from the World Trade Organization.

Table 26.3 summarizes China's efforts to liberalize trade and investment with a view to gaining entry into the WTO.

FIGURE 26. 4 Trends in Proportionate Share of Foreign Invested Enterprises in China's Trade

Sources: 1980-1991 figures from *China Foreign Economic Statistics;* 1992-1995 figures from
China Statistical Yearbook 1995, 1996 editions; 1996 figures from *Customs Statistics
Yearbook of China*.

TABLE 26.3 China's Steps Toward Joining the World Trade Organization

1996

April. Implementation of import tariff reductions (reduction from average of 35 percent to 23 percent)
on over 4,000 items.

July. Offered a detailed plan incorporating, among other things, a plan for abolishing import quotas.

October. Expressed intention henceforth not to adopt and implement any policies or laws not in
conformity with WTO principles.

November. Announced a broad set of measures at the APEC meeting in Manila: (1) the existing
average 23 percent import tariff rate to be reduced to 15 percent by 2000; (2) review remaining
nontariff barriers on 384 products and abolish all non-tariff barriers not in conformity with the WTO;
(3) provide greater market access in such fields as banking, insurance, securities, retail commerce,
transport, telecommunications, and tourism; (4) implement policy measures including amending and
adopting new customs laws and regulations to further promote protection of intellectual property.

December. Implementation four years in advance of schedule of IMF article 8, meaning abolishing
restrictions on convertibility of the RMB for settlement trade and service transactions on current
account.

1997

March. Announced intention to reform "foreign trade rights" system to expand rights to engage in
foreign trade and directly import and export without prior approval or consent to all enterprises--up
from present 12,000 enterprises--within three years of joining WTO.

March. Announced that immediately after accession China would apply the WTO principle of
nondiscrimination between domestic and foreign entities and accept the duty of legal review. In this
connection the two-price system (higher prices for foreigners) for hotel rates, airfares, raw materials,
and service fees was abolished.

October. Implemented import tariff reduction (reduction from average 23 percent to 17 percent) for
4,874 items. In six duty reductions since 1993 tariffs had been reduced by 60 percent (from average
42.5 percent in 1992 to 17 percent in 1997).

November. At the APEC Vancouver meeting State Pres. Jiang Zemin announced that the Chinese
government had decided to lower the average tariff rate on industrial products to 10 percent by 2005.

Source: JETRO, *White Paper on International Trade* 1997, pp. 174-175.

In December 1996 China brought itself into compliance with the International Monetary Fund's article 8 by abolishing restrictions on convertibility of RMB to foreign exchange in transactions under current account (trade and services). This step was implemented four years earlier than originally planned.

In March 1997 China announced its intention, within three years of joining WTO, to grant all enterprises the right to engage directly in importing and exporting (currently only 12,000 Chinese enterprises enjoy that right). Based on this principle of "national treatment," the dual-price system previously applied to such services as airline and train tickets and hotels was abolished. It is obvious that "one item, one price" is one of the most important principles within a market economy.

In October 1997 the rates of import duties on 4,874 products were reduced to an average of 17 percent. This amounted to a 60 percent decrease from an average rate of 42.5 percent in 1992. The rate is scheduled to drop to 10 percent by 2005.

Apart from tariff rates, the problem spans such issues as nontariff barriers, intellectual property rights, and liberalization of trade in agricultural products. Within six to eight years of acceding to WTO membership, nontariff barriers must be abolished. Factories violating intellectual property rights by illegally pirating and producing protected works should be closed. Export subsidies for agricultural products should be abolished.

The Chinese government has continued negotiating for WTO membership while working out measures to deal with the problems discussed above. At the same time, it has been conducting parallel bilateral negotiations with WTO member countries. Nineteen ninety-eight will be the fiftieth anniversary of the start of the General Agreement on Tarrifs and Trade (GATT). It will be a happy event if 1998 is the year China's entry into WTO is resolved.

—Yabuki

27

Foreign Capital

Foreign-Invested Companies Are Transforming the Chinese Economy

Foreign Capital Driving the Transition to a Market Economy

In China, the real meaning of the *opening policy* is bringing foreign capital into Chinese territory. Unlike normal trade in goods, the import-export of capital has a direct bearing on productive relations. This meant that the decision to "open" China's policy required a willingness to accept significant change as well.

Introducing foreign capital comprises borrowing from abroad, receiving direct investment, and "other" investment. *Other investment* includes international leases, compensation trade, and commission processing. From 1979 through 1991 in terms of actual funds received, borrowing from abroad greatly exceeded receipt of direct investment. During this period the Chinese government used foreign loans to finance infrastructure projects. This may be seen as a stage in improving the investment environment for foreign enterprises. After ten years of efforts, foreign confidence in reform and liberalization policies rose, and progress in developing infrastructure was noticed. Suddenly massive amounts of foreign capital targeted China. Deng Xiaoping's Southern Excursion Talks were a turning point. Looking at actual funds received, we see that foreign direct investment in China, only US$4.4 billion in 1991, jumped to more than US$10 billion in 1992 and reached US$27.5 billion in 1993. Thereafter it steadily rose, reaching US$40 billion in 1996 and US$45.3 billion in 1997. However, the "leading indicator" of the contracted base foreign investment peaked in 1993 and has declined since, indicating declines in actual investment lay ahead (Table 27.1 and Figure 27.1).

TABLE 27. 1   Trends in China's Use of Foreign Capital

(unit: cases, US$ billion)

Year	Loans			Direct Investment			Other Investment	
	No.	Contracted	Actual	No.	Contracted	Actual	Contracted	Actual
1979-1983	79	15.1	11.8	1,392	7.7	1.8	1.2	0.9
1984	38	1.9	1.3	1,856	2.7	1.3	0.2	0.2
1985	72	3.5	2.7	3,073	5.9	1.7	0.4	0.3
1986	53	8.4	5.0	1,498	2.8	1.9	0.5	0.4
1987	56	7.8	5.8	2,233	3.7	2.3	0.6	0.3
1988	118	9.8	6.5	5,945	5.3	3.2	0.9	0.6
1989	130	5.2	9.3	5,779	5.6	3.4	0.7	0.4
1990	98	5.1	6.5	7,273	6.6	3.5	0.4	0.3
1991	108	7.2	6.9	12,978	11.9	4.4	0.5	0.3
1992	94	10.7	7.9	48,764	58.1	11.0	0.6	0.3
1993	158	11.3	11.2	83,437	111.4	27.5	0.5	0.3
1994	97	10.7	9.3	47,549	82.7	33.8	0.4	0.2
1995	173	11.3	10.3	37,011	91.3	37.5	0.6	0.3
1996	117	8.0	12.7	24,556	73.3	41.7	0.4	0.4
1997	137	5.9	12.0	21,046	51.8	45.3	0.4	0.7
1979-1996 (a)	1,391	115.9	104.1	283,344	469.1	174.9	7.9	5.0
1990-1996 (b)	84.5	64.2	64.8	261,568	435.3	159.4	3.4	2.0
(b) / (a) (%)	6.1%	55.4	62.2	92.3	92.8	91.1	43.1	40.1

Note: Other investment includes (1) international leases, (2) compensation trade, (3) processing
and assembling.

Sources: *China Statistical Yearbook* 1997; 1997 figures from MOFTEC.

FIGURE 27. 1   Trends in China's Use of Foreign Investment

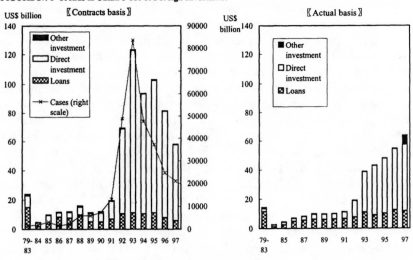

Sources: *China Statistical Yearbook* (each year); 1997 figures from MOFTEC.

Sources and Destinations
of Foreign Investment

Table 27.2 presents findings of a study on sources of direct foreign investment by country and region in the years 1985, 1990, and 1995. In 1985 some US$2 billion was received, 49 percent coming from Hong Kong and Macao followed by the United States and Japan.

In 1990 the total amount increased to US$3.75 billion, and the share of Hong Kong and Macao increased to 56 percent. The shares of the United States and Japan slightly declined. At this time, because of political considerations, investment from Taiwan was included in "other" investments. It was announced to be 6 percent in the 1996 *China Industrial Development Report*. In 1995 Taiwan's share had increased to 8.4 percent, on a par with the United States and Japan. Including Taiwan, investment from the Greater China Economic Region topped the important 60 percent mark. The respective shares of the United States and Japan decreased and were being approached by ASEAN and the EU. In 1995 the growing power of Asia, including the influences of the lifting of martial law and liberalization of trade restrictions in Taiwan, the normalization of relations between China and South Korea, and the development of Southeast Asia, is reflected in the expanding investment in China. Of course, the situation has been somewhat altered by the financial and economic crises of the late 1990s, but the long-term trend is still strong.

The official political position is that Taiwan, Hong Kong, and Macao are part of China, yet their investment is still classified as foreign investment. Notwithstanding that fact, what regions of China are receiving foreign capital? In 1985, 90 percent went to the eastern region, whereas the

TABLE 27. 2 Changes in Direct Investment in Selected Countries and Regions

Country / Region	1985 US$ million	%	1990 US$ million	%	1995 US$ million	%
China	955.7	48.8	2,118.5	56.4	23,790.1	62.9
Hong Kong, Macao	955.7	48.8	2,118.5	56.4	20,624.9	54.6
Taiwan	-	-	-	-	3,165.2	8.4
Japan	315.1	16.1	520.5	13.9	3,212.5	8.5
U.S.	357.2	18.2	461.2	12.3	3,083.7	8.2
ASEAN	22.4	1.1	64.1	1.7	2,625.3	6.9
EU	158.1	8.1	157.9	4.2	2,057.5	5.4
South Korea	-	-	-	-	726.1	2.1
Others	150.2	7.7	432.7	11.5	3,762.7	10.0
Total	1,958.7	100.0	3,754.9	100.0	37,805.7	100.0

Sources: China Foreign Economic Statistics; China Statistical Yearbook 1996.

FIGURE 27. 2 Changes in Destinations of Foreign Direct Investment by Region

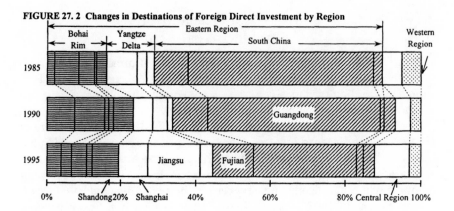

Sources: *China Foreign Economic Statistics; China Statistical Yearbook* 1996.

central and western regions received about 5 percent each. In terms of economic zones, we see that the South China economic zone received 60 percent (Guangdong province alone nearly 50 percent), the Bohai Rim economic zone received 16 percent, and the Yangtze economic zone received 13 percent (Figure 27.2).

In 1990 the eastern-region share reached 93 percent, with the central region at 4 percent, and the western region at only 3 percent. The share of the South China economic zone was slightly below 60 percent, that of the Yangtze economic zone declined to 10 percent, whereas that of the Bohai Rim economic zone was 23 percent. In 1995 the share of the eastern region declined to 88 percent, whereas that of the central region doubled to 9 percent. The western region remained at a low 3 percent. The South China economic zone now captured about 40 percent, whereas the share of the Yangtze economic zone jumped to 25 percent. This reflected the dynamic growth of Shanghai municipality and Jiangsu province. Viewing the trends during the ten-year period beginning in 1985, we see a shift within the coastal region from South China to the Yangtze and Bohai Rim areas and a lesser, gradual movement from the eastern region to the central region.

The Position of Foreign-Invested Enterprises in the Chinese Economy

Let us look at the position of FIEs in China's industry by referring to the industrial census. According to the Third National Industrial Census, in 1995 the total number of foreign-invested industrial enterprises was 59,000, a mere 0.8 percent of the national total of industrial enterprises.

Employees numbered 8.99 million, a 13.6 percent share. Total value of industrial output was RMB 1.2 trillion, 13.1 percent of the total national industrial output. Total assets value constituted a 16.2 percent share.

Comparing these 1995 results against the situation in 1985, we can appreciate how far FIEs have come during this ten-year period. Take the data for production units at or above the village level, which means 49,500 enterprises (59,000 total enterprises less 10,000 very small-scale enterprises). *Village level* refers to "villages" as they are defined by government administrations in the countryside. Not included in the village-level classification and higher are individual enterprises and village-run enterprises, which are too small and numerous to be included in the analysis.

According to the census data, among the 49,000 village-level and higher enterprises, some 29,000, or about 60 percent, were invested from Taiwan, Hong Kong, and Macao. U.S., Japanese, and other FIEs totaled 20,000, about 40 percent. This constitutes a classification by national origin. Now let us classify the enterprises by the business forms taken by Chinese and foreign capital. Equity joint ventures totaled 34,000, for a 68 percent share. Wholly owned foreign enterprises totaled 10,200, some 20 percent of the whole. Cooperative joint ventures numbered slightly more than 5,300, about a 10 percent share.

Looking at the position of the 49,000 foreign-invested industrial enterprises within all village-level and above industrial enterprises, we see that the former occupy a 16.7 percent share based on value added, with the share of total sales being slightly less than 20 percent. Separating domestic sales and exports, we observe slightly more than 60 percent in domestic sales, slightly less than 40 percent in exports. Foreign industrial companies earn about one-fourth of total profits but pay less than 10 percent of total tax. From this we can understand the complaints of local enterprises against the tax concessions given to foreigner investors.

Table 27.3 presents an analysis of the types of products produced by foreign-invested industrial enterprises. Electronics and telecommunications equipment occupies the top position, with 60 percent of total production being supplied by FIEs. Next is apparel and fibers at roughly 50 percent. Transportation equipment and electrical machinery FIEs account for roughly one-fourth of total production.

If we look at the product share within FIEs only, we see that electronics and telecommunications equipment occupies the top position, with a 14.2 percent share, followed by textiles at 7.7 percent, transportation equipment at 7.6 percent, and apparel and fibers at 6.9 percent.

China's policy toward foreign investment and foreign-invested projects and sectors provides for five kinds of treatment and selection, which are,

TABLE 27. 3 Main Sectors of Foreign Invested Industrial Enterprises According to the PRC 1995
              Third National Industrial Census

Kinds of Industry	Total Industrial Production Value (billion RMB)	Share of Total FIEs %	Share of Total Chinese Industry %	Export Sales %
Electronics and telecommunications equipment	151.8	14.2	60.0	59.1
Textile industry	82.4	7.7	17.9	
Transportation equipment manufacturing	81.3	7.6	24.6	
Garments and other fiber products	73.7	6.9	50.2	71.7
Electronic equipment and machinery manufacturing	63.1	5.9	24.3	
Food industry	62.3	5.8	20.5	

Source: *The Data of the Third National Industrial Census of the People's Republic of China in 1995.*

from most open to closed: encouraged, restricted "A," restricted "B," approval required, and prohibited. This policy has been adjusted many times to reflect China's changing economy and priorities. The trend now is toward promoting foreign investment that supports infrastructure development, technical upgrading of the industry, and development of interior regions.

—Yabuki

28

The Asian Financial Crisis and the RMB

China's Balance of Payments and the Power of US$140 Billion in Foreign Exchange Reserves

The Asian Financial Crisis and China

During late summer and fall 1997 a financial typhoon struck Asia. The cause was the financial weakness of a number of countries—including Thailand, Indonesia, Malaysia, the Philippines, and South Korea—that had fixed currencies to the U.S. dollar and had allowed current account balances and net external asset balances to fall deeply into deficit. When international speculators saw this weakness, they attacked the currencies and the financial markets—particularly stock markets—of these countries. Thereby depleted of foreign currency reserves and no longer able to withstand the attack, the countries were forced to devalue their currencies and to seek financial support from the IMF.

Is there a chance that China, Asia's biggest developing country, will experience a similar crisis in international payments and foreign exchange? The short answer is that it will not. Although China's economy does have many serious weaknesses similar to those in Thailand and Korea—the fundamentally weak financial position of banks, a real estate bubble, vast misallocation of borrowed capital into unprofitable or lossmaking ventures—China's international payments position, foreign currency reserves, and international debt levels are far better than the crisis countries that required an IMF rescue. Moreover, China has yet to open its financial system to international capital movements (except for direct investment), and thus its exposure in the international financial system is largely indirect—through trade and services. Thanks to these conditions, China will

TABLE 28. 1 Comparison of Crisis Countries and China

(Unit: %)

Country	Current Account Balance / GDP			Net Foreign Assets (liabilities) / GDP		
	1994	1995	1996	1994	1995	1996
Indonesia	-1.7	-3.3	-3.3	-36.2	-29.6	-31.7
Malaysia	-7.8	-10.0	-4.9	-25.5	-27.3	-22.3
Philippines	-4.6	-4.4	-4.7	-55.4	-49.0	-46.5
South Korea	-1.2	-2.0	-4.9	-18.4	-20.5	-25.4
Thailand	-5.6	-8.0	-7.9	-37.3	-39.2	-47.0
China	1.3	0.2	0.9	10.9	11.0	13.6

Sources: Deutsche Morgan Grenfell; IMF, *International Financial Statistics*.

not suffer the same kinds of attack and crises that hit Southeast Asia and
South Korea.

Current Account and Foreign Debt Trends

Table 28.1 offers a comparison of the current account balances and net external asset/liability positions of Indonesia, Malaysia, Philippines, South
Korea, Thailand, and China. All of the crisis countries ran chronic current
account deficits (for Thailand, up to 8 percent of GDP) from 1994 to 1996.
During the same period, China consistently achieved current account surpluses of 0.2–1.3 percent of GDP. An even greater difference is seen in the
net external assets. By the end of 1996 the crisis countries had allowed net
external liabilities to grow to enormous levels (from 22 percent of GDP in
Malaysia to 47 percent of GDP in Thailand). In contrast, China has been
building net assets abroad, which by year-end 1996 had reached only
some 14 percent of GDP. China's net external assets, which is the net
value of foreign assets against liabilities consisting of state foreign exchange reserves, gold, and PBOC's net position with international financial institutions, grew to some US$142.6 billion by the end of June 1997.
Official foreign exchange reserves had grown to US$140 billion by the end
of 1997. It is estimated that an amount of foreign exchange equivalent to
official reserves is in the hands of private Chinese individuals and de-
posited in Chinese banks.

China's Prudent Management of Foreign Debt

China has been exceptionally careful in managing its foreign debt and has
a strict system for setting and allocating annual foreign borrowing quotas
(see Chapter 23). As a consequence of this tight foreign debt control, at the
end of 1997 China had healthy ratios for foreign debt principal and inter-

TABLE 28. 2 Indicators of Foreign Debt Risk

(unit: %)

Year	Debt Service Ratio (a)	Liability Ratio (b)	Foreign Debt Ratio (c)
1985	2.8	5.6	53.4
1990	8.5	14.8	87.0
1991	8.0	15.0	87.0
1992	7.3	14.1	90.7
1993	9.7	14.0	94.5
1994	9.1	17.6	77.8
1995	7.3	15.5	69.9
1996	6.7	14.3	75.6
1997	7.3	14.1	63.2
Int'l warning line	20.0	25.0	100.0

Notes: [1] Debt service ratio refers to the ratio of the payment of principal and interest of foreign debts to the foreign exchange receipts from exports and nontrade services of the current year.

[2] Liability ratio refers to the ratio of the balance of foreign debts to the gross national product in the current year.

[3] Foreign debt ratio refers to the ratio of the balance of foreign debts to the foreign exchange receipts from exports and nontrade services in the current year.

Sources: *China Statistical Yearbook* 1997, p. 257; 1997--*Economic Daily*, April 7, 1998.

est repayments to trade and service receipts (7.3 percent), for foreign debt to GDP (14.1 percent), and for foreign debt to foreign exchange receipts from exports and services (63.2 percent). Such ratios are well below accepted international warning lines (Table 28.2).

A major problem for the crisis countries, notably South Korea, was a concentration of foreign debt in short maturities, meaning they were vulnerable to refinancing risk if foreign creditors refused to roll over existing loans and asked for repayment. This is exactly what happened, yet China would not be so vulnerable. The key indicator is the debt service ratio, which, as indicated, was very low at the end of 1997. Table 28.3 shows that throughout the 1990s China has managed its debt service carefully, with the proportion of short-term debt generally remaining below 15 percent of total debt. The outlook for the next five years is also favorable.

China's Closed Capital Market

Another difference between China and the crisis countries—and more important, of the insulation of the Chinese financial system—is experience in the foreign exchange market. The RMB is not freely convertible for capital account transactions. The specific approval of the State Administration of Foreign Exchange is required before any RMB can be sold or

TABLE 28. 3 Balance of China's Foreign Debt

(unit: US$ billion)

Loans	1990	1991	1992	1993	1994	1995	1996
Foreign government loans	8.39	9.51	11.50	14.32	19.59	22.06	22.16
International financial organizations' loans	6.29	7.07	8.42	10.47	12.94	14.80	16.74
Commercial loans	29.18	31.59	35.48	41.08	47.34	52.63	56.94
Others	8.69	12.39	13.93	17.71	12.94	17.11	20.43
Total	52.55	60.56	69.32	83.57	92.81	106.59	116.28

Source: China Statistical Yearbook 1997, p. 257.

bought for foreign currency if the transaction is not for settlement of a trade or service transaction (and even for trade or service settlements, documentary proof is required by the bank before it will buy or sell RMB for foreign currency). Portfolio investment into China—that is, the purchase of RMB-denominated securities—by nonresidents is forbidden. Unless they receive special permission from SAFE, Chinese residents are forbidden to have accounts outside China and to purchase overseas securities. Most Chinese companies must also sell any foreign exchange earned from exports to Chinese banks. Foreign currency loans are not generally allowed to be converted to RMB; they should be used only to settle import transactions. And though foreign direct investment capital may be converted to RMB, this is strictly monitored and subject to approval and verification by the banks. All these restrictions and rules have the effect of insulating the RMB from any speculative pressure, so that its exchange rate versus other currencies—particularly the U.S. dollar—is "managed" by PBOC. Table 28.4 shows what happened to the currencies of the crisis countries during 1997, with devaluations versus the U.S. dollar in some cases reaching nearly 60 percent of previous highs. The RMB (called CNY in international markets) remained essentially stable, with some upward movement during 1997.

US$/RMB Exchange Rate Movement Since 1990

But if the RMB is to be "managed" so, what should the "real" exchange rate be? Figure 28.1 shows the RMB/US$ rate movement from 1990 to June 1998. A dual exchange rate system existed before 1994 in which an "official" rate and a "market" rate existed side by side, with most transactions—particularly for state-owned companies—being settled at the official rate. At approximately RMB 5–6 to US$1, the official rate was an overvaluation, something that benefited Chinese importers. The dual rate system was abolished effective January 1, 1994, at which time the com-

TABLE 28. 4 Devaluations of the Asian Currencies During the Asian Financial Crisis

(unit: each country's currency to one dollar)

	MYR	THB	IDR	KRW	PHP	CNY
Feb. 28, 1997	2.48	25.9	2,398	861	26.3	8.30
Dec. 17, 1997	3.81	46.3	5,445	1,483	40.3	8.28
Change rate (%)	-35	-44	-57	-42	-34	1.9

Source: The Economist, Dec. 20, 1997

FIGURE 28. 1 Trends in RMB / US$ Exchange Rate

US$ to RMB 100

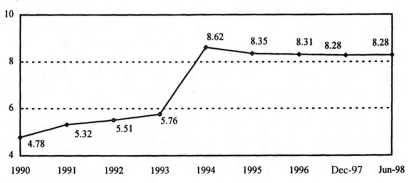

Note: Average annual rate.
Source: IMF, *International Financial Statistics*.

bined rate immediately sank to about RMB 10 to US$1. But after a few months a new level of about RMB 8.5 to US$1 was reached. Since then, the trend was of slight appreciation, reaching a level of some RMB 8.28 to US$1 in early December 1997. The appreciation trend continued through the first half of 1998, but signs of weakening (and market speculation about devaluation) were seen repeatedly in 1998.

The RMB appreciated through 1996 and 1997 because U.S. dollars were in relatively greater supply than RMB in the market. The reasons include (a) China's strong current account surpluses, driven by net exports; (b) a strong inflow of direct foreign investment funds; and (c) the requirement for Chinese companies to sell all foreign exchange to the banks. These factors put upward pressure on the RMB, which the PBOC tried to control, since it did not want to see pronounced appreciation of RMB. What about 1998 and beyond? Many market participants, including the author (Harner), think that the situation described above will change in 1998: that the RMB will begin to devalue moderately and that moderate devaluation could become the trend through the year 2000.

Trends in China's Balance of Payments

The reasons for the pressure to devalue relate to China's overall balance of payment situation. Table 28.5 (based on Figure 28.2) presents balance of payments data from 1990 to 1997. The data show that China's overall balance was strongly positive for six of the eight years. Most of the net credits have come from the capital account, especially from net direct investment (foreign direct investment in China minus Chinese investment abroad), which was US$32 billion, US$34 billion, US$38 billion, and US$42 billion in 1994, 1995, 1996, and 1997 respectively. (Gross foreign investment into China was US$45.3 billion in 1997.) Most observers think the boom in foreign direct investment is largely over and that foreign investment will decline rapidly from 1998 forward. Contracted investment peaked in 1993 and has been falling. It declined from US$73.3 billion in 1996 to US$57.8 billion in 1997. The reasons are (a) most of the companies seeking to invest in China have already done so; (b) the experience of many foreign investors has been disappointing, so that they will not be making new investments; (c) many of the major investors are companies in crisis countries, who will be restructuring and postponing new investment for several years to come; and (d) the Asian debt crisis has frightened many institutional investors (who provide capital to direct investment funds) away from Asia, and they will not return for some time.

Historical Trade Account Volatility

China's trade account was strongly positive in 1995 and 1996, with US$18 billion and US$20 billion in net earnings (exports minus imports) respec-

TABLE 28. 5 Trends in China's Balance of Payments

(unit: US$ million)

	1990	1991	1992	1993	1994	1995	1996	1997
Current account	11,999	13,272	6,401	-11,609	6,908	1,618	7,243	29,717
Trade and Service account	10,668	11,601	4,998	-11,497	7,611	11,957	17,551	40,497
trade account	9,165	8,743	5,183	-10,654	7,290	18,050	19,735	46,222
service account	1,503	2,858	-185	-843	321	-6,093	-1,984	-5,725
Income account	1,055	840	248	-1,284	-1,038	-11,774	-12,437	-15,922
Transfer account	274	831	1,155	1,172	335	1,435	2,129	5,143
Capital account	3,255	8,032	-250	23,474	32,645	38,673	39,966	22,959
Direct investment	2,657	3,453	7,156	23,115	31,787	33,849	38,066	41,674
Portfolio investment	-241	235	-57	3,049	3,543	789	1,744	6,804
Other investment	839	4,344	-7,349	-2,690	-2,685	4,035	156	-25,498
Errors and Omissions	-3,205	-6,767	-8,211	-10,096	-9,100	-17,822	-15,504	-16,952
Overall account	12,047	14,537	-2,060	1,769	30,453	22,469	31,705	35,724
Total reserves minus gold	29,586	43,674	20,620	22,387	52,914	75,377	107,039	141,901

Sources: IMF, *International Financial Statistics* November 1997; 1997 data from *Xinhua Financial News*, June 8, 1998.

FIGURE 28. 2 Trends in China's Balance of Payments

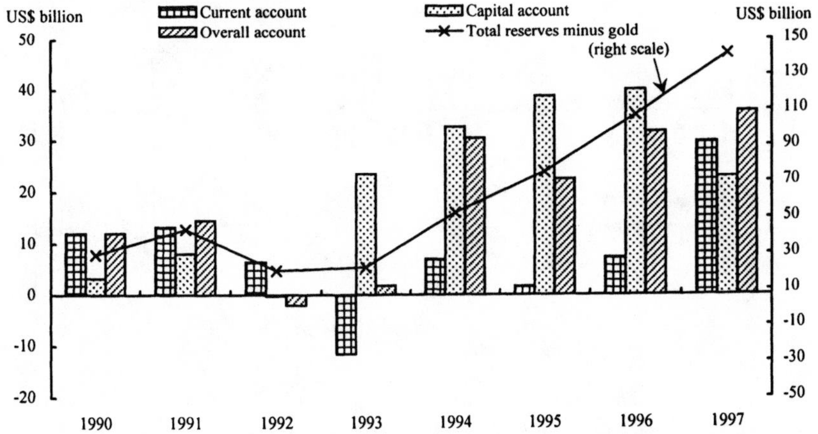

Source: Table 28. 5.

tively. The next surplus, in 1997, was US$46.2 billion. However, we note that China's trade account has been somewhat volatile, as it registered an US$11 billion deficit in 1993. There is concern that exports will suffer from a combination of (a) reduced competitiveness in foreign markets (especially the United States, Japan, and Europe) vis-à-vis the crisis countries (plus Taiwan and Japan), which substantially devalued currencies in 1997; and (b) reduced sales to Southeast Asia itself, a major market for Chinese goods. China's record is one of carefully controlling the trade account to prevent repeated deficits. The deficit in 1993 was followed by the devaluation of the RMB and tight controls on imports, which produced a surplus of US$7.3 billion in 1994.

Balance of Payments "Leakage": Trends Income, Errors and Omissions, and Other Investment Accounts

Three items in the balance of payments are worth additional mention. The first is the income account under the current account (Figure 28.3), which from 1995 to 1997 has been a significant negative factor. This figure is a measure of payments to foreign equity and debt capital and illustrates how much China is now relying on foreign capital for development. The second noteworthy item is errors and omissions (Figure 28.4). This huge figure, US$17.8 billion in 1995, US$15.5 billion in 1996, and US$17.0 billion in 1997, is a measure of the "leakage" from the tight controls of capi-

FIGURE 28. 3 **Changes in Income Account Under Current Account**

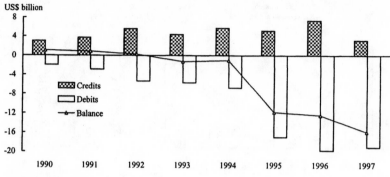

Source: Table 28. 5.

FIGURE 28. 4 **Errors and Omissions in Balance of Payments Accounts**

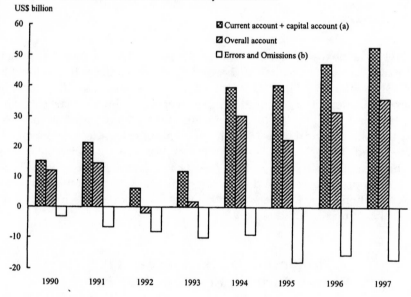

Source: Table 28. 5.

tal into the international market. It is undoubtedly true that the value of overseas investments by Chinese companies and individuals is vastly larger than the US$2 billion carried in the statistics for each 1995 and 1996 and the US$2.6 billion recorded for 1997. It is known that money from China has played a huge role in stock market and property speculation in Hong Kong (and even in the United States), and much of this capital has evaded official channels or monitoring. Hence, it appears as errors and omissions. In 1997 and 1998 the investment climate in China cooled dramatically, and many Chinese began to believe that the Asian financial crisis might also affect them. This kind of sentiment could be expected to increase the amount of capital leaving China through unofficial channels.

A third remarkable figure in the 1997 balance of payments data is the huge US$25.5 billion negative figure under "other investment" in the capital account. Since the figure appeared, economists have been trying to understand it. Little help has been given by PBOC. It seems to reflect increases in foreign assets of Chinese commercial banks as a consequence of (1) PRC enterprises stopping the conversion of foreign currency earned from exports or obtained from other sources to RMB, as would normally be required by PBOC regulations, and keeping these funds in the banks, and (2) Chinese individuals converting RMB holdings to foreign currency—overtly or through the black market—and depositing the proceeds into Chinese banks. Both activities would reflect a lack of confidence in the RMB.

Such behavior—combined with actual capital flight—caused foreign reserves to register a US$400 million decrease in June 1998 and to rise by a negligible US$600 million during the first six months of 1998, notwithstanding a strong reported trade surplus and substantial foreign direct investment inflows during the period. This all shows that Chinese balance of payments figures are "soft" and that China's capital account is not really as "closed" as the government would hope.

—Harner

29

Hong Kong and Taiwan

Economic Relations
Among the "Three Chinas"

The Repatriation of Hong Kong

On July 1, 1997, the ceremony for the handover of Hong Kong to China (Hong Kong's "return to the motherland," or *Xianggang huigui*) was held, and the last British governor, Mr. Chris Patton, regrettably departed. Patton's tenure was that of a lame duck in two senses. When Patton arrived five years earlier, the basic terms for the return of Hong Kong had already been agreed, and there was little he could do in this regard. In this context, the several issues he raised, and particularly his democratic reform proposals, drew strident protests and opposition from China, in the end producing no results. Moreover, in the spring 1997 British elections the Conservative government led by John Major, which had appointed Patton, was defeated. This development dashed Patton's hopes that his performance as governor would underpin his comeback in British politics. Thus, although Patton might have been expected to play a pivotal role in the Hong Kong repatriation drama, his part was that of a politician's reluctant withdrawal into retirement.

The island of Hong Kong was ceded to Britain after the Opium War of 1842. After the Second Opium War in 1860 the southern tip of the Kowloon Peninsula (Kowloon City) was ceded. In 1898 the New Territories were "leased" for a period of ninety-nine years. That lease expired in 1997. And whereas it can be said there was a legal requirement to return the leased New Territories to China, no such obligation existed as to Hong Kong and the Kowloon Peninsula. However, the ceded territory and leased territory had long since become economically indivisible. They were organic parts of a whole, so it was practically impossible that Britain should control one while losing control over the other. Thus, the

1985 Joint Sino-British Declaration, which established a policy of complete repatriation, was the natural development. After repatriation, Tung Qihua became the first executive of the Hong Kong Special Administrative Region (SAR), founded on the principles of "one country, two systems" (*yiguoliangzhi*) and "Hong Kong people governing Hong Kong" (*gangrenzhigang*).

Hong Kong's Indigenous Exports and Reexports

Hong Kong performs six key functions. It is a world-class center of financial, trade, transport, tourism, and information services and of light industry. Let us focus here on trade. Figure 29.1 graphs local exports, reexports, and ratio of reexports to local exports (Table 29.1). In the 1990s the ratio of reexports to local exports has risen to 5.6 times, occupying an 85 percent share of total exports.

Figure 29.2 presents the results of a study into the sources and destinations of reexport goods. The "place of origin" of slightly more than 50 percent of export goods is China, followed by Japan, Taiwan, and the United States. And where do reexported goods go? In 1996, 35 percent were "destined for China." Largest destinations thereafter were the United States, Japan, and Germany.

What can we deduce about statistics that give China as both the "place of origin" and the "place of destination"? This riddle is solved by looking at Figure 29.3. Here are cases where Hong Kong capital has moved production facilities to the mainland, and where these facilities are now engaged in "consignment processing." A third country is using Hong Kong as a base from which raw materials are reexported into China. After these raw materials are processed on a consignment basis in China, Hong Kong serves as a reexport base to export them to the third country. In short, for a large volume of trade, goods enter China through the southern window of Hong Kong and, after processing, are exported through Hong Kong.

Within local exports from Hong Kong to China, consignment processing goods occupy more than 40 percent. Within local exports from China to Hong Kong, such goods exceed 70 percent. In reexports from China to Hong Kong, they exceed 80 percent (Table 29.2).

These statistics show clearly that under the reform and liberalization policy the Chinese economy has taken full advantage of Hong Kong's function as a connecting base to source capital, technology, and management know-how, as well as raw materials on beneficial terms, and to expand exports using consignment processing as a mainstay. Table 29.3 provides figures for the share of Chinese products in Hong Kong's reexports. On a value basis the largest items were apparel at HK$85.5 billion and electrical machinery at HK$52.3 billion.

FIGURE 29. 1 Hong Kong's Exports and Reexports

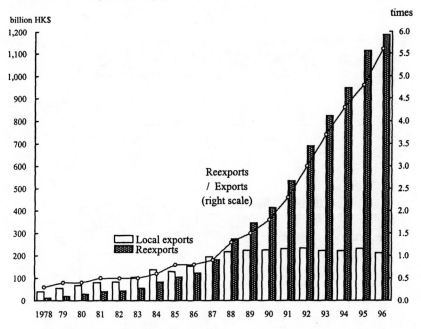

Source: Table 29. 1.

TABLE 29. 1 Hong Kong's Exports and Reexports

(unit: million HK $)

Year	Total Exports (a)	Local Exports (b)	Reexports (c)	(c) / (a) %	(c) / (b) times
1978	53,908	40,711	13,197	24.5	0.3
1979	75,934	55,912	20,022	26.4	0.4
1980	98,243	68,171	30,072	30.6	0.4
1981	122,162	80,423	41,739	34.2	0.5
1982	127,385	83,032	44,353	34.8	0.5
1983	160,699	104,405	56,294	35.0	0.5
1984	221,440	137,936	83,504	37.7	0.6
1985	235,152	129,882	105,270	44.8	0.8
1986	276,529	153,983	122,546	44.3	0.8
1987	378,034	195,254	182,780	48.4	0.9
1988	493,069	217,664	275,405	55.9	1.3
1989	570,509	224,104	346,405	60.7	1.5
1990	639,872	225,875	413,997	64.7	1.8
1991	765,886	231,045	534,841	69.8	2.3
1992	924,952	234,123	690,829	74.7	3.0
1993	1,046,251	223,027	823,224	78.7	3.7
1994	1,170,013	222,092	947,921	81.0	4.3
1995	1,344,127	231,657	1,112,470	82.8	4.8
1996	1,397,918	212,160	1,185,758	84.8	5.6

Source: Hong Kong Trade Statistics (each year).

FIGURE 29. 2 Original Regions and Destinations of Hong Kong's Reexports
〖 Original regions 〗

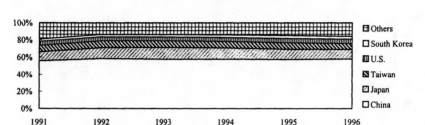

〖 Destination 〗

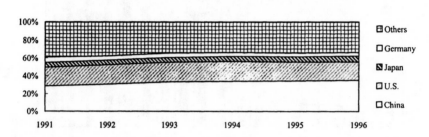

Source: Government Census and Statistics Dept., *Hong Kong Annual Digest of Statistics* 1996.

Taiwan's Dependence on China

Here let us broaden our view slightly to include the Taiwan economy in Hong Kong–China relations. At the top of Figure 29.4 we see the trend of Hong Kong's exports to Taiwan and, within this figure, the proportionate weight of products reexported from the Chinese mainland. In recent years the share of reexports from the mainland has been near 40 percent. In the bottom part of Figure 29.4 we see the trends in Hong Kong's imports from Taiwan and, within this figure, the proportionate weight of products reexported to the mainland. The share within reexports is more than 60 percent.

Against Hong Kong's exports to Taiwan in 1996 of US$4.0 billion, imports from Taiwan were US$16.0 billion, fourfold greater. In other words, from Taiwan's perspective, Hong Kong (mainland China) as a source of imports is not of great importance, whereas Hong Kong (mainland China) as an export market now is of a serious size.

Table 29.4 looks at the dependency of Taiwan on trade with China and, likewise, that of China with Taiwan. From the left column we see that in the middle of the 1990s the degree of Taiwan's dependency on exports to China was 8–9 percent. At the same time, dependency on imports from

FIGURE 29. 3 Status of Hong Kong Trade in China's Processing Trade, 1995

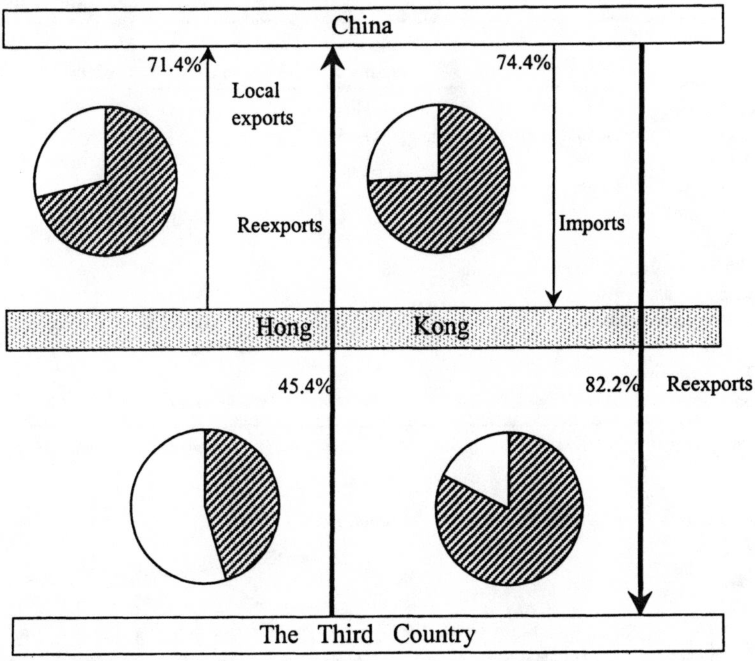

China

71.4%   Local exports   74.4%

Reexports   Imports

Hong   Kong

45.4%   82.2%   Reexports

The Third Country

Source: Table 29. 2.

TABLE 29. 2 Position of China-Directed Processing Trade in Hong Kong Total Trade

(unit: million HK$)

	1990	*1991*	*1992*	*1993*	*1994*	*1995*
China-directed local exports	36,418	40,369	44,271	45,141	41,959	43,890
	79.0%	76.5%	74.3%	74.0%	71.4%	71.4%
China-directed share of reexports	55,496	73,562	97,368	115,037	139,221	173,722
	50.3%	48.2%	46.2%	42.1%	43.3%	45.4%
China-source share of imports	145,103	197,384	254,013	295,203	354,912	399,567
	61.8%	67.6%	72.1%	73.8%	75.9%	74.4%
China-products share of reexports	n.a.	221,450	299,833	364,536	422,544	492,461
		74.1%	78.3%	80.8%	82.0%	82.2%

Source: Government Census and Statistics Dept., *Hong Kong Annual Digest of Statistics*, 1996.

TABLE 29. 3 Ratio of Chinese Products in Reexports from Hong Kong, 1995

(unit: million HK$)

Goods	Volume of Reexports	Of Which: Made in China	Share of Products Made in China (%)
Apparel	90,951	88,531	97.3
Electronic equipment and electrical machinery	114,628	52,394	45.7
Textiles	92,840	41,596	44.8
Baby buggy, toys, games, and sporting goods	83,117	80,615	97.0
Footwear	60,107	58,564	97.3
Radio, television, and communications equipment and apparatus	60,042	32,991	54.9
Travel supplies, gloves	35,010	32,597	93.1
Watches	33,543	14,648	43.7
Office, accounting, and computing machinery	37,220	21,231	57.0

Source: Government Census and Statistics Dept., *Hong Kong Annual Digest of Statistics* 1996.

FIGURE 29. 4 Share of Hong Kong-Taiwan Trade in China's Reexports

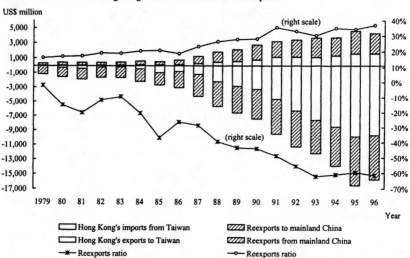

Source: *Cross-Straits Economic Statistics Monthly*, June 1996.

China was about 1.5 percent. The average for two-way trade was slightly more than 5 percent. This calculation is based on statistics from the Taiwan Ministry of Finance. Because of the political sensitivity of dependency on trade with the mainland, these figures understate the reality. Chinese figures for Taiwan-China trade give a value twice as high, that is, in the middle of the 1990s Taiwan's dependency on exports to China was slightly less than 20 percent, whereas dependency on imports from China

TABLE 29. 4 Degree of China-Taiwan Mutual Trade Dependency

	Degree of Taiwan's Dependence on Trade with China [1]			Degree of China's Dependence on Trade with Taiwan [2]		
	Export	Import	Trade	Export	Import	Trade
1981	1.70	0.35	1.05	0.34	1.75	1.04
1982	0.88	0.44	0.68	0.38	1.01	0.67
1983	0.63	0.44	0.55	0.40	0.74	0.67
1984	1.40	0.58	1.06	0.49	1.55	1.03
1985	3.21	0.58	2.17	0.42	2.34	1.58
1986	2.04	0.60	1.49	0.47	1.89	1.29
1987	2.28	0.83	1.71	0.73	2.84	1.83
1988	3.70	0.96	2.47	1.01	4.06	2.65
1989	4.38	1.12	2.94	1.12	4.90	3.12
1990	4.88	1.40	3.32	1.23	6.14	3.50
1991	6.10	1.79	4.16	1.57	7.32	4.27
1992	7.72	1.55	4.83	1.32	7.80	4.47
1993	8.93	1.43	5.36	1.20	7.30	4.44
1994	9.15	1.51	5.50	1.07	7.36	4.14
1995	8.85	1.52	5.32	1.06	7.48	4.08
1996	8.35	1.56	5.20	1.05	7.00	3.90

Notes: [1] Degree of Taiwan's export and import dependence on China = Taiwan's exports to and imports from China / Taiwan's total volume of exports and imports.

[2] Degree of China's export and import dependence on Taiwan = China's exports to and imports from Taiwan / China's total volume of exports and imports.

Source: *Cross-Straits Economic Statistics Monthly*, June 1997 (original data from Hong Kong customs statistics, Taiwan Ministry of Finance import-export trade statistics, Chinese customs statistics).

was 3–4 percent. The average for two-way trade was somewhat more than 10 percent. The author (Yabuki) believes this approximates reality.

Looking at the right column of Table 29.4 we see that China's dependency of exports to Taiwan was slightly more than 1 percent, whereas that for imports from Taiwan was 7 percent. The average for two-way trade was roughly 4 percent. This is based on Chinese customs statistics.

Comparing the two sets of statistics we can appreciate the relative weight of importance of "Taiwan for China" and "China for Taiwan." Whereas Taiwan is apprehensive about its rapidly rising dependency on exports to China, China would like to see this dependency grow.

Direct Investment from Taiwan and Hong Kong in China

Economic exchange has a tendency to develop from trade to investment. Table 29.5 juxtaposes the shares of Taiwan and Hong Kong as sources of foreign direct investment in China. Putting aside the leading indicator of contracted investment, let us look at the hard numbers of actual investment. It is relatively well known that from the time China began to accept foreign investment in 1979 until the end of 1996 Hong Kong and Macao carried out aggregate investment amounting to US$101.8 billion. The Tai-

TABLE 29. 5 China's Receipt of Direct Investment from Hong Kong and Taiwan

Country/ Region	No. of Cases (case)	(%)	Value of Contracts (bil. US$)	(%)	Actual Investment Value (bil. US$)	(%)
Hong Kong, Macao	168,318	59.4	269.8	54.4	101.8	58.2
Taiwan	34,964	12.3	34.5	7.0	14.9	8.5
U.S.	22,240	7.8	35.2	7.1	14.3	8.2
Japan	14,991	5.3	26.4	5.3	14.2	8.1
Singapore	6,693	2.4	23.6	4.8	6.2	3.5
South Korea	8,116	2.9	11.0	2.2	3.6	2.1
England	1,798	0.6	11.8	2.4	3.5	2.0
Germany	1,500	0.5	5.4	1.1	1.7	1.0
Others	24,724	8.7	78.4	15.8	14.7	8.4
Total	283,344	100.0	496.1	100.0	174.9	100.0

Note: Case and value is cumulative amount from 1979 to 1996.
Source: *Cross-Straits Economic Statistics Monthly*, June 1997 (original data from MOFTEC).

wan government's acceptance of direct investment in China dates only from the 1990s, and as such may be considered recent, but by 1996 it had already reached US$14.9 billion, putting Taiwan ahead of the United States and Japan. Looking at the shares of the value of foreign investment received by China, Hong Kong and Macao account for slightly less than 60 percent, whereas Taiwan, the United States, and Japan are each 8–9 percent.

The large share claimed by Hong Kong and Macao, apart from local capital, is attributable to the use of "Hong Kong resident companies" capitalized for political reasons by interests from ASEAN countries and Taiwan to invest in China. This factor is huge. Rather more astonishing is the speed with which Taiwan's investment in the mainland is increasing. By scale of GNP, Taiwan is much smaller than the United States or Japan, but in the scale of investment in China, it is bigger than the United States or Japan. This shows irrefutably the strength of the complementary economic relationship between the Taiwan and Chinese economies. The image of China held by Taiwanese is complex, but in the limited aspect of economics, the degree of mutual dependency is rising and broadening daily.

According to data compiled in the *China Foreign Economic Yearbook* 1996, 50 percent of the direct investment from Hong Kong went to Guangdong, 10 percent to Fujian. In contrast, Taiwan invested 35 percent each in Guangdong and Fujian. Most residents of Taiwan—the native Taiwanese—are descendants of immigrants from the southern part of Fujian province. In business, then, half of investment has gone to Guangdong province and half to the ancestral home. Taiwan's investment in Shanghai, Jiangsu, and other parts of the Yangtze River Delta region is also greater than Hong Kong's. We may postulate that this is in part a reflection of the close ties maintained with Shanghai and the surrounding region by Taiwan's mainlanders—residents who fled to Taiwan with the Kuomintang government in 1948–1950—sometimes referred to as the Jiangsu-Zhejiang *zaibastu*. However, much, if not most, of the investment—particularly in such places as Kunshan in Jiangsu province—is by native Taiwanese companies and entrepreneurs.

—Yabuki

30

U.S.-China Relations

Realpolitik Between "Equal" Powers

Frequent Public Sparring Between U.S. and PRC Leaders

China's sense of its own importance and uniqueness—as the greatest of the ancient civilizations, as the world's most populous country, as the fastest growing economy in Asia—and the traditional sense of hierarchy in the Chinese mind combine to cause Chinese leaders to feel that only one country in the world, the United States—the richest and largest country in the West—is truly on the same level in terms of national stature and prestige. (Is the same view held, we are sometimes compelled to ask, by the United States with respect to China?) In this sense, from the Chinese perspective, across the globe only China and the United States are "equals." This appreciation for the United States as an equal means that Chinese leaders tend to pay particular attention to opinions expressed by U.S. leaders. It does not mean, however, that Chinese leaders feel that they should defer in any way to the United States. On the contrary, it is often observed that Chinese leaders—speaking directly or through propaganda—consider it particularly important to refute U.S. opinions, to exaggerate offense and injury caused by U.S. words and actions, and otherwise to publicly highlight and accentuate the differences between U.S. and Chinese views. Indeed, it is observed that Chinese leaders find refuting and challenging the United States as the most face-enhancing way to defend and enhance their own stature and authority. (Again, one can point to many cases of U.S. leaders seeking the same kind of advantage at the expense of China.)

The willingness—indeed inclination—of Chinese and U.S. leaders to publicly challenge and refute each other means that Chinese-U.S. relations—more than perhaps any other bilateral relationship for either country—are buffeted by public disputes and controversies. Some of these disputes are serious, some are simply politics being played by either side to

265

satisfy domestic political interests. On the whole, however, it is clear that leaders in China and the United States are acutely aware that there are important benefits to their countries in maintaining a positive and constructive relationship and that there would be serious dangers in allowing the relationship to become hostile.

An Emerging "Strategic Partnership"?

As was evidenced in the state visit of Jiang Zemin to the United States in October 1997, in which the term *strategic partnership* was officially used, and in the state visit of U.S. Pres. Bill Clinton in June 1998, both sides perceive important national interests being served by close cooperation. And two gestures in specific, China's release of dissident Wei Jingsheng after the conclusion of Jiang's trip, and its release of dissident Wang Dan in advance of President Clinton's visit, can be seen as designed to encourage reciprocal actions (such as granting permanent most-favored-nation status) by the United States. In 1998 China's new leadership team, highly confident in itself and its plans, and sure of what it wants, presents a worthy counterpart to the U.S. Clinton administration.

For both sides, as befitting real powers, what has been, what is, and what will continue to be the essence of the relationship is pure national interests—and the mode of communication is the language of realpolitik. As indicated, the interests of China and the United States are shared in many areas, yet they are not shared equally. Benefits and costs, opportunities and dangers are viewed differently by both sides. The essence of diplomacy and realpolitik is that each side measures and judges what it wants and what it has that the other side wants, and, during negotiations, concessions are given and taken as each side attempts to advance its respective interests. Of course, each side attempts to give as little and to gain as much as possible in this exchange. Also it tries to disguise weaknesses (particularly dependence on or vulnerability to the other party) and to emphasize its strengths (particularly its attractiveness and importance for the other side). Of course, in the end, for any real progress there must be a win-win result.

Where do we find the most fundamental common national interests between China and the United States? Without a doubt, they are (1) economics and trade, and (2) security issues and Taiwan.

PRC-U.S. Economic and Trade Relations: China the Big Winner

Figure 30.1 shows figures for merchandise trade between the U.S. and China from 1986 to 1997, according to U.S. Department of Commerce sta-

FIGURE 30. 1 Trends in Total U.S. Trade and Trade Deficits with China

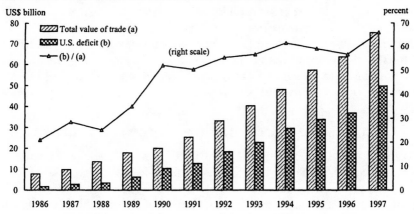

Source: U.S. Department of Commerce.

tistics. During this decade, total trade increased from less than US$10 billion to more than US$75 billion. More important, China's exports to the United States have exploded to more than US$62.5 billion, meaning that the U.S. market has become a critical source of foreign exchange earnings.

There are huge discrepancies between Chinese and U.S. statistics for trade, as seen in Table 30.1. Whereas the U.S. deficit figure in 1997 is US$49.7 billion, China shows a deficit of only US$16.4 billion. U.S. customs statistics count, as "China-origin" goods, those shipped directly from China as well as Chinese goods reexported from third countries or

TABLE 30. 1 Statistical Gap in Chinese and U.S. Statistics for Deficits in Trade

(unit: US$ billion)

Year	U.S. imports		U.S. exports		Disparity	
	Chinese Statistics (a)	U.S. Statistics (b)	Chinese Statistics (c)	U.S. Statistics (d)	Chinese Statistics (c) - (a)	U.S. Statistics (d) - (b)
1986	2.6	4.7	4.7	3.1	2.1	-1.6
1987	3.0	6.3	4.8	3.5	1.8	-2.8
1988	3.4	8.5	6.7	5.1	3.3	-3.4
1989	4.4	12.0	7.9	5.8	3.5	-6.2
1990	5.2	15.2	6.6	4.8	1.4	-10.4
1991	6.2	19.0	8.0	6.3	1.8	-12.7
1992	8.6	25.7	9.0	7.4	0.4	-18.3
1993	17.0	31.5	10.7	8.7	-6.3	-22.8
1994	21.5	38.8	14.0	9.2	-7.5	-29.6
1995	24.7	45.5	16.1	11.8	-8.6	-33.8
1996	26.7	51.5	16.2	12.0	-10.5	-39.5
1997	32.7	62.5	16.3	12.8	-16.4	-49.7

Sources: China's statistics from MOFTEC; U.S. statistics from U.S. Department of Commerce.

regions like Hong Kong. China counts as exports to the United States only those goods that are shipped directly. There are other discrepancies, some no doubt justifiable from a technical standpoint for both countries. But one point must be clear: From a negotiating standpoint it is clearly in China's interest to minimize the appearance of dependency on the U.S. market, because by some measures that dependency—meaning the importance of the U.S. market—is massive.

China's Huge Dependency on the U.S. Market

According to statistics from the Ministry of Foreign Trade and Economic Cooperation (MOFTEC), total Chinese exports in 1997 were US$182.7 billion. Exports to the United States, at US$32.7 billion, constituted 18 percent of total exports. This is a large share, but still less than exports to Hong Kong and Japan. The picture changes dramatically if we look at a figure (based on U.S. statistics and found in the IMF *Direction of Trade Statistics Yearbook*) of US$62.5 billion for U.S. imports from China and, from this, calculate the share of China's total exports (Figure 30.2). We find that the U.S. share is 34 percent, a striking level of Chinese dependency on and vulnerability to the U.S. market.

Against the huge importance of the United States as a market and source of foreign exchange earnings, China relies on the United States for relatively few of its imports. Of total Chinese global imports in 1997 of US$142.4 billion (MOFTEC figures), imports from the United States according to U.S. figures were only US$12.8 billion, or 9 percent. Even using the bigger Chinese import figures, the U.S. share comes to only 11.4 percent of China's total.

FIGURE 30. 2 Share of U.S. Trade in Chinese Exports and Imports

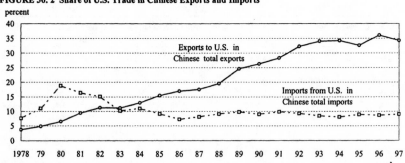

Source: China Foreign Economic Statistics Yearbook 1995-1996, 1997-1998; IMF, *Direction of Trade Statistics Yearbook.*

U.S. Companies' Approach:
Investment, Not Trade

Looking at trade and economic relations from the U.S. side, the imbalance in relative importance is evident. In 1997, out of total U.S. global exports of US$678 billion, exports to China accounted for a mere 1.9 percent. China accounted for 7.1 percent of U.S. global imports, big but not huge (Figure 30.3). In reality, except for Boeing, Motorola, and—depending upon the year—U.S. fertilizer, cotton, vegetable oil, or grain producers, the China market is still of negligible importance for the United States.

Table 30.2 presents U.S. Department of Commerce statistics for trade with China in 1997. The top U.S. exports to China were aircraft, fertilizer, telecommunications equipment, cotton, and vegetable oil, constituting, re-

FIGURE 30. 3 Share of Chinese Trade in U.S. Exports and Imports

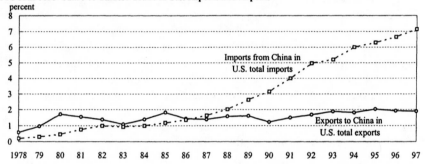

Source: *China Foreign Economic Statistics Yearbook* 1995-1996, 1997-1998; IMF, *Direction of Trade Statistics Yearbook*.

TABLE 30. 2 The Ten Largest U.S. Export and U.S. Import Categories with China

(unit: US$ millions)

	1997 U.S. Exports			1997 U.S. Imports		
		amount	% of world		amount	% of world
Total		$12,805	1.9%	Total	$62,552	7.2%
1	Aircraft	2,122	5.2	1 Toys, etc.	9,922	57.1
2	Fertilizer	1,049	34.1	2 Footwear	7,415	52.9
3	Telecom. equipment	629	2.8	3 Apparel--women's	2,458	20.9
4	Cotton	580	21.0	4 Telecom. equipment	2,206	11.6
5	Vegetable oil	413	5.2	5 Computers and peripherals	2,068	4.6
6	Scientific instruments	375	2.2	6 Computer parts	2,030	8.0
7	Specialized equipment	295	2.6	7 Stereos	1,943	33.8
8	Engineering equipment	293	3.0	8 Luggage	1,928	50.2
9	Semiconductors	258	0.6	9 Apparel--textile fabric	1,857	13.5
10	Heating/cooling equip.	242	3.5	10 Plastic goods	1,716	30.2

Source: Bureau of the Census, U.S. Department of Commerce.

spectively, 5.2 percent, 34.1 percent, 2.8 percent, 21.0 percent, and 5.2 percent of U.S. global exports of these products. The numbers for sales of other products, particularly in global perspective, are unimpressive. (This is in contrast to the huge importance of the United States for many categories of Chinese exports.)

Of course, China could be a bigger market, especially in areas like computer software, entertainment (films and music), and media. In these areas, however, for protectionist and political reasons Chinese laws keep out foreign investment, control, and direct distribution, on the one hand, and are lax at preventing intellectual property piracy on the other.

Despite periodic, politically inspired "noise," neither the trade imbalance nor lax intellectual property protection is actually a major political or economic problem between the United States and China. In general, U.S. companies that want to be active in China are doing so through direct investment. The biggest U.S. companies—General Motors, Ford, DuPont, IBM, General Electric, and Procter and Gamble—are significant investors in manufacturing facilities, usually targeting the domestic market. And even though the U.S. government continues to claim to be exerting strenuous efforts to open China's market to U.S. exports, the reality is that most Chinese barriers to importing have been removed, and the remaining ones (like high tariffs and restrictions on automobiles) are accepted by U.S. officials as being justified by China's level of development (the "infant industry" argument) and in any event will be phased out as a condition for China's entering the WTO.

U.S.-PRC Security Relations:
Cooperation on Korea and Japan

When U.S. officials consider the potential benefits or dangers of relations with China, they think first and foremost of security issues. A positive rather than neutral or negative role for China in maintaining stability in East Asia is what is desired. The key areas of concern are Korea, U.S.-Japanese security relations, and, of course, the exceptionally complex problem of Taiwan.

With respect to Korea, in the likely event that reunification becomes a possibility due to North Korea's collapse, China and the United States will have to agree on a security structure for a united country: total foreign troop withdrawal, limited U.S. security role, joint U.S.-Chinese "protection," Korean "neutrality," or some other arrangement. A positive and constructive Chinese role will be essential. This role is actually being seen in the Four Part Talks being held in Geneva. The United States desires—and to a large extent is seeing—the same constructive Chinese attitude with respect to the maintenance of the U.S.-Japan security treaty, which the United States still considers essential for East Asian stability.

The Key Bilateral Issue: Taiwan

China says it wants the United States to stop interfering in its internal affairs—meaning the United States should stay out of China's way as it tries to solve the "Taiwan problem" (Table 30.3). China claims that in the series of U.S.-PRC communiqués covering relations the United States undertook to sever all ties with Taiwan and to reduce sales of advanced arms to Taiwan. The United States has its own interpretation of its rights and obligations under the communiqués as well as under the U.S.-Taiwan Relations Act, which was passed in April 1979 after the United States and China normalized diplomatic relations and the United States severed diplomatic relations with the government on Taiwan. Beijing protested a violation of agreements in the mid-1980s when the United States sold advanced fighter aircraft to Taiwan. It reacted violently with live-missile exercises in the Taiwan Strait (Map 30.1) in March 1996, claiming that the U.S. granting of a visa for a personal U.S. visit by Taiwan President Lee Teng-hui was encouraging Taiwan independence. In reality, the missile tests were designed to frighten the Taiwan electorate into rejecting outwardly proindependence candidates in national elections. The gambit succeeded but provoked an unwelcome dispatch of U.S. aircraft carriers (one on them, ironically, the USS *Independence*) to the Taiwan Strait.

Although claiming to oppose U.S. interference, China wants the United States to put pressure on Taiwan to negotiate reunification. By agreeing to the "three no's" policy toward Taiwan—no recognition of "one China, one Taiwan," no backing for Taiwan independence, no support for Taiwan rejoining the United Nations—the United States is cooperating with China. The quid pro quo for this U.S. cooperation is that China must not use force to pressure Taiwan into reunification. It is another injury to Chinese pride and a cause of great umbrage, but the reality is that in any settlement of the Taiwan question, the United States will be a participant.

—Harner

TABLE 30. 3 Jiang Zemin's Eight-Point Proposal to Taiwan, January 30, 1995

1. [Taiwan must] uphold the "One China" principle.
2. China will not object to the development of Taiwan's people-to-people economic and cultural relations with foreign countries. China opposes expansion of Taiwan's international activities aimed at independence.
3. Pursue peaceful negotiations aimed at unification. Representatives of all political parties and groups may participate in the negotiations.
4. Strive for unification through peaceful means. [China's] refusal to disavow resort to force is not directed against Taiwan compatriots, but rather against the foreign interests plotting "Taiwan independence."
5. The legitimate rights of Taiwanese enterprises will be protected. Free, direct communications by air, sea, and telecommunications should be realized as soon as possible.
6. [The Chinese mainland and Taiwan] should perpetuate and develop the superior traditions of Chinese culture together.
7. [China] welcomes visits from the people of Taiwan. We also hope to be able to accept the invitations from the Taiwan side to visit Taiwan.
8. The Chinese people should resolve their own problems. There is no reason to take matters into international forum.

Source: People's Daily, January 31, 1995.

MAP 30.1 Military Exercises Conducted Around Taiwan in March 1996

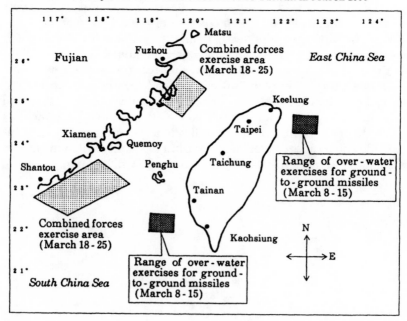

31

Japan-China Relations

An Ambivalent Relationship Between Neighboring Countries

Trends in Japan-China Trade

Japan-China diplomatic relations were normalized in 1972. During the 1970s, Japan-China annual exports and imports were about US$2 billion each way, or a combined two-way figure of US$4 billion. In 1997, Japan's exports to China totaled US$21.8 billion, imports from China US$42.1 billion, for a two-way total of some US$63.9 billion. This is a some sixteenfold increase in twenty-six years. Looking at the lower panel of Figure 31.1 we see that until the early 1980s the trade was roughly balanced. This is because China's orientation was to control trade by using foreign exchange earned from goods exports to Japan to purchase Japanese industrial products. In the mid-1980s there occurred in China a "reform leap import boom," during which China registered a deficit. However, during the 1990s Japan has had a consistent import surplus. As we will observe in the next section, this is because China has become a production base for Japan for agricultural products and light industrial manufactures.

We see in Figure 31.2 that China's share of Japan's trade has fairly consistently increased, reaching 8.9 percent in 1997. What, then, is Japan's share of China's trade? It was in the 20–25 percent range from the mid-1970s to the mid-1980s, that is, from China's perspective one-fourth of all trade was with Japan. In 1984–1985 an unprecedented export boom (in such products as automobiles and household appliances) occurred, and the reaction in 1986–1987 was a year-on-year decline in growth rate. Before full recovery, the aftereffects of the Tiananmen Incident were felt, and the growth rate become negative again. Thus, from 1987 to 1992 the share of Japan-China trade in China's total trade dropped below the 20 percent level. However, in 1993–1997 the 20 percent level was exceeded again.

273

FIGURE 31.1 Trends in Japan - China Trade

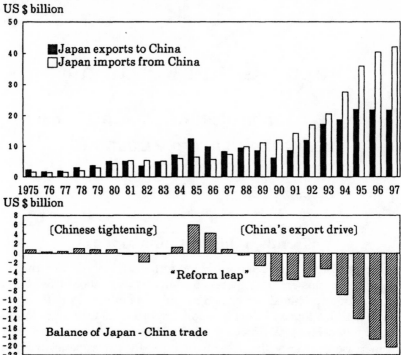

Source: MOF, *Ministry of Finance Customs Statistics*, various issues.

Commodity Composition of Japan-China Trade

The upper panel of Figure 31.3 presents the general categories of Japan's exports to China based upon Japanese government statistics. In the 1970s there were times when steel occupied more than 50 percent, but in recent years it has fallen to about 10 percent. In juxtaposition to steel's decline, we see remarkable growth in general machinery and electrical machinery. In recent years these two categories of machinery and equipment have taken up some 50 percent of the total. Transportation equipment generally refers to trucks and automobiles. The graph also illustrates a perspective on the automobile smuggling incident of the mid-1980s, when Hainan Island was used as a base. In the second half of the 1970s, chemical products (largely chemical fertilizer) began to become a larger share. Afterward, China's domestic chemical fertilizer plants were built, and their production began to substitute for imports.

FIGURE 31.2 Trends in Japan-China Trade

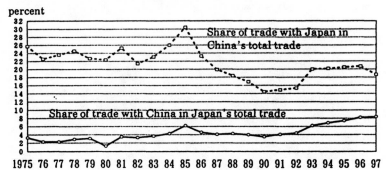

percent

Sources: China Foreign Economic Statistics 1979–1991; China Statistical Yearbook 1992–1998.

The lower panel of Figure 31.3 presents the composition of Japan's imports from China. Through the first half of the 1980s the largest share, sometimes more than 50 percent, was taken by petroleum and petroleum products. Afterward, as the Daqing oil field began to show signs of depletion and lower-cost supplies became available from the Middle East, oil imports from China drastically declined. In recent years it has occupied only some 5 percent.

Substituting for oil, and registering a remarkable increase, has been textile products, in 1996 some 30 percent of the total. Textiles are an export product in which China has traditionally been competitive. However, in recent years a new impetus has been added for the growth of textile products. This is the success in producing products welcomed in the Japanese market through consignment processing and production in joint venture enterprises based on designs, capital, and technology supplied from Japan. The same generalization is applicable to food products. Formerly Japan was simply importing agricultural products in the form of raw materials. In recent years companies have appeared that are importing Japanese sake, miso, and soy sauces processed in China. From fried eels, to string beans, to tofu, the share of Chinese foods on Japanese dinner tables is increasing. Whether it be food products or textile products, as a result of enhanced processing in China the share of raw materials in exports has declined.

In recent years, with the increased commissioning of FIEs, the share of machinery and equipment in exported goods has been increasing. Such products as standard-feature TVs have become a typical export of China.

FIGURE 31.3   Trends in the Commodity Composition of Japan

percent   (Japan's exports to China)

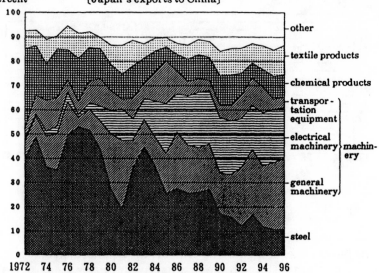

percent   (Japan's imports from China)

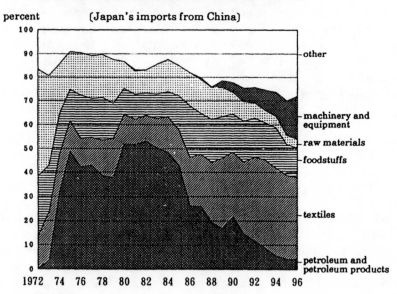

Note: Composition basis is U.S. dollar value.
Source: JETRO, *White Paper on International Trade*, each year.

Direct Investment of Japan and Other Countries in China

Foreign investment is divided into securities investment (indirect investment) and direct investment. The former involves taking ownership of stocks and other securities with a view to earning dividends and trading profits, whereas the latter is aimed at direct operation of an enterprise. Figure 31.4 presents trends in Japanese direct investment in China. The line graph plots the number of investment cases by investment contracts signed. It is apparent that there was a boom in investment in China from 1992 to 1995. During this period the contracted value of investments rises in parallel with number of cases, but finally in 1996 there is a decline. In 1997 a turning point is reached as the leading indicator of contracted investment (US$3.4 billion) falls substantially below actual investment (US$4.3 billion) for the first time. The number of new cases fell to 1,402. This decline in contracted investment is typical, and the same pattern is seen with other major investors. In 1996 Japanese actual aggregate investment reached US$14.2 billion. This was about the same level as the United States and slightly below the figure of US$14.4 billion for Taiwan.

FIGURE 31.4 Trends in Japanese Direct Investment in China

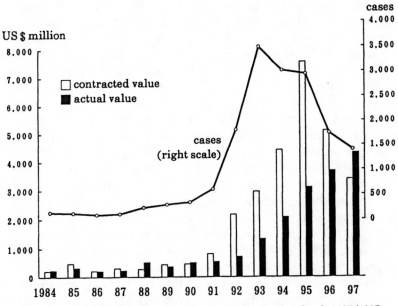

Source: MOFTEC, *Foreign Economic and Trade Yearbook*, 1996/1997.

Notwithstanding the differences in scale of GNP, these three countries were neck and neck in investing in China.

In terms of sales in 1996, the top Japanese enterprise operating in China was Qingling Motors, a joint venture of Isuzu Motors producing small trucks in Chongqing. In the automotive sector, there are also joint ventures with Honda, Nissan, and Suzuki. In second place is Shanghai Mitsubishi Elevator, a joint venture of Mitsubishi Electric. In third place is Beijing Matsushita Color Tube, a joint venture making vacuum picture tubes. Electrical equipment makers were among the first to enter China. Other names jostling in the market include Sanyo Electronics, Hitachi, and NEC. In fourth place is Canon Zhuhai, a joint venture in Zhuhai City, Guangdong province, making cameras and printers. Other office equipment makers competing in the market include joint-venture investments from Epson, Sharp, and Ricoh.

Japanese Economic Cooperation with China

As we see in Table 31.1 the Japanese government has implemented four yen loan programs for China, that is, the first yen loans (over five years, 1979–1983) totaling ¥330.9 billion, the second yen loans (over six years, 1984–1989) totaling ¥470 billion, the third yen loans (over six years, 1990–1995) totaling ¥810 billion, and the fourth yen loans (first half over three years, 1996–1998) totaling ¥580 billion. In each case, terms are thirty years for repayment, ten years' grace period, and a low (below market) rate of interest. Notwithstanding the low interest rate, the repayment burden for China depends much more on the RMB/¥ exchange rate, and the Chinese have pointed out that previous appreciation of the Japanese yen has increased the burden of servicing these loans.

The first yen loans financed six projects in sectors including railways, ports, and electric power. The second yen loans financed seven projects in sectors including railways, ports, telecommunications, electric power, and urban improvement. The third yen loans, in addition to financing forty projects in sectors including electric power, railways, ports, airport improvement, telecommunications, urban improvement, and agriculture, also financed two projects using funds received from repayments. The fourth yen loans will finance forty projects in sectors including agriculture, railways, aviation, ports, roads, telecommunications, energy, urban transportation, and environmental protection.

In total, Japanese yen loans exceed ¥2 trillion in four programs. It is appropriate to credit these loans with making a great contribution to the building of China's infrastructure. By virtue of these projects, China's in-

TABLE 31.1   Trends in Japanese Yen Loans to China

	First Yen Loans	Second Yen Loans	Third Yen Loans	Fourth Yen Loans
Commitment made	December 1979,	March 1984,	August 1988,	December 1994,
	Prime Minister Ohira	Prime Minister Nakasone	Prime Minister Takeshita	Prime Minister Murayama
Projects	Six projects including transport (railways, ports) electric power	Seven projects including railways, ports, telecom, electric power, urban improvement	Forty projects including railways, ports, electric power, airport access roads, telecom, urban improvement, agriculture. Additional two projects from repaid funds.	For first three years (FY96-98), forty projects including agriculture, railways, aviation, ports, roads, telecom, energy, urban transportation, and environmental protection
Period	Five years FY79-83 (including commodity loans of Yen 30.9 billion provide in FY84)	Six years FY84-89 completed one year ahead of schedule. Nine projects added in FY88, FY89	Six years 1990-1995	5 years FY96-2000
Amount	Total amount Yen 330.9 billion Project loans Yen 200.9 billion Commodity loans Yen 130 billion	Yen 470 billion for 16 projects. Additional Yen 70 billion in FY88 from funds repaid.	Yen 810 billion (to 1995) (general repayable Yen 770 billion; from funds repaid Yen 40 billion)	for the first three year portion (FY96-98) Yen 580 billion
Amount provided per FY	1979: Yen 50 billion 1980: Yen 56 billion 1981: Yen 60 billion 1982: Yen 65 billion 1983: Yen 69 billion	1984: Yen 71.5 billion 1985: Yen 75.1 billion 1986: Yen 80.6 billion 1987: Yen 85 billion 1988: Yen 161.5 billion 1989: Yen 97.2 billion	1990: Yen 122.5 billion 1991: Yen 129.6 billion 1992: Yen 137.3 billion 1993: Yen 138.7 billion 1994: Yen 129.6 billion 1995: Yen 141.4 billion	1996: Yen 170.5 billion 1997: Yen 202.9 billion
Interest rate	3 percent	FY84 portion 3.25 percent FY85-86 portion 3.5 percent FY87 portion 3 percent FY88-89 portion 2.5 percent	FY90 portion 2.5 percent FY91-95 portion 2.6 percent	1996 2.3 percent 1997 2.5 percent (2.1 percent for environment projects)
Repayment period	Ten-year grace for principal Thirty years to final repayment	Ten-year grace for principal Thirty years to final repayment	Ten-year grace for principal Thirty years to final repayment	Ten-year grace for principal Thirty years to final repayment

Source: Japanese Ministry of Foreign Affairs, Economic Cooperation Bureau, Repayable Funds Cooperation Section.

vestment environment has been remarkably improved, and a firm foundation has been laid for the boom in investment in China during the 1990s.

The conceptual basis for Japan's economic cooperation with China is the "Ohira three principles": (1) coordination with Europe and the United States; (2) balance with ASEAN; and (3) no cooperation in the military field. In 1991 a study group chaired by Saburo Okita was established by Japan's aid agency to formulate new guidelines for aid to China. The group offered four principles that continue to guide policy: (1) to promote Japan-China friendship and world peace; (2) to support China's economic reform and opening to the outside world; (3) to militate to correct imbalances resulting from economic development; and (4) to take into consideration China's geographic scale and large population (Japan International Cooperation Agency, 1992). Dating from the late 1970s, the Ohira three principles need to be updated in light of the realities of the 1990s.

—Yabuki

Appendix A:
A Chronology of China's Liberalization and Reform, 1978–1998

1978

August 12   Signing of the Japan-China Treaty of Peace and Friendship.

December 16   Resumption of U.S.-China diplomatic relations (from January 1, 1979) announced. (U.S. official relations with Republic of China on Taiwan severed effective January 1, 1979.)

December 18–22   Third Plenum of the Eleventh Party Central Committee. The Deng Xiaoping faction achieves dominance.

1979

January 28–   Deng Xiaoping makes a state visit to the United States.
February 5

February 15   The State Council decides that Shenzhen municipality in Guangdong province should be built up as an "export products production base."

February 17–   China-Vietnam War (Deng Xiaoping's decision).
March 16

March 28–29   U.S. Congress passes the U.S. Taiwan Relations Act (signed by Pres. Jimmy Carter on April 10).

April   Suppression of "Democracy Wall" movement in Beijing. Wei Jingsheng arrested.

July 1   The Law of the People's Republic of China on Joint Ventures Using Chinese and Foreign Investment (Joint Venture Law) is enacted at the second session of the Fifth National People's Congress.

July 30	Decision to establish the Foreign Investment Control Committee is established.
August 26–29	Vice Pres. Walter Mondale visits China.
October 4	The China International Trust and Investment Company is established (Rong Yiren, chair).
December 5–9	Japanese Prime Minister Ohira Masayoshi makes a state visit to China and commits to provide the first of several yen loans.

1980

April	The IMF reinstates China's representative status.
May	The World Bank reinstates China's representative status.
May	Decision of the Party Central Committee to change the name of the initiative called "export products production bases" to "special economic zones."
August 26	The fifteenth session of the Standing Committee of the Fifth National People's Congress approves "Regulations for the Special Economic Zones of Guangdong Province." Establishment of special economic zones in Shenzhen, Zhuhai, and Shantou is announced.
September 10	The Income Tax Law of the People's Republic of China relating to Sino-Foreign Joint Ventures and the People's Republic of China Individual Income Tax Law adopted, with immediate effect.
December 18	The State Council promulgates "Provisional Regulations Governing Foreign Exchange Control."

1981

Spring	Japanese plant cancellation incidents occur.
October 15	Construction begins on the 2.5-square-kilometer Huili export processing zone of the Xiamen special economic zone.
November 24	The State Council approves the private placement in the Japanese market of a ¥10 billion bond issue by CITIC.
December 22	Veteran leader of the conservative faction, Chen Yun, issues statements designed to put a brake on the special economic zones ("A Few Important Policies for Economic Construction")—included in *Since the Third Plenum*.
December 24	"Provisional Regulations on the Entry and Exit of Personnel of the Special Economic Zones in Guangdong Province," "Provisional Regulations on Registration of Business Enterprises of the Special Economic Zones of Guangdong Province," "Provisional

Regulations Governing Labor Wages of Enterprises in the Guangdong Province Special Economic Zones," and "Provisional Regulations governing Land in the Shenzhen Special Economic Zone" promulgated. All regulations effective January 1, 1982.

1982

January 1   The State Administration of Exchange Control promulgates "Implementing Rules for Audits of Foreign Exchange Applications from Individuals" and "Implementing Rules for Control of Foreign Exchange with Individuals."

February 21   The Ministry of Finance promulgates "Detailed Rules and Regulations for the Implementation of the Income Tax Law of the People's Republic of China for Foreign Enterprises."

September 21   The State Council issues "Notice of the State Council regarding the Question of Taxation of Sino-Foreign Joint Ventures and Cooperative Enterprises."

1983

May 1   The State Council decides to accord preferences to Taiwan compatriots investing in the special economic zones.

May 16   The State Council issues its "Decision on Expanding the Autonomy of Shanghai Municipality in Foreign Trade."

June 26   Publication of Deng Xiaoping's "Initiative on Peaceful Unification of Taiwan and the Chinese Mainland" (*Selected Works of Deng Xiaoping*).

July 11   The Party Central Committee and the State Council decide to accelerate development of Hainan Island (in April, "Minutes of Discussions on Issues Relating to Accelerating Development and Construction of Hainan Island" has been approved and circulated).

October 10–12   After the Second Plenum of the Twelfth Party Congress Central Committee, the Central Committee launches the campaign against "spiritual pollution." Persons associated with the special economic zones are shaken.

November 23–30 General Secretary Hu Yaobang visits Japan.

November 27   The State Council grants Dalian municipality expanded authority in the introduction and management of technology.

November   Shenzhen municipality establishes the Labor Services Corporation.

1984

January 24–29   Deng Xiaoping, Wang Zhen, Yang Shangkun, and other officials make inspection tours of the Shenzhen and Zhuhan special economic zones in Guangdong province.

February 1   The General Administration of Customs establishes "Regulations of the General Administration of Customs, the Ministry of Finance, the Ministry of Foreign Economic Relations and Trade of the People's Republic of China Concerning the Supervision and Control Over, and the Imposition of, or Exemption from Tax on, Imports and Exports by Sino-Foreign Cooperative Ventures."

February 7–10   Deng Xiaoping makes an inspection visit to the Xiamen special economic zone and pens a dedication: "Develop special economic zones more quickly and splendidly."

February 7   The Guangdong provincial people's government promulgates "Regulations on Foreign Economic Contracts of the Shenzhen Special Economic Zone" and "Provisional Regulations on the Introduction of Technology in Special Zones."

March 23–26   Japanese Prime Minister Nakasone Yasuhiro makes a state visit to China, commits to providing the second yen loan, and inaugurates the Japan-China 21st Century Friendship Committee.

March 26–   The Party Central Secretariat and the State Council convene a
April 6   "Symposium on Selected Coastal Cities" (decision is taken to open fourteen coastal cities to foreign investment).

June 22 and 23   Publication of Deng Xiaoping's "One Country, Two Systems" (*Selected Works of Deng Xiaoping*).

July 12   The responsible person of the State Council answers questions posed by the Xinhua News Agency about certain policies for the fourteen open coastal cities.

July 14   The eighth meeting of the Standing Committee of the Sixth Fujian Provincial People's Congress adopts "Regulations of the Xiamen Special Economic Zone Governing the Entry and Exit of Personnel"; "Regulations of Xiamen Special Economic Zone on the Registration of Enterprises"; "Regulations on Xiamen Special Economic Zone on Labor Management"; and "Regulations of Xiamen Special Economic Zone on Land Use." It also approves "Regulations of Xiamen Special Economic Zone on Economic Association with Interior Areas."

July 24   The Economic and Technical Development Corporation for the open coastal cities is established in Beijing.

September 26   China and Britain initial an agreement on the question of Hong Kong (officially signed December 19).

November 15   The State Council promulgates "Provisional Regulations of the State Council of the People's Republic of China Regarding the Reduction of, and Exemption from Enterprise Income Tax and Consolidated Industrial and Commercial Tax in the Special Economic Zones and the Fourteen Port Cities."

1985

January 19   The journal *Economic Reference* reports that per capita income within the Shenzhen special zone has surpassed U.S. $1,000.

January 25–31   The State Council convenes the "Symposium on the Yangtze River, Zhujiang Delta, and Minnan Delta Regions."

March 28   Yao Yilin, speaking with a Hong Kong journalist, complains that "less than one-third of the products of the special export zone are exported. . . . Exports are insufficient."

June 25   Deng Xiaoping warns that "the liberalization policy must not be misapprehended" (*Selected Works of Deng Xiaoping*, vol. 3).

August 1   *People's Daily* reports approval by the Party Central and the State Council of "The Report of the Investigation of the Material Issues of Automobile Importation and Reselling on Hainan Island."

September 18   A student demonstration in Beijing protests the attendance of Japanese Prime Minister Nakasone Yasuhiro at a ceremony for war-dead at the Yasukuni Shrine.

December 25   A conference on work of the special economic zones is convened in Shenzhen. The Party Committee secretary of Shenzhen municipality, Liang Xiang, delivers a summary report on the Shenzhen zone at the "Conference of Cadres of Organizations Directly Under Central."

1986

January 15   The State Council promulgates "Regulations Concerning the Question of Balance of Foreign Exchange Receipts and Expenditures for Joint Ventures Using Chinese and Foreign Investment."

March 28   The People's Bank of China and the Japanese Ministry of Finance agree on the establishment of branches in Shenzhen for Bank of Tokyo, Sanwa, and Takugin banks (branches opened May 16).

April 12   The fourth session of the Sixth National People's Congress adopts the Foreign-Invested Enterprises Law.

July   The State Council Leading Group on Foreign Capital Work (headed by Gu Mu) is established.

1987

January 16   General Secretary Hu Yaobang resigns.

July 15   Martial law lifted in Taiwan.

October 19   The State Council approves the State Planning Commission's "Methodology for Substitution of Imports of Products of Sino-Foreign Equity Joint Ventures or Cooperative Joint Ventures."

October 25–   The Thirteenth Party Congress adopts the "Theory of the Initial
November 1   Stage of Socialism."

1988

January 5   *Economic Daily* publishes "A New Great Choice: Economic Development Strategy in the Context of International Cycles," by Li Delai (*Economic Daily* reporter).

January 13   Taiwan Pres. Chiang Chingguo dies. Li Denghui elevated to presidency (and leadership of Kuomintang).

January 23   *People's Daily* carries Zhao Ziyang's "Comments on the Economic Development Strategy of the Coastal Region."

April 13   The first session of the Seventh National People's Congress elevates Hainan Island to province level and designates Hainan Island as a special economic zone.

April 13   The first session of the Seventh National People's Congress adopts the Sino-Foreign Joint Venture Law of the PRC.

July 6   The State Council promulgates "Provisions Concerning Encouragement of Investment from Taiwan."

August 25–30   Japanese Prime Minister Takeshita Noboru pays a state visit to China and commits to providing the third yen loan.

December 2   Zhao Ziyang stresses the coastal region economic development strategy at a national planning meeting.

1989

January 3   *People's Daily* carries the article "Our Country Has Already Become a Net Aid Receiving Country."

April 15   Hu Yaobang dies; democracy movement begins.

May 15–18   Soviet leader Mikhail Gorbachev visits China; Sino-Soviet leadership discussions are held.

May 20   Martial law is declared in some sections of Beijing municipality.

June 3–4   Suppression by military force is begun against the democracy movement.

June 23–24	The Fourth Plenary Session of the Thirteenth Party Central Committee dismisses Zhao Ziyang; Jiang Zemin assumes position as general secretary.
November 6–9	At the Fifth Plenum of the Thirteenth Party Central Committee, Deng Xiaoping retires from the position of chairman of the Party Central Military Affairs Commission. His successor is Jiang Zemin.
November	Berlin Wall falls.
December	The Communist regime in Romania collapses.

1990

January 11	Martial law is lifted.
March 9–12	The Sixth Plenum of the Thirteenth Party Central Committee adopts the "Decision on the Mass Line."
May 1	Martial law is lifted in Lhasa City.
July 1	The fourth population census is taken.
September 22–October 7	The Asian athletic games are held in Beijing.
October 20	Agreement reached to establish the China–South Korean Trade Office.
December 25–30	The Seventh Plenum of the Thirteenth Party Congress Central Committee adopts "Outline of the Eighth Five Year Plan."

1991

January 17–February 28	U.S.-led coalition defeats Iraq in Gulf War. China realizes arrival of "high-tech" war and obsolescence of "people's war."
March 2	Publication of Huang Puping's "New Thinking Required for Reform and Liberalization."
April 8	Zhu Rongji is promoted to State Council vice premier from his position of mayor of Shanghai.
June 1	Rehabilitation of persons purged after the Tiananmen Incident: Hu Qili (Politburo Standing Committee member); Yan Mingfu (Communist Party Central United Front Department head); and Rui Xingwen (Communist Party Central Secretariat secretary).
July	Deng Xiaoping advances his "New Cat" theory.
August	In the former Soviet Union an attempted coup d'etat by the old conservative faction fails; the Soviet Communist Party is disbanded.

August	China announces accession to the Nuclear Nonproliferation Treaty.
August 31	An article by the commentator of Shanghai's *Liberation Daily* insists that it will be impossible to overcome difficulties by "sticking to old conventions" and calls for courage and determination in pursuing reform and liberalization.
September 1	Chen Yeping's commentary indirectly criticizes Deng Xiaoping's "White Cat, Black Cat" doctrine and "New Cat" theory.
September 2	*People's Daily* editorial "Cut Out Disturbances" rehashes the issue of "socialist in name, capitalist in name" (a rebuttal to Huang Puping's March 2 commentary).
October 9	Yang Shangkun delivers a commemorative address on the eightieth anniversary of the Xinhai revolution and makes no reference to opposing "peaceful evolution." This signals a thaw in the conservative mood.
November 25–29	At the Eighth Plenum of the Thirteenth Party Congress Central Committee, Deng Xiaoping's "productive forces" theory ("New Cat" theory) manages to achieve acceptance, but the conservative faction achieves a dominant position in the party organization.

1992

January 20	Deng Xiaoping visits Shenzhen. He calls for speeding up reform and liberalization.
March 1	Communist Party Central Document No. 2 (1992), Deng Xiaoping's Southern Excursion Talks, is disseminated.
March	Foreign investment and border trade is approved for thirteen border cities and areas, including Heihe and Suifanghe in Heilongjiang province; Hunchun in Jilin province; Manzhouli and Erenhot in Inner Mongolia; Yining, Tacheng, and Bole in Xinjiang Autonomous Region; Ruili, Tianwanding, and Hekouxian in Yunnan province; and Pinxiang and Dongxingzhen in Guangxi Autonomous Region.
May 2	*People's Daily* reports a statement of Chen Yun supporting the development of Pudong.
May 22	Deng Xiaoping visits the Capital Iron and Steel Works in Beijing and encourages reform of SOEs.
Late May	Communist Party Central Document No. 4 (1992), "Views of the Communist Party Central on Expanding Reform and Liberalization, and Striving to Take the Economy to a Higher and More Splendid Stage," is issued.
June 12	The Production Office of the State Council is abolished and reorganized into the State Council Office of Economic Trade, with

Vice Premier Zhu Rongji in charge. This is an expansion of Zhu's authority.

June 30 Communist Party Central Committee and State Council "Decision Regarding Speeding Up the Development of Tertiary Industry" is published in *People's Daily* (decision dated June 16).

June–July Five Yangtze River riparian cities (Chongqing, Yueyang, Wuhan, Jiujiang, and Wuhu); and seven border province cities (Kunming, Nanning, Urumchi, Harbin, Changchun, Huhehot, and Shijiazhuang) are opened to foreign investment and economic relations. Eleven interior cities (Taiyuan, Hefei, Lanzhou, Nanchang, Zhengzhou, Changsha, Chengdu, Guiyang, Xian, Xining, and Yinchuan) are opened to the outside (*People's Daily*, August 13).

July 21 Chen Yun, in an article mourning Li Xiannian's death, for the first time sanctions economic zones (*People's Daily*).

July 25 *People's Daily* publishes "Rules and Regulations Governing Transformation of the Management System of Industrial Enterprises Under Ownership of the Whole People."

August 13 The State Council decides to establish "coastal open cities" in five Yangtze River riparian cities including Chongqing, four border and coastal-area cities including Harbin, and in eleven interior cities including Taiyuan.

August 24 China establishes diplomatic relations with the Republic of Korea.

September U.S. sells 150 F-16 fighter aircraft to Taiwan; Beijing claims "violation of joint communiqués."

September 28 Commemoration of the twentieth anniversary of normalization of Japan-China diplomatic relations.

October 12–18 Convening of the Chinese Communist Party's Fourteenth Party Congress. The theory of "the socialist market economy" is embraced. Jiang Zemin is elected general secretary.

1993

March 15 The State Administration of Exchange Control issues "Regulations Governing Management of the Foreign Exchange Adjustment Markets."

March 29 Zhu Rongji is reelected vice premier at the National People's Congress.

April 19 The State Council initiates a reform of government institutions (directly supervised institutions are reduced to thirteen from nineteen, offices are cut to five from nine).

April 29 Wang Daohan (chair of the Cross-Straits Relations Association) and Gu Zhengpu (chair of the Straits Exchange Fund) meet in Singapore.

July 2	Li Guixian (governor of the People's Bank of China) is dismissed; Vice Premier Zhu Rongji becomes governor concurrently. Financial rectification begins.
November	European Union officially formed.
November 11–14	The Third Communist Party Central Committee Plenum adopts "Fifty Articles for a Market Economy."
Continuing	A boom in establishing development zones is seen nationwide.

1994

January 1	The foreign exchange system is overhauled as the "official" rate is abolished and trading is unified against a managed floating rate (initially RMB 8.7 to US$1). Foreign Exchange Certificates are abolished. All settlements are in RMB. State enterprises are prohibited to hold foreign currency, which must be surrendered immediately to Chinese banks.
January 19	Announcement of the "Outline for Development of China's Agriculture in the 1990s."
February 2–4	Decision on "Outline of National Environmental Protection Work, 1994–1998."
February 5	Commencement of commercial operation of the Daya Bay nuclear power plant in Guangdong province.
February 9–12	Deng Xiaoping sojourns in Shanghai during the Spring Festival and is seen on television to be old and frail.
March 25	The State Council approves a white paper entitled "China's Population, Environment, and Development in the 21st Century."
May 18	The China real estate market is established in Beijing.
June 23	Announcement of "Outline of Policy for State Industries in the 1990s."
October 17	Work begins on the second phase of the Taishan nuclear power plant.
November 19	The Agricultural Development Bank of China is established.
December 7	Completion of the forty-eight-kilometer inner ring elevated expressway in Shanghai.
December 8	The Ministry of Labor mandates so-called Itinerant Employment Certificates.
December 12	Shanghai's first subway line (16.1 kilometers) is completed.
December 14	Three Gorges dam project officially started.

1995

February 1	Jiang Zemin offers an eight-point initiative on the Taiwan question.
March 18	Law of the People's Bank of China promulgated.
April 27	Chen Xitong, party secretary of Beijing, is dismissed from office; his successor is Wei Jianxing.
May 5–10	The Standing Committee of the National People's Congress adopts the Commercial Bank Law and the Commercial Bills Law.
June 6–12	Taiwan Pres. Li Tenghui visits Washington, D.C.; Beijing protests "violation of joint communiqués."
June 23	Zhu Rongji resigns as governor of the People's Bank of China; the soft landing has been achieved.
July 5	Promulgation of the "Rules and Regulations Governing Protection of Intellectual Property in the PRC" (effective from October 1).
July 21–26	Missile-firing exercises conducted in the Taiwan Strait.
August 4	Opening of the Beijing-Tianjin expressway (142.7 kilometers).
September 25–28	The Fifth Plenum of the Fourteenth Communist Party Central Committee adopts the Ninth Five Year Plan and recommendations for the long-range plan to 2010.
November 16	The State Council releases the white paper on "China's Arms Control and Arms Reduction."

1996

January 12	China's first shareholding bank, China Minsheng Bank, established.
January 15	Connection of a 2,052-kilometer optical cable network between Beijing, Huhehot, Yinchuan, and Lanzhou.
March 5–17	The National People's Congress adopts the Ninth Five Year Plan and Long Term Plan to 2010.
March 23	Li Tenghui elected president of the Republic of China by popular vote.
March 8–25	Missile exercises in the Taiwan Strait (March 8–15), "live" ammunition exercises (March 12–20).
June 2	Work begun on installation of generators (2x600MW) in the second phase of Taishan nuclear power plant.
June 3	State Environmental Protection Bureau releases "Communiqué on China's Environmental Situation in 1995."

October 1	The Beijing-Guangzhou railway line (2,553 kilometers) is opened to traffic.
October 11	The State Council accepts "State Environmental Protection Ninth Five Year Plan and Long Term Plan for 2010."
October 25	The Information Office of the State Council releases "China's Food White Paper."
December 16	Booming Chinese stock markets drop after *People's Daily* editorial warns of risks (hinting of government cooling measures). Market participants joke of three types of market: a bear market, a bull market, and a "pig" market. *Pig* in Chinese is pronounced the same as *Zhu*, a reference to Zhu Rongji.
December	Implementation of RMB foreign exchange convertibility for current account transactions (compliance with IMF article 8).

1997

February 13	Commissioning of the Lijiaxia power plant, the largest electric power–generating plant on the Yellow River.
February 18	The State Statistical Bureau releases results of the Third National Industrial Census.
February 19	Deng Xiaoping dies.
April 14	The State Council decides to extend until year's end an import duty exemption for equipment imported for foreign-invested projects.
May 15	Work begins on installation of main generating units of the Guangdong Fengau nuclear power plant.
May 16	Decision to expand from 57 to 120 the number of large experimental group companies.
July 1	Hong Kong reverts to Chinese sovereignty; Hong Kong Special Administrative Region is established.
July 1	Chinese domestic airlines abolish premium tariffs for foreigners, unify ticket prices.
July 18–24	Zhu Rongji inspects SOEs in Liaoning province, says "three years from now most of the SOEs should manage to get themselves out of serious trouble."
September 12–18	Fifteenth Communist Party Congress held in Beijing. Limited-liability share ownership companies officially sanctioned (previously "experimental"). Theory of "early stages of socialism" revived (formerly advanced in 1987, then unmentioned).
October 28–November 11	Jiang Zemin makes a state visit to the United States.

November 16	Political criminal Wei Jingsheng is released, allowed to take refuge in the United States.
November 17–19	Central Financial Work Conference.
December 9–11	Central Economic Work Conference.
December 19	Seventh anniversary of the founding of the Shanghai Securities Exchange; the exchange moves to its new building in Pudong.

1998

March 5–19	Ninth Chinese National People's Congress convenes in Beijing; Zhu Rongji elected premier; decision to restructure government agencies; number of ministries reduced from forty to twenty-nine.
March 19	At news conference Premier Zhu Rongji promises to "exert my utmost efforts to the task until my dying day."
March 21	PBOC lowers reserve ratio from 13 percent to 8 percent.
March 25	Commercial bank lending and deposit rates and PBOC's rediscount rate are lowered to counteract deflationary pressures.
March 31–April 7	Zhu Rongji attends Asia–European Union Conference in London and makes an official visit to France.
April 2	State Council Securities Commission absorbed by the China Securities Regulatory Commission (Zhou Zhengqing, chair).
April	Party Central Document No. 3, "GDP 8 Percent, Inflation Under 3 Percent," on economic targets disseminated.
April 19	Political criminal Wang Dan released, allowed to take refuge in the United States.
June 25–June 30	U.S. Pres. Bill Clinton pays a state visit to China. Asserts "three no's" policy toward Taiwan.
August 11	PBOC announces that an additional ten foreign banks will be licensed to conduct RMB business in Pudong, Shanghai. Also, the Shenzhen special economic zone is designated as the second experimental location for foreign banks to be licensed to conduct RMB business.
August–September	The most destructive flooding in four decades devastates large areas of the Yangtze River basin and the northeast province of Heilongjiang. Thousands lose their lives.

Appendix B:
Key Indications for
China's Economy, 1978–1997

TABLE Appendix 2. 1 Population and Employment

unit: million persons

Year	Population End of Year	Population Middle of Year	Number of Employed Persons	Primary Industry (%)	Secondary Industry (%)	Tertiary Industry (%)
1978	963	956	402	70.5	17.4	12.1
1979	975	969	410	69.8	17.7	12.6
1980	987	981	424	68.7	18.3	13.0
1981	1,000	994	437	68.1	18.4	13.5
1982	1,017	1,009	453	68.1	18.5	13.4
1983	1,030	1,023	464	67.1	18.8	14.2
1984	1,044	1,037	482	64.0	20.0	16.0
1985	1,059	1,051	499	62.4	20.9	16.7
1986	1,075	1,067	513	60.9	21.9	17.2
1987	1,093	1,084	528	59.9	22.3	17.8
1988	1,110	1,102	543	59.3	22.4	18.3
1989	1,127	1,119	553	60.0	21.7	18.3
1990	1,143	1,135	639	60.0	21.4	18.6
1991	1,158	1,151	648	59.7	21.4	18.9
1992	1,172	1,165	656	58.5	21.7	19.8
1993	1,185	1,178	664	56.4	22.4	21.2
1994	1,199	1,192	672	54.3	22.7	23.0
1995	1,211	1,205	679	52.9	23.0	24.8
1996	1,224	1,218	689	50.5	23.6	26.0
1997	1,236	1,230	696			

Sources: *China Statistical Yearbook* 1997; *China's Regional Economy Through Seventeen Years of Reform and Opening-Up*; "Bulletin on National Economic and Social Development for 1997," *Economic Daily,* March 5, 1998.

TABLE Appendix 2. 2 GNP and GDP

Year	GNP			GDP		
	At Current Prices (billion RMB)	Index (1978=100)	YoY Growth (%)	At Current Prices (billion RMB)	Index (1978=100)	YoY Growth (%)
1978	362	100.0	11.7	362	100.0	11.7
1979	404	107.6	7.6	404	107.6	7.6
1980	452	116.0	7.8	452	116.0	7.8
1981	486	122.0	5.2	486	122.1	5.2
1982	530	133.3	9.3	530	133.1	9.1
1983	596	148.2	11.1	593	147.6	10.9
1984	721	170.9	15.3	717	170.0	15.2
1985	899	193.5	13.2	896	192.9	13.5
1986	1020	209.9	8.5	1020	210.0	8.8
1987	1196	234.1	11.5	1196	234.3	11.6
1988	1492	260.5	11.3	1493	260.7	11.3
1989	1692	271.5	4.2	1691	271.3	4.1
1990	1860	283.0	4.2	1855	281.7	3.8
1991	2166	308.8	9.1	2162	307.6	9.2
1992	2665	352.2	14.1	2664	351.4	14.2
1993	3456	398.4	13.1	3463	398.8	13.5
1994	4667	448.7	12.6	4676	449.3	12.6
1995	5750	489.1	9.0	5848	496.7	10.5
1996	6756	536.5	9.7	6859	544.2	9.6
1997				7477	592.1	8.8

Sources: China Statistical Yearbook 1997; China's Regional Economy Through Seventeen Years of Reform and Opening-Up; "Bulletin on National Economic and Social Development for 1997," *Economic Daily,* March 5, 1998.

TABLE Appendix 2. 3 Composition of GDP

Year	Primary Industry (billion RMB)	(%)	Secondary Industry (billion RMB)	(%)	National Industry (billion RMB)	(%)	Tertiary Industry (billion RMB)	(%)
1978	102	28.1	175	48.2	161	44.3	86	23.8
1979	126	31.2	191	47.4	177	43.8	87	21.4
1980	136	30.1	219	48.5	200	44.2	97	21.4
1981	155	31.8	226	46.4	215	44.2	106	21.8
1982	176	33.3	238	45.0	216	40.8	115	21.7
1983	196	33.0	265	44.6	238	40.0	133	22.4
1984	230	32.0	311	43.3	279	38.9	177	24.7
1985	254	28.4	387	43.1	345	38.5	256	28.5
1986	276	27.1	449	44.0	397	38.9	295	28.9
1987	320	26.8	525	43.9	459	38.3	351	29.3
1988	383	25.7	659	44.1	578	38.7	451	30.2
1989	423	25.0	728	43.0	648	38.3	540	32.0
1990	502	27.0	772	41.6	686	37.0	581	31.3
1991	529	24.5	910	42.1	809	37.4	723	33.4
1992	580	21.8	1170	43.9	1029	38.6	914	34.3
1993	688	19.9	1643	47.4	1414	40.8	1132	32.7
1994	946	20.2	2237	47.8	1936	41.4	1479	31.6
1995	1199	20.5	2854	48.8	2472	42.3	1795	30.7
1996	1388	20.2	3361	49.0	2908	42.4	2110	30.8
1997	1367	18.3	3677	49.2	3175	42.5	2433	32.5

Sources: *China Statistical Yearbook* 1997; *China's Regional Economy Through Seventeen Years of Reform and Opening-Up*; "Bulletin on National Economic and Social Development for 1997," *Economic Daily*, March 5, 1998.

TABLE Appendix 2. 4 GDP Per Capita and Composition of National Output

Year	GDP Per Capita			Composition of National Output				
	At Current Prices (RMB)	Index (1978=100)	YoY Growth (%)	National Output (billion RMB)	Total Consumption (billion RMB)	(%)	Net Investment (billion RMB)	(%)
1978	379	100.0	10.2	361	224	62.1	138	38.2
1979	417	106.1	6.1	407	262	64.3	147	36.1
1980	460	113.0	6.5	455	298	65.4	159	34.9
1981	489	117.4	3.9	490	331	67.5	158	32.3
1982	526	126.4	7.7	549	364	66.3	176	32.1
1983	582	138.5	9.5	608	402	66.2	201	33.0
1984	695	157.6	13.8	716	470	65.5	247	34.5
1985	853	175.5	11.9	879	577	65.7	339	38.5
1986	956	188.2	6.9	1,013	654	64.6	385	38.0
1987	1,104	206.6	9.8	1,178	745	63.2	432	36.7
1988	1,355	226.3	9.5	1,470	936	63.7	550	37.4
1989	1,512	231.9	2.5	1,647	1,056	64.1	610	37.0
1990	1,634	237.3	2.3	1,862	1,137	61.0	644	34.6
1991	1,879	255.6	7.7	2,128	1,315	61.8	752	35.3
1992	2,287	288.4	12.8	2,586	1,595	61.7	964	37.3
1993	2,939	323.6	12.2	3,450	2,018	58.5	1,500	43.5
1994	3,923	360.4	11.4	4,711	2,722	57.8	1,926	40.9
1995	4,854	394.0	9.3	5,941	3,453	58.1	2,388	40.2
1996	5,634	427.1	8.4	6,850	4,017	58.6	2,687	39.2
1997	6,079	462.5	8.3					

Note: Disparities in figures for total output and total production due to calculation errors.

Sources: China Statistical Yearbook 1997; *China's Regional Economy Through Seventeen Years of Reform and Opening-Up;* "Bulletin on National Economic and Social Development for 1997," *Economic Daily,* March 5, 1998.

TABLE Appendix 2. 5 Cultivated Area and Food Production

Year	Cultivated Area Year-End (mil. ha)	Sown Area of Food Crops (mil. ha)	Cultivated Area Per Capita (ha)	Food Production (mil. ton)	Food Production Per Capita Crops (kg)	Unit Yield of Cultivated Area (kg)
1978	99.4	120.6	0.10	304.8	318.7	2,527
1979	99.5	119.3	0.10	332.1	342.7	2,785
1980	99.3	117.2	0.10	320.6	326.7	2,735
1981	99.0	115.0	0.10	325.0	327.0	2,827
1982	98.5	113.5	0.10	354.5	351.5	3,124
1983	98.0	114.1	0.10	387.3	378.5	3,396
1984	98.1	112.9	0.09	407.3	392.8	3,608
1985	96.9	108.9	0.09	379.1	360.7	3,483
1986	96.2	110.9	0.09	391.5	367.0	3,529
1987	96.0	111.3	0.09	403.0	371.7	3,622
1988	95.7	110.1	0.09	394.1	357.7	3,579
1989	95.7	112.2	0.08	407.6	364.3	3,632
1990	95.7	113.5	0.08	446.2	393.1	3,933
1991	95.7	112.3	0.08	435.3	378.3	3,876
1992	95.4	110.6	0.08	442.7	380.0	4,004
1993	95.1	110.5	0.08	456.5	387.4	4,131
1994	94.9	109.5	0.08	445.1	373.5	4,063
1995	95.0	110.1	0.08	466.6	387.3	4,240
1996		112.6		504.5	414.4	4,483
1997	95.5		0.08	492.6	400.4	

Sources: China Statistical Yearbook 1997; *China's Regional Economy Through Seventeen Years of Reform and Opening-Up*; "Bulletin on National Economic and Social Development for 1997," *Economic Daily,* March 5, 1998.

TABLE Appendix 2. 6 Industrial Production

Year	Gross Industrial Output Value (bil. RMB)	Of Which: State-Owned (bil. RMB)	(%)	Collective (bil. RMB)	(%)	Urban Individual (bil. RMB)	(%)	Others (bil. RMB)	(%)
1978	424	329	77.6	95	22.4				
1979	468	367	78.5	101	21.5				
1980	515	392	76.0	121	23.5	0.1	0.0	2.4	0.5
1981	540	404	74.8	133	24.6	0.2	0.0	3.1	0.6
1982	531	433	81.5	144	27.2	0.3	0.1	3.9	0.7
1983	646	474	73.3	166	25.7	0.8	0.1	5.0	0.8
1984	762	526	69.1	226	29.7	1.5	0.2	7.7	1.0
1985	972	630	64.9	312	32.1	18	1.9	12	1.2
1986	1,119	697	62.3	375	33.5	31	2.8	16	1.5
1987	1,381	825	59.7	478	34.6	50	3.6	28	2.0
1988	1,822	1,035	56.8	659	36.1	79	4.3	50	2.7
1989	2,202	1,234	56.1	786	35.7	106	4.8	76	3.4
1990	2,392	1,234	51.6	852	35.6	129	5.4	105	4.4
1991	2,663	1,496	56.2	878	33.0	129	4.8	160	6.0
1992	3,460	1,782	51.5	1,214	35.1	201	5.8	263	7.6
1993	4,840	2,273	47.0	1,646	34.0	386	8.0	535	11.1
1994	7,018	2,620	37.3	2,647	37.7	708	10.1	1,042	14.8
1995	9,189	3,122	34.0	3,362	36.6	1,182	12.9	1,523	16.6
1995	(8,230)	(2,684)	(32.6)	(2,925)	(35.5)	(1,197)	(14.5)	(1,423)	(17.3)
1996	9,960	2,836	28.5	3,923	39.4	1,542	15.5	1,658	16.6

Note: The numbers in ( ) for 1995 and numbers for 1996 are calculated according to a new definition.
Sources: China Statistical Yearbook 1997; *China's Regional Economy Through Seventeen Years of Reform and Opening-Up.*

TABLE Appendix 2. 7 Government Finances

Year	Fiscal Revenue (a) (billion RMB)	(a) / GDP (%)	Fiscal Expenditures (b) (billion RMB)	Fiscal Balance (a) - (b) (billion RMB)	Defense Expenditures (d) (billion RMB)	(d) / (b) (%)
1978	113	31.2	112	1	17	15.0
1979	115	28.4	128	-14	22	17.2
1980	116	25.7	123	-7	19	15.4
1981	118	24.2	114	4	17	14.8
1982	121	22.9	123	-2	18	14.3
1983	137	23.0	141	-4	18	12.6
1984	164	22.9	170	-6	18	10.6
1985	200	22.4	200	0.6	19	9.6
1986	212	20.8	220	-8	20	9.1
1987	220	18.4	226	-6	21	9.3
1988	236	15.8	249	-13	22	8.8
1989	266	15.8	282	-16	25	8.9
1990	294	15.8	308	-15	29	9.4
1991	315	14.6	339	-24	33	9.8
1992	348	13.1	374	-26	38	10.1
1993	435	12.6	464	-29	43	9.2
1994	522	11.2	579	-57	55	9.5
1995	624	10.7	682	-58	64	9.3
1996	741	10.8	794	-53	72	9.1
1997	864	16.7	920	-56	81	9.3

Sources: China Statistical Yearbook 1997; China's Regional Economy Through Seventeen Years of Reform and Opening-Up.

TABLE Appendix 2. 8 Prices

Year	National Retail Price		Consumer Prices	Urban Consumer Prices	Rural Consumer Prices
	YoY Change (%)	1978=100	YoY Change (%)	YoY Change (%)	YoY Change (%)
1978	0.7	100.0		0.7	
1979	2.0	102.0		1.9	
1980	6.0	108.1		7.5	
1981	2.4	110.7		2.5	
1982	1.9	112.8		2.0	
1983	1.5	114.5		2.0	
1984	2.8	117.7		2.7	
1985	8.8	128.1	9.3	11.9	7.6
1986	6.0	135.8	6.5	7.0	6.1
1987	7.3	145.7	7.3	8.8	6.2
1988	18.5	172.7	18.8	20.7	17.5
1989	17.8	203.4	18.0	16.3	19.3
1990	2.1	207.7	3.1	1.3	4.5
1991	2.9	213.7	3.4	5.1	2.3
1992	5.4	225.2	6.4	8.6	4.7
1993	13.2	254.9	14.7	16.1	13.7
1994	21.7	310.2	24.1	25.0	23.4
1995	14.8	356.1	17.1	16.8	17.5
1996	6.1	377.8	8.3	8.8	7.9
1997	0.8	380.8	2.8	3.1	2.5

Sources: *China Statistical Yearbook* 1997; *China's Regional Economy Through Seventeen Years of Reform and Opening-Up.*

TABLE Appendix 2. 9 Trade and Foreign Exchange Reserves

Year	Import and Export (bil. US$)	Export (bil. US$)	Import (bil. US$)	Balance (bil. US$)	Foreign Exchange Reserves (bil. US$)	Rate to US$ (RMB per 100 US$)
1978	20.6	9.8	10.9	-1.1	1.6	168.36
1979	29.3	13.7	15.7	-2.0	0.8	155.49
1980	38.1	18.1	20.0	-1.9	-1.3	149.84
1981	44.0	22.0	22.0	-0.01	2.7	170.50
1982	41.6	22.3	19.3	3.0	7.0	189.25
1983	43.6	22.2	21.4	0.8	8.9	197.57
1984	53.6	26.1	27.4	-1.3	8.2	232.70
1985	69.6	27.4	42.3	-14.9	2.6	293.67
1986	73.9	30.9	42.9	-12.0	2.1	345.28
1987	82.7	39.4	43.2	-3.8	2.9	372.21
1988	102.8	47.5	55.3	-7.8	3.4	372.21
1989	111.7	52.5	59.1	-6.6	5.6	376.59
1990	115.4	62.1	53.4	8.8	11.1	478.38
1991	135.6	71.8	63.8	8.1	21.7	532.27
1992	165.6	84.9	80.6	4.4	19.4	551.49
1993	195.7	91.7	104.0	-12.2	21.2	576.19
1994	236.6	121.0	115.7	5.4	51.6	861.87
1995	280.9	148.8	132.1	16.7	73.6	835.07
1996	289.9	151.1	138.8	12.2	105.0	831.42
1997	325.1	182.7	142.4	40.3	139.9	828.98

Sources: China Statistical Yearbook 1997; China's Regional Economy Through Seventeen Years of Reform and Opening-Up.

TABLE Appendix 2. 10 Utilization of Foreign Capital

Year	Contracts Total (no.)	Total (bil. US$)	Foreign Loans (no.)	Foreign Loans (bil. US$)	Direct Investment (no.)	Direct Investment (bil. US$)	Actual Use Total (bil. US$)	Foreign Loans (bil. US$)	Direct Investment (bil. US$)
1978							0.3		
1979				3.6		0.05	0.4		
1980				17.2		0.2	0.6		
1981				36.3		0.5	0.8		
1982				31.4		0.5	0.8		
1983	522	3.4	52	1.5	470	1.7	2.0	1.1	0.6
1984	1,984	4.8	38	1.9	1,856	2.7	2.7	1.3	1.3
1985	3,145	9.9	72	3.5	3,073	5.9	4.6	2.7	1.7
1986	1,551	11.7	53	8.4	1,498	2.8	7.3	5.0	1.9
1987	2,289	12.1	56	7.8	2,233	3.7	8.5	5.8	2.3
1988	6,063	16.0	118	9.8	5,945	5.3	10.2	6.5	3.2
1989	5,909	11.5	130	5.2	5,779	5.6	10.1	6.3	3.4
1990	7,371	12.1	98	5.1	7,273	6.6	10.3	6.5	3.5
1991	13,086	19.6	108	7.2	12,978	12.0	11.6	6.9	4.4
1992	48,858	69.4	94	10.7	48,764	58.1	16.2	7.9	11.0
1993	83,595	123.3	158	11.3	83,437	11.4	39.0	11.2	27.5
1994	47,646	93.8	97	10.7	47,549	82.7	43.2	9.3	33.8
1995	37,184	103.2	173	11.3	37,011	91.3	48.1	10.3	37.5
1996	24,673	81.6	117	8.0	24,556	73.3	54.8	12.7	41.7
1997	21,183	61.7	137	5.9	21,046	51.8	64.0	12.0	45.3

Sources: China Statistical Yearbook 1997; China's Regional Economy Through Seventeen Years of Reform and Opening-Up; "Bulletin on National Economic and Social Development for 1997," *Economic Daily,* March 5, 1998.

Selected References

Brown, Lester. 1995. *Who Will Feed China?* New York: Norton.

CCP Organization Department. 1990. *Chart of Cadre Assignments for Positions Under Control of Party Central.* (Doc. 2, 1990) [internal distribution].

China Finance Society, ed. 1997. *Almanac of China's Finance and Banking.* Beijing: Editorial Department, Almanac of China's Finance and Banking.

China Market Research Institute. 1996. *China Market Statistics.* Tokyo: China Market Research Institute.

Chinese Academy of Social Sciences Industrial Economic Institute. 1996, 1997. *China's Industrial Development.* Beijing: Economic Management Press.

Central Committee of the CCP and State Council of the PRC. "Notice from the Chinese Communist Party Central Committee and the State Council: Report on Opening of a New Phase for Commune and Brigade Enterprises of the State Council Ministry of Agriculture, Animal Husbandry, and Fisheries." *People's Daily,* March 18, 1984.

_____. October 23, 1996. "Decisions by Party Central and the State Council on Solving the Problems of the Poor Rural Population." *People's Daily,* January 8, 1997.

Chen Jinhua. "Earnestly and Thoroughly Implement the Spirit of the Fifteenth Party Congress, Actively Promote the Strategic Adjustment of the Economy's Structure." *People's Daily,* December 17, 1997.

China Statisticians' Office, ed. 1997. *Report on China's National Affairs, 1978–1996.* Beijing: China Planning Press.

Customs Administration of the People's Republic of China. Annual in December. *Customs Statistics Yearbook of China.* Beijing: Customs Administration of the People's Republic of China.

Deng Xiaoping. 1993. *Selected Works of Deng Xiaoping.* Vol. 3 (October). Beijing: People's Press.

Deutsche Morgan Grenfell. April 1998. *DMG China Digest.* Hong Kong: Deutsche Morgan Grenfell.

Economic Daily. Various issues. Beijing: Economic Daily Press.

Finance Year Book of China Editorial Committee. 1997. *Finance Year Book of China.* Beijing: China Finance Publishing House.

Fourteenth CCP Congress Third Plenum. "Fifty Articles on the Socialist Market Economy." *People's Daily,* November 17, 1993.

Gan, Luo. "Luo Gan Is Entrusted by the State Council to Deliver to the First Session of the Ninth NPC an Explanation of Reform of State Council Institutions." *People's Daily,* March 7, 1998.

General Office of the State Council. 1995. *Organization and Institutions of the Central Government*. Beijing: China Development Press.

Guo Jinping, ed. 1995. *A Comprehensive View of China's Social Security System*. Beijing: China Democratic Legal System Press.

Guo Qingsong and Yang Guang. 1997. "Research into China's Unemployment Insurance System Under the Market Economy." *Population and Economics*, vol. 4.

Government Census and Statistics Department. 1996. *Hong Kong Annual Digest of Statistics*. Hong Kong: Government Census and Statistics Department.

Government of Hong Kong. Annual. *Hong Kong Trade Statistics*. Hong Kong: Government Printing Office.

Hu Zhanghong. 1996. *The Competitive Strategy of Chinese Commercial Banks*. Beijing: Economic Management Press.

IFR Asia. Various issues, 1997, 1998. Hong Kong: IFR Publishing.

International Financing Review. Various issues. London: IFR Publishing.

International Monetary Fund. *International Financial Statistics*. Washington, D.C.: International Monetary Fund.

_____. Annual. *Direction of Trade Statistics Yearbook*. Washington, D.C.: International Monetary Fund.

Japan External Trade Organization. 1997. *White Paper on International Trade*. Tokyo: Japan External Trade Organization.

Japanese Economic Planning Agency. 1997. *Scenario for China in the Twenty-First Century*. Tokyo: Ministry of Finance Printing Bureau.

Japanese Overseas Economic Cooperation Fund. Annual. *China's Regional Development Strategy: Status and Issues*. Tokyo: Overseas Economic Cooperation Fund.

Japanese Science and Technology Agency, Science and Technology Policy Research Institute. 1993. "Energy Use and Volume of Emissions of Materials Affecting the Earth's Environment in the Asian Region." Tokyo: Japanese Office of Science and Technology Agency, Science and Technology Policy Research Institute.

Jiang Zemin. "Political Work Report at the Fifteenth CCP Congress." *People's Daily*, September 22, 1997.

Jie Zhenhua, ed. 1996. *China Environment Yearbook*. Beijing: China Environment Yearbook Press.

Li Peng. 1997. *Qiushi*, vol. 1. Beijing: *Quishi* Press.

_____. "Li Peng Discourses with Delegates to the Work Meeting of Experimental Enterprise Groups." *People's Daily*, June 25, 1997.

Li Weiyi. 1991. *China's Wage System*. Beijing: China Labor Press.

Liu Changming, He Dingmeng, and Zhao Xiyu. 1997. "Unemployment: Need for Reassessment of a Social Economic Phenomenon." *Literature, History, and Philosophy*. Special edition.

Ma Hong, ed. 1995, 1996. *Almanac of China's Economy*. Beijing: Almanac of China's Economy Press.

Ma Licheng and Lin Zhijun. 1998. *Cross Swords* (original Chinese: *Jiaofeng*). Beijing: Today's China Press.

Mao Zedong. 1956. "On the Ten Great Relationships." 1992. *Literary Works of Mao Zedong Since the Establishment of the Country*, Vol. 6. Beijing: Central Literary Press.

_____. 1974. *Long Live Mao Zedong Thought*. Tokyo: Gendai Hyorunsha (reprint).

_____. 1974. "Talks on Some Philosophical Questions." In *Long Live Mao Zedong Thought*. Tokyo: Gendai Hyorunsha (reprint).

Ministry of Foreign Trade and Economic Cooperation. 1997. *Foreign Economic and Trade Yearbook, 1996–1997*. Beijing: Ministry of Foreign Trade and Economic Cooperation.

_____. *International Trade News*. Beijing: International Trade News Press.

Ministry of International Trade and Industry. Various years. *White Paper on International Trade*. Tokyo: Ministry of International Trade and Industry.

Mitsubishi Research Institute. 1997. *China Information Handbook*. Tokyo: Sososha Ltd.

_____. Monthly. *Chugoku Joho* (China Information). Tokyo: Mitsubishi Research Institute.

Office of the Third Industrial Census, ed. 1997. *The Data of the Third National Industrial Census of the People's Republic of China in 1995*. Beijing: China Statistics Press.

People's Bank of China. 1997, 1998. *The People's Bank of China Quarterly Statistical Bulletin*, vols. 8–10. Beijing: People's Bank of China.

People's Liberation Army. 1988. *Summary of the Cadre System*. Beijing: Military Science Press [internal distribution].

People's Republic of China. "Outline of the Ninth Five Year Plan and Goals for the Long Term Plan for the Year 2010." *People's Daily*, March 20, 1996.

People's Republic of China, Ministry of Agriculture. 1996. *Report on China's Agricultural Development*. Beijing: China Agriculture Press.

"Provisional Regulations Governing State Public Servants," *People's Daily*, August 19, 1993.

Republic of China, Legislative Yuan, Statistics Bureau. 1997. *Taiwan Statistical Data Book, 1997*. Taipei: Legislative Yuan Statistics Bureau.

Republic of China, Mainland Commission. Monthly. *Cross-Straits Economic Statistics Monthly*. Taipei: Mainland Commission.

Shanghai Economic Monthly. 1998, vols. 1–3. Shanghai: Shanghai Modern Statistics Development Center.

Shanghai Securities News. Various issues.

Shanghai Statistics Bureau. 1997. *Shanghai Statistics Yearbook*. Shanghai: China Statistical Publishing House.

Shanghai Stock Exchange. 1996. *Shanghai Stock Exchange Annual Report*. Shanghai: Shanghai Stock Exchange.

State Council Development Research Center. *China Economic News*. Beijing: China Economic News Press.

State Council Information Office. October 1996. White Paper: "China's Food Problem." Beijing: State Council Information Office.

State Statistics Bureau. Various years, including 1995, 1996, and 1997. *China Statistical Yearbook*. Beijing: China Statistical Yearbook Publishing House.

State Statistics Bureau, Department of Trade and Materials, ed. 1992. *1979–1991 China Foreign Economic Statistics*. Beijing: Statistical Information and Consultancy Service Center.

_____. "Bulletin on National Economic and Social Development for 1997." *Economic Daily*, March 5, 1998.

State Statistics Bureau, Population and Employment Statistics Department, ed. 1989. *China's Commercial and Foreign Economic Statistical Materials, 1952–1988*. Beijing: China Statistics Press.

_____. 1993. *National Key Social and Economic Indicators Ranking Yearbook*. Beijing: China Statistics Press.

_____. 1996. *China's Regional Economy Through Seventeen Years of Reform and Opening-Up*. Beijing: China Statistics Press.

_____. 1996, 1997. *China Population Statistics Yearbook*. Beijing: China Statistics Press.

_____. March 4, 1998. "Bulletin on National Economic and Social Development Statistics for 1997." *Economic Daily*, March 5, 1998.

_____. Annual. *China Foreign Economic and Trade Yearbook*. Beijing: China Statistics Press.

_____. Annual. *China Industrial Statistics Yearbook*. Beijing: China Statistics Press.

_____. Annual. *China Market Statistics Yearbook*. Beijing: China Statistics Bureau.

_____. Annual. *China Population Yearbook*. Beijing: China Statistics Press.

Sun Benyao et al. 1992. *Record of the Fourteenth Party Congress*. Beijing: CCP Central Party School Press.

Sun Haiming. 1997. *Financial and Economic Research*, vol. 10. Shanghai: Shanghai University of Finance and Economics.

Ta Kong Pao. "Special Dispatch" from Beijing. "The CPC Issues Document Number Four, Fully Expounding Expansion of Opening Up." In Chinese, June 18, 1992. FBIS-CHI–92–118, June 18, 1992.

Tozai Boeki Press. 1997. *China's Petroleum Production and Petrochemical Industry*. Tokyo: Tozai Boeki Press.

United Nations. 1994 (rev.). *World Population Prospects*. New York: United Nations.

Wang Hanmin and Harima Mikio (trans.). 1967. *China's Atmospheric Pollution and Its Countermeasures*. Tokyo: Heavy Chemical Industry Press.

Wang Maoling. "Actively Search for Various Forms of Realizing Public Ownership." *Economic Daily*, October 6, 1997.

Wei Houkai. 1996. "An Analysis of China's Regional Income Disparities." *Economic Research*, vol. 11.

World Bank. 1994. *The East Asian Miracle*. New York: Oxford University Press.

_____. 1997. *World Bank Atlas*. New York: Oxford University Press.

_____. 1997. *World Development Indicators, 1997*. New York: Oxford University Press.

_____. 1998. *China 2020: Development Challenge in the New Century*. New York: Oxford University Press.

Wu Guoguang and Zheng Yongnian. 1996. *A Discussion of Central-Local Relations*. Hong Kong: Oxford University Press.

Wu Houkai. November 1996. "An Analysis of China's Regional Income Disparities." *Economic Research*. Beijing: Industrial Economy Research Institute, Chinese Academy of Social Sciences.

Wu Jiesi. August 1996. *Research on the Behavior of State-Owned Commercial Banks in China*. Beijing: China Financial Press.

Xinhua Financial News. Various issues, 1997–1998. Beijing: Xinhua News Agency.

Xu Kuangdi. "Report Concerning Shanghai's Economic and Social Development During the Ninth Five Year Plan and Long Term Objectives for 2010 (Excerpts)." *Liberation Daily*, February 11, 1996.

Yan Changle, ed. 1997. *Report on China's Energy Development*. Beijing: Economic Management Press.

Yan Xiaoming. Untitled article. *People's Daily*, March 23, 1992.

Yang Peixin. 1990. *Inflation: A Catastrophe for the People*. Beijing: Chinese Economic Press.

Index

Printed in the United States
112684LV00002B/105/A